MAYWOOD PUBLIC LIBRARY
459 Maywood Avenue
Maywood, NJ 07607
201-845-2915
maywood.bccls.org

The Inn of a
Thousand Days

For All the READERS
at MAywood LiBRARy —
HAppy READING!

The Inn of a
Thousand Days

A MEMOIR OF A
COUNTRY B&B

Alan Tongret

[signature]
26 Oct 2015

The Inn of a Thousand Days
A Memoir of a Country B & B

Published by

SINGULARITY PRESS

an Imprint of Star Cloud Press
6137 East Mescal Street
Scottsdale, Arizona 85254-5418

www.StarCloudPress.com

ISBN: 0-9765711-0-2 — cloth — $ 24.95

Library of Congress Control Number: 2005920539
Set in Adobe Garamond Pro font

Printed in the United States of America on acid-free paper

Also by Alan Tongret

PLAYS

Brontë
The World Aflame
Memories of the Lost Acres
Shakespeare and the Gospels — Primetime!
Poor Richard's Revolt
MVP
The Aurora Cycle:
"Treasure at the Devil's Backbone"
"Aurora"
"Arbor Day"
"The River Arno"

SCREENPLAYS

Thunder on the Moor
The Night Manager
Memories of the Lost Acres

NOVELS

Heaven Will Bleed
Endless Night

RADIO PLAY
Buccaneers

NON-FICTION

The Book of Lamps: A Pathway for Playwrights

ILLUSTRATIONS

Foreword

Every now and then one is asked that dog-eared question, "Where do you get the ideas for your stories?" If the company is friendly one answers, "I steal them." This is a good answer. It has the happy effect of putting a quietus to the subject. If the question must be taken soberly, however, one answers, "Everyone has a story. Whether it's someone else's or your own, first you must dig it out, and then you must be able to write it."

I have known Alan Tongret for some time without knowing this story or that he had the ability to write it. I knew him as a colleague, a playwright, living as I do in territory which is not only dry climatically but equally arid for playwrights. And I knew and had worked with his wife, the talented Jo Ann Yeoman, whose direction and choreography of musical shows are known and applauded nationally. I even knew that Alan and Jo Ann had met while performing in a musical play of my authorship, "Man of La Mancha," Jo Ann starring as my "splendid alley cat," Aldonza, with Alan playing the stiff-necked Dr. Carrasco. While this by no means confers upon me the mantle of Marriage Broker, it does pique my interest in two good people who have sustained their relationship through some times which were bad and some others which were worse. In the absence of the authority to hand out medals, I offer my applause; they have fought the wars of Show Business, and they have prevailed.

Now Alan has written a book. I have read it with absolute fascination; it is surely one of the most harrowing accounts of obsession — in this case obsession to achieve an objective — since Moby-Dick. In this case the Great White Whale was a hotel, or more accurately the renovation and revival of a hotel in an obscure Kentucky town, the adopted home of Alan's family. It was a hotel to which termites had long since claimed title. It was decayed, desiccated, utterly infirm. Dry rot ran riot. Plumbing was antique and electricity in literally shocking condition. Mysterious tenants drifted in and out of rooms long since condemned. And these were merely the beginning.

To put it mildly, there were problems. To put it more realistically, there were obstacles so various, so horrendous, even, that they would have persuaded any sensible person to cut and run. Not merely once, but again and again. Alan and his father, whose dream this was, undertook to become carpenters, plumbers, dry-wall installers, electricians, loan-negotiators, town planners and general contractors. There were penalties for such hubris: mashed thumbs, falls from ladders, broken bones, deep and despairing fatigue, lack of money and a constant and maddening coping with the bureaucracy of town, county and state. The budget quadrupled. The allotted ten months for completion turned into three years. In order to keep the project afloat, Alan was compelled to earn money from outside employment teaching high school — in the process employing all his various talents as well as others he didn't know he had. And finally, when all seemed lost, to invent a delicious *coup de theatre* which saved the day and the hotel as well. It's too improbable a happening to give away here; read and enjoy it for yourself.

And yet . . . a question troubles my mind. America is attuned to a set of clichés which seem as immutable as the Ten Commandments. They're expressed in catchwords and epigrams: Stick-to-itiveness. Never Give Up. Persist and You Will Prevail. What You Can Perceive You Will Achieve . . . and so on. You know all these and more; they are underlying assumptions of our culture. But allow a touch of apostasy here —

How does one know when a sustained commitment is worth the price? The major price to pay, of course, is one's time. We are allotted a limited number of days for our lives, and a limited number of chances, as well, to discover and express the best that may be in us. Is a given objective worth the cost in time and, perhaps more importantly, in spirit? The clichés do not answer questions which may be more disturbing and tortuous than would first appear.

Alan Tongret's account is more than merely a suspenseful story; it carries implied questions of character and commitment, and how they may be most wisely fulfilled.

Dale Wasserman

For Mom & Dad

Prologue

There is a stretch of the Ohio River as straight as a ten-mile mirror. It forms the bottom of a vast basin that intensifies the greens and browns of the rolling terrain, returning to heaven its own image, and inflaming the valley with soul-shaking beauty where Ohio and Kentucky rub shoulders. But to really appreciate how splendid the valley is you must climb to the top of a nearby hill, a hill that rises above Augusta, Kentucky. Tranquil beside the rushing waters, Augusta occupies one of the loveliest spots in America.

As you examine Augusta from your perch on the hilltop you realize that it's distant enough that you lose sight of its modern trappings. Cars and trucks might be wagons and carriages, and power cables fade from view. Lawn mowers whisper like cicadas beneath avenues of cedar trees, and TV antennas become motes in the sunlight. Even the mobile homes — lined up like oversized cracker boxes on the south side of town — are too distant to mar the view. On the east end of town is a plastics factory whose acres of roof mimic the sprawling shoe factory that burned down in the 1950s, and nearby is the Victorian facade of another factory where carriage parts were once crafted. You imagine a nickering horse harnessed to a wagon, and a boy releasing a pebble from a slingshot.

Carved out by the Ice Age, the river has the power of the *Odyssey's* sirens to lure houses and line them up like shells along its banks. Illustrious houses, like the Tomlinson place where you can almost hear

Stephen Foster composing a melody, inspired by a gospel tune borne on the wind from a neighboring church. You imagine President William Henry Harrison sitting down as a dinner guest at the Payne House on Riverside Drive, and Rosemary Clooney entertaining in her yellow brick summer house farther down the street. You picture her nephew George Clooney, scrawling his name on a piece of scenery at the high school where he was a student, and Heather Renee French, Miss America 2000, visiting the old house where she was born.

Some of the river houses date from the 1790s, and they stare at you with a stubborn tenacity. James Michener's *Centennial* was filmed in front of them, after the houses had survived countless floods and the gunfire of John Hunt Morgan's Confederate Raiders. The seven Confederate soldiers killed in Morgan's attack rest in the cemetery at the west end of town. Augusta was cast in Michener's film because it looks more like early St. Louis than any of the towns on the Mississippi River where Michener's story is set. The Ohio River owes much of its charm to this chameleon ability to out-mimic its larger sister: There's a house on the west edge of town where Huck Finn escaped from the Widow Douglas' second-story window in a recent filming of Mark Twain's novel, and part of Neil Simon's *Lost in Yonkers* was shot in front of the abandoned Augusta Farm Supply building on Elizabeth Street, showing that the thespian-like Ohio can also mimic the Hudson River. Augusta is the birthplace of Stuart Walker, whose portable theatre toured America before he sought Hollywood fame as director of the 1934 *Great Expectations*. All of this activity has made Augusta a cinematic curiosity, an exporter of illusions.

Augusta was also an early magnet for scholars. In 1798 Bracken Academy was built on the corner of High and Elizabeth streets, and beneath the clock tower in the middle of town is the present-day schoolhouse, whose towering brick walls have shaded the same slate sidewalks for over a century. On the same site stood Augusta College, founded in 1822 as the world's first Methodist institution of higher learning with a faculty that included John P. Durpin, later to become Chaplain of the U.S. Senate, and Henry Bascom, Chaplain of the House of Representatives. Schoolboys 12 years old arrived by saddle and bruising wagon ride, and among its alumni were the presidents of universities, an Iowa governor, and Thornton F. Marshall, who cast the deciding vote that kept Kentucky in the Union during the Civil War. The dormitories where students once crammed for exams on Shakespeare and the Bible are now private homes.

Long after the arrival of the college, the carriage factory, and Augusta's 300 residents — a population that's grown by about six people a year in two centuries — came KY Route 8, dodging the knobby hills and linking Augusta with Cincinnati to the northwest, and antebellum Huntington, West Virginia, to the southeast. Two blocks north of Route 8 is the Chesapeake & Ohio Railway. Until a few years ago passengers alighted from the trains at the depot on Third Street, where they came to buy a hat in one of Augusta's millinery stores, or to see a movie at the picture house. Occasional steam trains resurrect the 19th Century by hustling excursion cars through town. The shriek of the whistle chills the spine of anyone within a mile of the tracks, as steam bursts angrily around the drive wheels to shroud the graveled banks.

But few steam trains come through nowadays, and you turn again to the river — Augusta's reason for being. The river brought Native Americans to hunt buffalo, and Augusta's black, alluvial soil continually pours forth their arrowheads and burial relics. In the mid-1700s the populous deer and beaver along the river attracted white trappers, as Daniel Boone and Simon Kenton pushed in from the Cumberland Gap, hacking out the Wilderness Trail and opening the way to the Northwest

Territory. Flatboats floated down with hogsheads of tobacco, corn, and sorghum molasses, and later generations traveled on the deck chairs of packet boats and steam wheelers. Bryant's *Showboat* gave its first performance on Augusta's riverfront, and William Jennings Bryan lectured there on the Chautauqua circuit. From the hilltop you can see a descendant of the steamboats in the giant Delta Queen as she shakes the valley with the thunder of her calliope. Barges a quarter of a mile long — drifting continents of coal — surge by with the black gold mined throughout Appalachia. A ferry boat — scion of the first ferry that operated in Augusta in 1793 — lays a ribbon across the water to the Ohio shore, ablaze with redbuds.

If it's a hot day you jog down the hill and soak your feet in the river. The current — conceived as a trickle near Lake Erie — nips at your toes and you dream of voyaging down the broad water. Think of it! You can jump in a boat and the current will take you clear to New Orleans. Without touching land you can sail all the way to Borneo.

The road, the railway, and the river created dreams by linking Augusta to other places and other times, while the appeal of the historic houses and painfully haunting scenery reversed this exodus by drawing a stream of settlers into the town. A few of these new inhabitants revived the old homes, including my parents — Charles and Doris Tongret — who bought a couple of derelict row houses on the riverfront that they renovated from cellar to attic. But they soon discovered a cancer more deadly than rotted wood — an attitude of complacency among many of the long-time residents that Augusta was just fine as it was, that the old houses ought to be allowed to sink into oblivion while mobile homes and tanning booths sprouted up around them like bread mold. Nowhere was this more evident than a cluster of decaying buildings on Main and Second streets, and the worst eyesore of all was the old Parkview Hotel. It had stood for decades, a festering wound. The hotel was so far gone my dad occasionally muttered that someone ought to do the town a favor and burn it down.

Then suddenly the man who owned the Parkview offered to sell it to my parents.

Part I

1. Among the Cicadas

The summer my parents bought the Parkview Hotel I was an actor in New York, but I'd wearied of the routine of wandering from summer stock to dinner theatre to small parts in TV and film, and decided I was more passionate about writing — for which I could abandon my gypsy lifestyle and stay in one place. I was agonizing about leaving the city for a quieter spot where I could live more cheaply. I'd written a novel that had attracted the attention of a couple of agents, and a radio script that was taped as a pilot for a public-radio series. I had a bundle of other projects I was anxious to begin when my parents phoned about the hotel.

"Why don't you help us renovate it?" said dad. "We're gonna do it as a bed-and- breakfast, and you can be the manager."

"Should leave you plenty of time for writing!" mom added.

My parents knew what they were talking about when it came to redoing old buildings. Dad was expert at wiring, masonry, and carpentry. He could plumb, build fireplaces with sensual patterns of brick, and make cabinetwork you'd take for museum pieces. Mom decorated, hung wallpaper, sewed drapes, and made old furniture glow like honey. They'd renovated their own house into a showplace by the river. Moreover, my sister and three brothers offered to help with the hotel — all of whom had remodeled their own houses.

That summer I flew to Kentucky to look over the hotel, and the clanging of the bell on the ferry boat echoed across the river as mom greeted me with a hug at their doorstep. She wore her brown hair short, and was tanned and fit from yard work and bicycle rides with my dad.

"He's already at work!"

She led me through the garden as their cat Osha dodged our feet, serenaded by the *tchew-wew! tchew-wew!* of the purple martins who lived in a birdhouse near a mulberry tree. We entered a two-story garage my parents had built the year before, where dad was bent over his drafting table. His handsome blue eyes lit up as he clapped me on the shoulder.

"How was the flight from New York?"

A drawing on the drafting table was marked PARKVIEW HOTEL RENOVATION, with rectangles labeled "Guest Room No. One," "Lobby," and "Coffee Shop."

He grabbed a measuring tape and bounded out the door as I ran to keep up. At sixty-one my father had the physique of a far younger man, kept trim by a regimen of Canadian Air Force exercises done each morning in front of the burning logs of the fireplace he'd built in their bedroom. We entered a dirt alley behind McCracken's Bar, where gunshots occasionally entertained the town. A huge dog lunged at us and I jumped back.

"It's all right, Duke," said dad. "We're not gonna trespass!"

Duke was leashed to a stake in the boiling sun, and his head snapped back as the leash drew tight. We were just below Second Street, and I stared speechless at what seemed to be a sharecroppers' tenement left over from the Depression — a sprawling heap of warped clapboards, tar paper, and asphalt siding manufactured to resemble bricks.

"That's the Parkview," said dad.

He's joking, I thought. Much of the building's asphalt had flaked off onto the ground. Ivy smothered its clapboards, etched by sun and rain, and it exuded a mood of desolation amid the drumming cicadas in the nearby trees.

"Gotta double-check some measurements," said dad.

He's *not* joking, I realized. He handed me one end of the tape, then we elbowed our way through a dense stand of weeds to an enclosed porch baking in the sun. A jagged crack ran through one of the porch's brick walls, and decaying windows bulged out from their frames.

"This'll be the coffee shop," said dad, using his shirt sleeve to rub a peep hole in the dust on a window. I pressed close to the window and amid the shadow saw a radiator resting on a broken concrete floor below walls of cracked plaster as dad explained. "Thought we'd build a small stage for weekend cabarets. Maybe put on *plays*."

Plays! Well, I knew lots of actors who'd kill to get away from the city for a few weeks, especially if it was somewhere as tranquil as Augusta. I nodded at a wall that blocked off one end of the porch. "What's that?"

"Gambling room," said dad. "Story goes they used to bring in tarts from Cincinnati. Best little whore house in Kentucky!"

Rusted tiles covered the porch roof, mashed flat by kids who'd climbed out the second-story windows, and there were nests of wrens and screech owls. A willow tree limb the size of a truck threatened to crash into the porch. Drain pipes sagged in their moorings, and electric fans sucked at the sultry air in a couple of the windows, where curtains lapped over the sills like the tongues of panting dogs.

I turned to dad. "There's somebody *living* up there?"

He spread his hands. "We inherited some tenants in three of the old guest rooms. But their rent will help pay for the renovation. Six hundred bucks a month!"

We continued our measurements to the front of the hotel, where lampposts with missing globes leaned over a sidewalk that was broken up as if by an earthquake. The clammy Kentucky air whistled through a pair of sway-back doors at the entrance, where sunlight flared around cardboard stuffed in to replace broken panes. Tea-green corrosion covered the doorknobs above a welcome mat of bird droppings.

Dad turned a key and we entered the lobby. The drumming of the cicadas stopped as if a switch had been thrown, and the nearest car might have been a hundred miles away. The silence held us like anesthesia, and we were surrounded by a forest of junk. Doors leaned against the walls; old carpeting, lumber, tool boxes, battered stoves and refrigerators stood every which way. A mummified pigeon lay inside a stone fireplace, its mantle carved *1800*. I felt the presence of people who were long dead and the hair rose at the back of my neck.

"Started out as a log cabin," said dad. "Then a tavern and livery stable." His eyes brightened at a pressed-tin ceiling, supported by massive twin columns. "That's what sold your mom and me on the place!"

An acne of rust and flaking paint spotted the floral patterns in the pressed tin, which curled away from the oak framing. Cobwebs hung in sheets from a chandelier with tarnish thick as paint.

Dad stepped over a mound of carpeting to an industrial sewing machine. "They had a factory here when the hotel closed. Made sleeping bags for Vietnam." A ledger book with hand-written entries lay on a table, and brass rivets glimmered like myriad eyes in the cracks of the floorboards. Dad turned to the transept at one end of the lobby. "That's where we'll put the front desk."

I tried to imagine the lobby as it used to be. One corner of the floor fell away into a void, and I made my way between a pair of old barber chairs to get a closer look as the floor bowed beneath me and a wall of cold air reeking of damp earth smote me in the face.

"Careful!" said dad.

He switched on a flashlight and aimed it into the void, revealing a cellar with stone walls and a cast-iron furnace with pipes trailing off like tentacles. The floor under my feet teetered on a solitary water pipe above this dank chasm. I retreated to safety, and we moved to another part of the hotel where nothing remained but a jungle of naked studs.

"This was the dining room," said dad. "Mrs. Parker at the funeral home belonged to a women's club that met here in the thirties. She showed me a picture of one of their dinners. There were beveled-glass windows, potted plants, and brass chandeliers polished to within an inch of their life. Waiters in white jackets and women done up in gowns and jewelry."

But the women had vanished in the mists of time. Fire-blackened joists spanned the ceiling above the old dining room, and something hissed in the shadows.

"Water heater," said dad.

The red eye of a gas flame winked at us from the water heater's belly. Wire from an electrical panel spilled onto the floor, inches from a puddle of water.

We trekked to the back of the hotel — taking what measurements we could among the trash — and came to the main work room of the sewing factory where former guest rooms had been replaced with a concrete slab the size of a bowling alley. A truck sat by the back door among stacks of roofing tin and plumbing supplies. Old toilets and sinks lined the walls, and doors lurked everywhere, in more styles than I thought possible.

"This'll be our workshop," said dad.

A staircase wide enough for only one person led to the second story on treads that yielded beneath our feet like twigs, then opened to a tunnel-like hallway where a couple of naked light bulbs spread a dismal twilight. Buckets filled with rancid water crouched on the floor.

"Leaky roof?"

Dad nodded. "But our purchase agreement requires Art Taylor to give the roof a new coating of tar."

Art Taylor was the realtor who'd sold my parents the hotel. Dad moved down the hall and knocked on a door. A latch disengaged and a pimply-faced woman appeared with hair like wind-blown straw.

"Hi, Dotty. Is Lem around?"

"Come on in!" cried a voice behind the woman.

We went in and found Lem Otley eating fried eggs. He was naked from the waist up, with a pink belly that rolled over his jeans. His cheeks bulged as he watched an *Andy Griffith* rerun. Dotty crept to the stove and stabbed a pan of bacon with her spatula. Grease snapped and popped, mingling with the odor of cigarettes.

"We'll come back later," said dad.

"Won't bother us," said Lem. "I'm just comin' off night shift."

"This is my son Alan. He's visiting from New York, but he's thinking about moving to Augusta."

Lem's mouth dropped. "Zat right? Don't think I ever knowed anyone from New York!"

The next apartment was rented by Leroy Raines, an unemployed factory worker. He was pale, tall, and thin as a tomato stake, and stared at us through a crack in the door. He had strabismus — a condition causing one eye to cross out from the other.

"We'd like to take some measurements," said dad.

Inside, a woman sprawled in front of a TV that crackled with cowboy-and-Indian gunfire. The mounds of her arms rolled from her halter top, her legs bulged inside slacks, and flip-flops pinched her mottled feet. An electric fan pushed at the air with a nervous tick.

"How are you, Ada Sue?" said dad.

"It's too damn hot!" she said, fanning herself with a paper bag. "I been cleanin' the tavern all mornin'!"

Leroy offered to hold one end of the measuring tape, and he nodded at the TV while we worked. "You like videos? We rented this at Kelsch's. They've got some *racy* ones, if ya know whadda mean!"

"Long as there ain't too much shootin'!" said Ada Sue, her eyes glued to the mayhem on the TV.

The final apartment was rented by Rawley Tate, McCracken's bartender, but our knock went unanswered, and we went on to measure the vacant rooms, their floors groaning beneath chunks of plaster fallen from the ceilings and walls. A skeleton of oak studs from Kentucky's ancient hardwood forests bristled with broken lath. Cast-iron radiators sat like rhinos amid rusted bed frames. Furniture from the hotel's past hovered around us like wraiths. There were chairs with broken backs and amputated legs, and dressers with twisted frames and fractured mirrors. Drawers yawned beneath peeling veneer. And doors everywhere, some with room numbers still tacked to them, green with age. Hinges were calcified with paint, and hardware dangled from loose screws. Doors exhausted from decades of opening and closing, bracing themselves against anything they could find like tired old men.

In spite of the shambles around me, something about the sad, wasted glamour and pent up energy of the old hotel seized hold of me and wouldn't let go.

In a corner of the room dad uncovered an oak chair with a delicately curved back. "Better put this one aside for your mom!"

2. Making a Start

I moved to Kentucky in December, throwing everything I owned in the smallest truck that U-Haul had and driving the 600 miles from Manhattan with my girlfriend, Jo Ann Yeoman. She was an actor, dancer, and director, and would be returning to the city in a few days for a choreography job. We'd met several years earlier in New Hampshire at Theatre-by-the-Sea, a small Equity house that was, alas, no longer operating. We'd been cast in a production of *Man of La Mancha* — where Jo Ann was a provocative and compelling Aldonza, and I an enthusiastic but less than sensational Dr. Carrasco and Knight of the Mirrors. We planned to get married, and one of the things we wanted was to buy a house some day with a yard large enough for a dog to run around in.

Snow began to fall as I turned off KY Route 8 into Augusta, and it blended with the wood-burning smoke from the houses on upper Main Street. They were a patchwork of styles, most of which had plenty of yard for a dog. The library slept below a cedar tree, and a light shone at Ike Weldon's porch, Augusta's mayor. The mayor's job didn't pay very much, and Weldon earned his living from a sporting goods store in Maysville, 17 miles upriver from Augusta. I guided the U-Haul truck over the train tracks as fresh-from-the-factory paint gleamed on the equipment at Wilson's Ford Tractor Sales. Mr. Mains leaned on the counter of his grocery store, obscured by windows that hadn't been washed since the Vietnam War. Next door to it, a strip of tape curled at the edges around a crack running through Dr. Milton Brindley's office window, the town's GP. Lights burned at the drugstore, but the building next to it was darker than a bucket of charcoal.

"Not very Christmas-like!" I said.

The darkened building had been a department store with a grand soda fountain, then a hardware store, and finally a warehouse for used appliances.

"I suppose everyone gets their appliances in Maysville," said Jo Ann.

"Or Cincinnati," I said, which was 42 miles down river.

I was hoping that in the six months since I'd visited Augusta things would have improved, since our bed-and-breakfast would rely on tourists drawn to the town's charming waterfront and historic houses. I searched for signs of change, and saw another dark building with an Art Taylor Realty sign on it. It had been boarded up so many years it was hard to tell what it used to be.

The U-Haul truck's muffler echoed against the storefronts as we passed the city building, where a lamp on Police Chief Phil Cummins' desk highlighted a shotgun on the wall. The volunteer fire department hibernated behind roll-up doors, and CLOSED FOR THE SEASON was pasted across the Creamy Freeze. But next door at Jeans n' Such a woman came out with a shopping bag.

"At least someone's spending some money!" I said.

Mr. Bach slumped in his own barber chair, asleep over a magazine, and the shell of an old blacksmith shop — also belonging to Art Taylor — tucked itself behind a vacant parking lot. The forge had vanished years earlier and the place was used for storage. I stopped at the corner of Main and Second, the town's chief intersection. My parents had told me that it used to have a stop light, but it was removed in the 1950s when Route 8 opened and siphoncd off shoppers to the larger towns.

Overlooking the intersection was Farmers Liberty Bank with WE TAKE PRIDE IN TOBACCO emblazoned above the entrance. A Christmas tree made of pine cones glowed in the window of Petal Pushers Flowers, where Sharon Graves waited on customers.

"*They're* open!" said Jo Ann.

We were the only ones on the street and I drove through the intersection. An antique shop shaped like a cheese wedge filled the opposite corner behind windows hung with soiled drapes. There was no sign on the shop, and the owner opened only two or three times a year — whenever he had enough furniture to make it worth his while. Next was the pool hall, in front of which stood Sambo, who'd dropped out of school the year before because his low grades kept him off the basketball team.

Sunlight broke through a rent in the clouds and threw a shadow from the mansard outline of another, much larger bank that had closed decades earlier. It was the only building on the street with genuinely impressive proportions, with slate shingles that towered above the Masonic Hall and McCracken's Bar. It was boarded up with plywood, and bricks — loosened from its crumbling walls — cluttered the sidewalk. This old bank also belonged to Art Taylor.

Opposite the bank stood a ratty-looking mobile home and the oily pavement of a gas station, another Taylor holding. The Rotary Club's plastic Santa and reindeer swung in the breeze above the garish lights of Yesterdays, the town's only restaurant.

"Augusta's really jumping!" I said. Jo Ann smiled and put her hand on my shoulder.

At the foot of Main Street hovered a group of empty buildings my parents had once owned, but had sold with the understanding that they be fixed up. But they remained in ruins, including a row house being redone as a restaurant by a Cincinnati chef, who was two years behind schedule.

I turned onto Riverside Drive and parked in front of my parents' house as the ferry rocked and dipped its way through the fog as it returned from the Ohio shoreline to Kentucky. The phantoms of tree limbs and other jetsam wrenched from a thousand creeks below Pittsburgh swept by in the current. Jo Ann and I unbent ourselves from the truck and the frosty air embraced us.

"You need some hot chocolate," said mom. "Then we've got something to show you!"

Dad came in, and few minutes later he led the way through my parents' green house to the garden. "There's a lot happening around town," he said, sensing our despondency over the town's moribund appearance. "John Parker's talking about opening a museum to show off his antique cars."

"And another furniture shop's about to open!" chimed in mom.

Thank God! I thought.

We crossed a footbridge in the garden that dad had built over a miniature brook that emptied into a pond. The pond was iced over and reflected the underside of the Catawba tree as its limbs nodded in the cold. A possum waddled across our path and disappeared in the shrubbery.

"The flower shop looked busy," said Jo Ann.

"Sharon's been very busy," said mom. "Swears she needs a larger shop!"

The path meandered past a mulberry tree by the purple martin house, deserted for the winter. We followed dad into the garage and up to an apartment they'd finished since my summer visit. Robin's-egg blue and maple woodwork, thick carpeting, a waterbed, and kitchenette. One window looked out at a cedar tree, and another onto the evergreens behind the local museum. My view in New York had been an air shaft.

"Hundred a month," said dad. "Including utilities."

"We'll take it!" said Jo Ann.

I was happy to be home, and went to the kitchenette where another window looked out on the Parkview Hotel, huddling in the shadow of Art Taylor's decomposing bank.

That night dad showed us the drawings he'd been working on during my visit the previous summer. The temperature had dropped, but a Russian furnace dad had built — a tower of tawny-colored bricks in the heart of the living room — warmed us with the scent of burning locust wood. Light from its fire box danced over an oak staircase my parents had salvaged and restored. Dad smoothed the drawings with hands nicked from countless wood-working projects and scarred from a German machine-gun bullet.

"The red lines show the changes we'll have to make," said dad. "The lobby's the only thing we can actually *restore*. Everything else is toast."

"Except the floors," said mom. "We can refinish those."

Dad grabbed a pencil. "Conference room goes here, in the old dining room, and the coffee shop on the porch, where I showed you last summer. We'll have to tear out the staircase."

"If it doesn't fall down first," I said.

Mom smiled. "We want a counter with several stools and two or three booths."

"Who's gonna cook?" Jo Ann asked.

"Alan's a good cook," said mom.

"I'll be at the front desk," I protested. "Raking in the money!"

Dad unrolled the second-floor ground plan as mom went on. "We'll give each room an individual decor. Shaker, something contemporary, and maybe a western room."

I counted the rooms. "*Nine* bathrooms. That's a lot of plumbing!"

"Eleven," said dad, pointing to the coffee shop. "Plus the laundry room."

My plumbing experience in New York was limited to pouring Drano down the sink.

"When do you open?" Jo Ann asked.

Dad disappeared through an archway to the library and returned with a sheaf of papers marked PARKVIEW REHAB OBJECTIVES that divided the work into ten steps, with a budget for everything from wiring to window cleaner. The total cost would be $73,500. It was more money than I'd ever handled, and I sucked in my breath.

"I think we can have one or two rooms ready for paying guests by September," said dad. "And maybe the coffee shop."

A rush of anticipation shot through my veins as I gazed at the drawings. "So we open in ten months!"

3. Patchwork

The first of the ten steps on our renovation was to stop winter from blasting its way through the hotel. A solitary gas heater was the only thing warming the first floor, making frozen water pipes a constant hazard. While Jo Ann curled up by the Russian furnace to make notes for her choreography job, I helped dad staple sheets of plastic over windows and wrap insulation around water pipes. Art Taylor had removed most of his things, giving us some elbow room, and by mid-morning we made enough progress to celebrate at Yesterdays restaurant with hot chocolate. But when we came back the hotel shivered, and we found the pilot light dead in the heater.

"Third time this month!" said dad, climbing a ladder and finding the gas line clogged.

He cleaned the line and re-lighted the pilot, but next morning the heater was out again and the hotel was an ice box.

He shook his head. "Better get John Bonfield!" He stuffed a note into a newspaper lying in front of the hotel. I'd seen the newspaper the day before and assumed it was one of our tenants'.

"Are you kidding?" said dad. "None of them *read*."

"Doesn't Bonfield have a phone?"

"He never answers it."

The newspaper vanished, and next morning a man in his late 60s pulled up in a panel truck. He was freckled, bow-legged, and had slicked-down coppery hair, redder than the flame of a blowtorch. Although it was well below freezing, his plaid shirt was unbuttoned, exposing his T-shirt and a .22 caliber derringer pistol clamped to his belt buckle. He examined me through a pair of red-tinted glasses.

"Zischarlesaroun'?"

"Sorry?" He repeated the question, and I gathered it was John Bonfield. His impenetrable drawl was made worse by his habit of talking through a clenched jaw. "Dad's at the hardware store," I said.

Bonfield examined the heater, drove away and returned an hour later with a metal box. "Thermocouple. Knew I had`un som'ers."

Bonfield muttered that he had stuff scattered all over Bracken County, wherever he was working on furnaces or plumbing. He fastened the thermocouple and fired up the heater.

"What do we owe you?" I asked.

He waved a hand in dismissal. "Maybeyou'll nee'me for'som'else sometime."

He got his newspaper and drove away.

Later that day our tacking-up-plastic chore was interrupted by one of our tenants, Lem Otley's girlfriend, Dotty, who padded like a mouse into the shop.

"It's about the stove," she whispered.

Dad got his electrical kit, and we found a bare-chested Lem sprawled on the sofa in cut-offs with his eyes glued to a *Gomer Pyle* rerun. The gas heater was turned up so high the windows were steamed like a Turkish bath.

"Having my breakfast `fore I go to bed," he said, winking at Dotty as she hovered over a frying pan.

"Still on night shift?" dad asked.

"Hell, yes!"

Lem's words whistled through a missing tooth. I asked what he did, and he said he ran a machine at Clopay, the local plastics factory that employed half the town.

"This won't heat no more," said Dotty, opening the oven as dad aimed his flashlight.

Lem roared at the TV. "Ole Gomer's pretty good!"

We speculated on how long it had been since the *Gomer Pyle* show first aired, and out of the blue Lem asked me to guess his age. I figured he was 45, but decided to err on the side of good manners.

"Forty-two?"

Lem looked surprised. "Guess again."

"Forty-four?"

His face fell. "I'm thirty-two!"

Dad told Dotty we'd have to order a new heating element, and he let out his breath as we went back downstairs. "These apartments eat up gobs of time. Leaky faucets, broken toilets. . . . And you notice how hot they keep it?"

"Could roast a turkey *without* the stove," I said.

Dad sighed. "Wish we could do without the apartments, but that's six hundred a month!"

Before Jo Ann returned to New York we exchanged Christmas gifts and went to McCracken's for a celebratory drink, where our tenant Rawley Tate tended bar. The bar was so dark that we stumbled on the floor matting, and numerous eyes made phosphorescent by cigarettes peered at us from the gloom. Smoke was thick as gauze and the air was heavy with a concoction of other smells we didn't want to think about.

Rawley grinned at us. "We ain't met. But I seen y'all at the *ho*tel."

He was about 40 with a paunch and brown hair in need of shampooing that he wore like Dagwood Bumstead. I ordered a beer and Jo Ann asked about mixed drinks.

"We don't do none of those," said Rawley, making a pass with his towel at a puddle of something on the counter.

"Do you have any liqueurs? Drambuie or Bailey's?" Rawley shook his head. "How about sherry?"

"Nope." He made another swipe at the puddle on the counter. "Holt on a minute!"

He disappeared into the dark maw behind the bar and returned with a bottle that he opened and poured into a twelve-ounce water tumbler, filling it to the brim. "We did have some! Nobody ever asks for any!"

We stared at the pink liquid as Rawley went on to his other customers. Jo Ann took a sip and her eyes crossed. "Cooking sherry!"

In the morning I borrowed my folks' car to drive Jo Ann to the airport for her flight back to New York.

"I'll try to come in February," she said. She'd be flying to Texas in January for the *Guys and Dolls* choreography job, and she fastened her brown eyes on me. "Are you sure this is what you want? It's gonna be awfully *quiet* down here!"

With the hotel reasonably intact from the frigid winter gusts we fixed up our workshop. We built lumber racks and shelves, installed work lights, and hauled in dad's tools from the garage, including the jigsaw he'd gotten as boy as a Christmas gift from Grandpa Tongret. Dad had taught me how to use it when I was six or seven, and we'd turned out countless projects on it as I grew up. As December settled over Augusta, calluses formed on my hands, and we cheered up the long hours by tuning in the National Public Radio station in Cincinnati for classical music, jazz, and the banter of old radio shows.

Evenings we buried ourselves in paperwork. Dad made more drawings and refined our budget, drew up lists of materials to buy, and drafted guidelines to send to contractors for furnaces and other equipment. Mom searched magazines for ideas on decor and furnishings. Because of the liability risk we'd be facing, we formed a family S corporation. I was appointed secretary and treasurer, and began studying the Kentucky Corporation manual. I was also responsible for keeping our accounts, and one evening I ran into a snag and went to ask dad's advice when I found mom putting coffee on a try in the kitchen.

"I want you to meet someone!" she said.

I found Ed McClanahan in the living room, a bespectacled, broad-chested man in his late 40s with a bristling mustache.

"So you're the *actor*," he roared.

"Now I'm the *carpenter*."

McClanahan roared again and played with Osha, purring on the sofa, as dad handed me a novel McClanahan had just published. A former Wallace Stegner Fellow at Stanford University, McClanahan was visiting his mother in Augusta when dad invited him over to autograph the novel. Dad and I eventually excused ourselves to the library.

"I've got a spreadsheet in my computer," I said. "But it's not much help."

Dad took some books from a shelf. "Try these."

They were textbooks he'd used in college. He was trained as an engineer at AT&T, but had taken business courses when he moved up to a management position. Then another volume caught my eye, an art book that had belonged to Grandfather Tongret. He'd been a gifted amateur painter whose sketch books were family treasures.

"OK if I borrow it? I wanna start designing our brochure."

The possum was nowhere in sight as I went back to the apartment, and I was anxious for the return of the purple martins outside my window and the redbuds on the Ohio shoreline. McClanahan had told me he had a nonfiction book coming out in addition to the novel, and I thought about my own novel, untouched in my apartment. I glanced out at the hotel, a specter in the deepening gray, and acknowledged that my novel would have to wait. I put on the lamp and cracked open an accounting book.

4. Mud Up My Sleeve

Dad poked at the door frame with his screwdriver and it sank in like a knife into corn bread. "Crap!" We were walling up the opening left by the rickety garage door we'd removed at the back of the hotel. "We'll have to replace all of these!"

We spent the rest of the day splicing in new 2x4s, and next day the wall was finished. A cold front bullied its way into town, but the building fought bravely and stayed warm.

"Not bad," I said, feeling cocky as I swept up the saw dust. "And that job wasn't even on our list!"

"And there'll be plenty more of those!" dad warned.

A few nights later it dropped to zero with a wind-chill factor 15 below. I was catching up on paper work in my apartment over the garage, and revising my radio play for the producer in New York who wanted to submit it to an agent. Dad suddenly knocked on my door.

"Thought we oughta see how the hotel's doing in this deep freeze!"

The night before someone had thrown a brick through the hotel's porch window, and we'd decided to make spot checks of the hotel at night to discourage vandalism.

The frigid air burned my throat under a starless sky. The river was invisible and the Ohio shore might have been a thousand miles away. The frost crunched beneath our feet as dad told me about the meeting he and mom had just attended at the museum down the street owned by SHARE, Save Historic Augusta Restoration Effort. The meeting was to arrange a Christmas candlelight tour of the old houses to raise funds.

"This is the time to stir up interest in Augusta! If we had more shops and galleries we'd get more tourists!"

The SHARE museum was run by volunteers like my parents, and opened only on special occasions. And Augusta had only one art gallery, the Piedmont, a couple of doors down river from my parents'. Dad's news was welcome, and it shored up my faith that my decision to move to Kentucky had been the right one.

We entered the back of the hotel where the light of the gas heater flecked the tools with orange, where it was at 42 degrees. It got colder as we walked to the front of the hotel, where a flame burned steadily in the water heater and another thermometer showed 38 degrees.

Dad took off a glove and waved his hand in front of the flame. "If we can make it through a night like *this*, we'll be home free!"

Then we heard the porch door thrown open and footsteps run up the dilapidated stairs. We went around and found the door wide open to the bitter cold. "I've warned them about this a dozen times!" said dad, angrily closing the door.

Someone shouted upstairs, and I went up and found Rawley Tate pounding on Leroy's door. He saw me approach and swayed against the door jamb.

"Maybe you oughta call it a night," I said, overpowered by the smell of liquor.

His door opened to my touch, releasing a stench of stale tobacco and something burning. Rawley leaned against me like a sack of cement and fell onto a coffee table, overturning an ashtray that hadn't been emptied in days. I rushed to the kitchen and found a pan of pork chops about to burst into flame. I removed them from the stove and turned off the burner, then checked to see if anything else hazardous had been left on.

Dishes encrusted with food covered the dining table, and dirty clothes floated like drowned bodies in the bathtub in water whose suds had gone flat. A ring circled the tub like a band of brown paint.

Rawley was sound asleep, and I closed his door and went downstairs to dad. I explained what had happened and dad bit his lip.

"We're sitting on a powder keg here! We could close out the apartments, but six hundred a month would leave a heck of a hole in our budget."

"We'll just have to keep an eye on the place," I said. "I'll talk with Rawley tomorrow, and make a habit of coming by every night to check on things."

"And there's something else to worry about!" said dad.

We went to the street corner below Art Taylor's disintegrating bank building, where a FOR SALE sign had just been nailed up.

"Maybe someone will buy it and fix it up," I said.

Dad's mouth tightened. "Taylor's let it go so long, it would cost a zillion dollars. Besides, I know at least one person who did offer to buy it, and Taylor said he wasn't interested."

For-sale signs had also been put up on the rest of Taylor's Main Street property. But more puzzling was a sign in huge red letters on the blacksmith shop.

"That'll look great for the house tour!" said dad.

THIS PROPERTY IS DYING
— ALONG WITH THE REST OF MAIN STREET!

The charred pork chops in Rawley's apartment and plummeting bricks from Art Taylor's bank were cautionary tales, reminding us that the hotel also had safety problems — most of all the solitary staircase that left us vulnerable to fire, and our first major job was to install an exit stairs from the back of the second story to the alley. But as soon as we started work we unearthed more rotted wood, and were discussing how to deal with it when a voice caused us to look up.

"Looks like you're onto something interesting!" It was Jerry Litzinger, a pleasant-looking man in his 30s with engaging gray eyes, dressed in a tradesman's jacket with lapels that flopped in the breeze.

"Hi, Jerry," said dad, before he introduced me. "What brings you out of the grocery?"

"Deliveries. Y'know, I think it's wonderful that you folks are fixing this place up. We could use a lot more of that kind of spirit." He glared at Taylor's bank before turning back to us. "Lemme know if I can help."

Dad nodded as Jerry disappeared up the alley. "He means it. He's one of the nicest guys around. Just elected to city council."

The new staircase cut through Lem Otley's apartment, and he stayed at his mother's a day or two while we worked, making more noise than a rock concert with our crowbars, hammers, and saws. Mom put a coat of bright blue paint on the new door we'd installed in the alley and people began noticing that we were up to something. Leroy and Ada Sue watched us work, and Mr. Black, an octogenarian who rented a room above McCracken's Bar, hobbled by on his cane and passed his watery eyes down the building.

"I remember when this became a *ho*tel in nineteen and twenty-three. I'm glad to see it fixed up!"

With the framework of 2x4s in place for the fire escape stairs we covered them with drywall, and dad showed me how to seal the seams with joint compound, commonly known as "mud." He loaded up a trowel of the gooey stuff and pressed it along the seam where two sheets of drywall met, covered it with a strip of joint tape, then smoothed down the tape with another layer of mud to create an invisible, fire-resistant joint.

"Looks like fun!" I said. But when I loaded up a trowel the mud fell in a glob onto my shoes.

"I've done that a hundred times," said dad.

I scooped up more mud and got it onto a seam, applied the tape, then added another layer of mud. The trowel dug into the tape, which fell to the floor like a piece of lasagna.

"It just takes practice," said dad.

My face reddened. I pressed the tape back into the seam and plastered it in place with mud. The tape held, but as I smoothed more mud over it, globules squeezed out the ends of the trowel, leaving a pair of ridges, and the tape crimped where the trowel snagged it.

"We can sand it down," said dad. "It'll be fine."

He diplomatically went on to another job as I tried feathering out the ridges. The mud squeezed out beneath the trowel and oozed down my sleeve. Twenty minutes later I finished the seam and stood back to appraise it. It was a mass of horizontal ridges, and the mud formed an unsightly mound. Compared with the seam dad had done, mine was something out of the Guggenheim Museum. I shuddered to think how much sanding it would take — and how much mudding there was to do throughout the hotel. Our materials chart estimated the renovation would require 200 of the 4x8-foot sheets of drywall — over 6,000 square feet with hundreds of seams.

I sighed and went on to the next seam, astonished at the skills I'd have to master to become a writer.

5. My Three Brothers

Our family gathered at my parents' house for Christmas, and I played the tape of my radio drama that had been recorded in New York for my three nieces, who demanded I hurry with the next episode. But there was no time for writing and I regretfully put all thoughts of the radio show at the back of my mind. Our new heat pumps arrived, with state-of-the-art air conditioning and climate control, and a truckload of Romex cable, receptacles, terminals, power panels, conduit, fuses, and hundreds of switches and connectors. The water heater that supplied our rental units sprang a leak that dad patched up, and Rawley Tate got drunk again, this time with a roast in his oven, but Leroy got to it before the hotel caught fire. The roof coating Art Taylor had put on failed to stop the rain from leaking in, and I crawled among the wilderness of rafters in the hotel's five attics in a futile search for the holes while dad hosed down the roof. I joined him on the roof to admire the view of the town, which stretched and yawned in the warmth of Indian summer. The river turned iridescent blue and darkened to indigo as daylight fled, and the sky became the color of champagne.

A week or so after Christmas, Rolland — second oldest of us four boys — drove down again from his home in Columbus, Ohio, to help me put in a tongue-and-groove floor for the new hallway.

"Reminds me of the farm," he said.

When my parents remodeled the Kentucky farm house we grew up in, Rolland and I got the assignment of flooring the main hallway. We horsed around but somehow finished the job. Only 155 pounds his senior year in high school, Rolland had mashed his way through countless footballers 50 pounds heavier than he to become All-State tackle, and like our oldest brother, Leon, was a former Marine.

"Floor's probably still there!" he said, measuring another board.

Rolland was vice president at a manufacturing firm in Columbus, and working with him was like turning back the clock.

Sid — my youngest brother — came from Indianapolis to help with the coffee shop. A former cop and hospital security supervisor who was nearing his final year in law school, he'd be working with a public prosecutor for the summer. We muscled a twenty-foot joist into place, then straightened up to rest our backs.

"What you gonna do for your first play?" he asked. He was himself a fine actor who could have gone into theatre, although his talent would certainly pay off in the courtroom.

"Something for a small cast," I laughed. "There's only me and Jo Ann!"

Then Leon, my oldest brother, came from California on business for his computer firm and stayed a few days to help. We went to Yesterdays for the chicken-and-dumpling special, where Cheryl greeted us with a cheerful "How're y'all?"

"We're all sold outta the chicken and dumplings," she added, in a drawl that stretched her vowels to ear-splitting lengths.

"How about a fishtail sandwich on rye?" I asked.

"I'm 'fraid we're outta rye. Ain't it terrible, the things we're outta!" She laughed, holding a hand in front of her mouth to conceal a broken tooth.

We settled for white bread, and Cheryl brought our salads, submerged in a sea of dressing. After she left dad turned to Leon, "See why we need a coffee shop?"

Leon chuckled. "I've got an idea about that. Rather than just breakfast, why not do lunch and dinner? Maximize the return on it."

"We'd have to hire extra help," I said, trying to spear some lettuce in the lake of dressing.

"But we'd have the income to do it," mom countered.

"You can have the best of both worlds if you *lease* it," said Leon.

Tall, muscular, and fit from training for a marathon, he had a crisp, no-nonsense manner that bespoke his seven years in the Marines. "Let's find a chef who wants to start his own place. We'll provide the building and utilities. The chef will provide the kitchen equipment."

I gave up on the lettuce. "It would certainly be great having a pro in the kitchen!"

Mom leaned in. "And if the Beehive doesn't open soon, we'll *have* to provide a place for our guests to eat."

The Beehive was the restaurant going into the building my parents had sold on the river, whose opening the owner had recently pushed back by another year.

Cheryl reappeared with her order pad. "Sorry, but we've only got *one* piece of fish tail!"

Leon helped us draft an income-projection analysis, which showed that a room occupancy of 25% at the Inn would allow us to break even, and 50% would yield a profit of $2,800 a month.

"Maybe Jo Ann and I can start looking for a house," I said.

Leon brought me back to reality. "Next thing's a market survey. Find out what prices people will pay, what kind of breakfast they want." He had an MBA from San Jose State and showed us how to go about it.

Then we moved to the living room by the Russian furnace to study dad's ground plan.

"We've only got enough room for five or six tables," I said. "But what if we expand the coffee shop into the yard?"

Dad got his pencil and sketched in a new wall that went eight feet beyond the existing one, adding 256 square feet of dining area.

"We need a really stunning window," he said. "A *bay* window. Framed with flowers and evergreens."

The hotel had been called the Parkview because of the city park across the street. But we thought it evoked an earlier age when hotels were oases of comfort in a pre-electric world, and decided to call it the *Lamplighter Inn*.

The next day dad called the state capitol at Frankfort to find out what we had to do to open the Lamplighter, and was referred to the Division of Building Codes Enforcement — which promised to send the code books.

"They want us to hire an architect before we start construction," dad said as soon as he hung up.

"But we've already started!" I said.

"As far as Frankfort's concerned, we've just made the building *safe*. Tenants were there when we bought it, and a fire-exit stairway should have been put in years ago."

Dad knew an architect who'd done restoration work for the SHARE museum, Robert Lape, who agreed to look at the Inn in a few months. Dad was a habitual doodler, and during the conversation he sketched a whimsical Dr. Seuss face with over-sized eyes and whispy hair.

"Lape's draftsman gets thirty-five an hour, and Lape charges fifty for himself."

"What'll this do to do our budget?" mom demanded.

Our budget was $73,500, but the coffee shop expansion and Lape's architectural fee would increase it significantly. I was growing uneasy about what we'd taken on, and went strolling by the river to clear my head. It was warm for January and a breeze carried the rumble of a diesel engine up from the water, where a spotlight flicked back and forth across the driftwood. It was a Coast Guard cutter, anchoring for the night on its tour of the river, and a crewman stood on the prow to call instructions in a soft, musical voice as the gangplank dropped. The water licked the stones as the odor of mud and decaying cattails washed over me.

February fogged the river so thickly that for some days the ferry vanished and reappeared like a lightning bug. Coal barges three football fields long surged by Augusta to heat the Midwest — one-eyed dragons churning their way through the frothing water. Snow blanketed Kentucky and I shoveled it from the walkway around the garage and worked up a sweat chopping firewood for the Russian furnace in my parents' house.

With the fire escape stairs completed we began clearing out the wreckage of the old guest rooms — hauling off lath and plaster, radiators and water pipe — then sorted through furnishings and fixtures to see what could be salvaged. My Uncle Ray and Aunt Margie came from Illinois to pitch in. Like dad, Uncle Ray had been an engineer with AT&T, and he helped install the first of our heat pumps in Leroy and Ada Sue's apartment. The heat pumps were a significant step in our work. They would make the building safer by allowing us to eliminate the quirky old gas heaters, and would heat the Inn more uniformly while reducing heating costs. But installing them was a mammoth undertaking that tried our skills, and occasionally forced us to negotiate our tenants' idiosyncrasies. While we put in the first heat pump, Leroy shut off his TV and wedged his wiry frame in beside Ada Sue's sprawling girth on the sofa to watch us work.

"Lemme know if you wanna go huntin' some time," he said to me, motioning at the shotgun leaning in the corner of the room.

"I certainly will."

"Do y'all have another set of springs for that bed?" Ada Sue asked, her hair bunched into a rubber band like the stem of a squash. "It's about to fall apart under all the weight!"

I picked up a louvered aluminum grille that was supposed to fit onto the exterior of the heat pump and held it up for my uncle to see. "I think it goes like this."

Leroy and Ada Sue leaned forward on the sofa as Ray read the instructions. "It's supposed to have clamps."

"But it's got several sets of holes," I said. "Which do we use?"

"Why don't we just try it?"

We hurried into our coats and went out to the scaffold we'd set up in the alley as Leroy and Ada Sue pressed their faces to the window. I held the grille against the heat pump.

"Do we use the square holes, or the round ones?"

Ray knelt closer. "These flanges oughta give us a clue."

Leroy got out a beer and Ada Sue opened a bag of potato chips.

"Maybe a part's missing," I offered.

Dad called from the foot of the scaffold. "Aren't you finished? I thought two geniuses would have that done by now!"

Ray chuckled. "There's room up here for another genius!"

Dad climbed up and took the instructions. "We oughta be able to figure this out."

"Sure oughta," said Ray.

It was now dark and I blew on my fingers to warm them in the nipping cold when mom and Aunt Margie came by. "I don't think there's any more room up here," I said.

"Why don't you guys take a break," mom replied.

We went to Yesterdays for muffins and hot chocolate, where mom and my aunt showed us a brass plate they'd found in one of the Parkview's former guest rooms.

STOP! HAVE YOU LEFT ANYTHING?

PLEASE TURN OFF THE LIGHTS!

They'd also found a 1937 newspaper with a Parkview ad that was lining a bureau drawer. It advertised unfurnished rooms for four dollars a week, and meal tickets for five dollars a week.

"What if someone shows up with a ticket?" Aunt Margie laughed.

We solved the dilemma of the grille cover, and dad switched on the breaker at the power panel. The heat pump hummed, spreading warmth into Leroy and Ada Sue's living room, while they parked themselves on the sofa and stared as if it were their newborn baby.

6. Ferry of Fortune

When *Guys and Dolls* opened in Texas I sent Jo Ann a dozen roses. She planned to visit her mother in Arizona before returning to Augusta, but phoned that the director who'd hired her for the upcoming season of summer stock wanted her to help audition in New York.

"I can't come to Augusta till *April*," she lamented.

"Well, the weather will be better then," I said. "It's downright dreary."

As the days sped by I got better at putting mud on drywall, and spent numberless hours installing heat pumps. When I worked in Lem's apartment, Dotty was napping in the bedroom with a liquor-soaked rag to ease a toothache, and Lem seized his chance to show me a clock he'd gotten for Dotty's birthday with a color picture of Jesus on the dial.

"We don't go to church like we oughta, but at least we'll have Jesus in the house!"

I moved on to Leroy and Ada Sue's bedroom, where they sprawled on the bed to watch. The subject got onto books and Leroy confided that he'd never read one.

"Too busy hunting?" I offered.

He unraveled a thread from his stocking cap. "Caint read."

I looked at him in surprise. "You can learn."

"We never done much readin' at my home, neither," said Ada Sue. "Too much fightin'."

"Sounds like you came from a big family."

"There was twenty-three of us. But eleven died."

Later that month Leroy and Ada Sue got into a brawl. He slugged her and she went after him with a butcher knife — making me wonder how her eleven siblings had died.

The day I finally got to Rawley's apartment to install a heat pump it had snowed enough to bury Augusta in its own ice age, and I put planks below the scaffold to keep it from being swallowed in the slush. Rawley came home from his shift at McCracken's Bar, lit a cigarette, and turned on his TV to a *Mayberry, RFD* rerun.

"Be out of your way soon," I promised.

"Do whatever you have to," he replied, running a hand through his Dagwood Bumstead hair. It was no secret that Rawley rarely made it past noon without boozing, which he expressed in brash conviviality, but at the moment he was sober. "Catherine McCracken bet me I couldn't go a year without taking a drink. I told her I could and we wagered fifty dollars. I'm gonna *win* that fifty dollars!"

I considered adding another fifty dollars on top of Catherine McCracken's fifty, in hopes that if Rawley stayed sober it would lessen the chances of him burning down the Inn.

As February wore on we cleared out so much plaster and lath that we had to rent a dumpster, which we crammed to the brim twice a week. Mom refinished chairs and tables, and dad kept the apartments afloat by repairing faucets, soldering leaks, and nursing the battered old water heater. Fuses blew and dad ran in temporary wiring until permanent lines could be laid down. Rain and snow sent more water cascading into the rooms, and we made frequent explorations below the maze of rafters in search of holes to patch.

March entered wet and raw. The TV production of *Huckleberry Finn* filmed in Augusta a year earlier was broadcast, with the legendary Lillian Gish in the role of Aunt Polly, and we knocked off to watch it. Outside, the Ohio River — masquerading as the Mississippi on my parents' TV — softened its stark winter colors to the blue-gray of a fine silk screen painting. The wind lashed Art Taylor's dilapidated bank, toppling more bricks to the sidewalk and threatening to send sheets of tin slicing into the Inn. Taylor was also creating fallout from the ferry, which belonged to a group of stockholders of which he was president. My parents were also stockholders, as was the local doctor, Milton Brindley — who discovered that Taylor had never obtained the ferry's insurance, for which he'd been paid $7,000.

"Damn ferry's been operating without insurance for *months!*" Brindley said as he ran by the house one day.

There was also evidence that federal funds paid to the ferry in a program to train new pilots may have been misused. My parents and other stockholders tried to recover the payments made to Taylor and remove him as president, but ran into stiff opposition from Taylor's numerous friends among the remaining stockholders.

"Taylor's father was a state representative," dad explained. "Very influential, and Taylor must know half the people in Kentucky."

Taylor's wife was a respected high school teacher. Taylor's son, now in college, was well liked, and his daughter was high school homecoming queen.

The ferry was such a powerful piece of Augusta lore that the legal wrangling stirred up considerable attention throughout the region. The stakes were higher for us: More than half of our future guests would come from Ohio, so if the ferry went under, we could kiss the

Lamplighter goodbye. By a stroke of good luck the ferry was bought by a man who promised to keep it operating whatever happened. And at the same time, Mayor Weldon warned Art Taylor to either make the bank safe, or risk having the city condemn it.

7. Rot Run Riot

Inspired by granddad's art book I drafted the lettering for our business stationery and ordered a thousand sheets and envelopes, printed in russet-colored ink on cream wove paper. We prepared a questionnaire and gave it to everyone we could, and learned that they wanted fresh-baked muffins with breakfast and rooms *without* TVs or phones. The returning questionnaires projected the kind of B&Bs Jo Ann and I had favored on our visits to New England and the British Isles, and I was getting excited about the guests we'd have. People interested in travel, music, books, museums, and antiques.

To brush up on our business skills dad and I attended a two-day seminar sponsored by the Small Business Administration at Northern Kentucky University. The seminar gave us a much-needed dose of reality, and made us realize that our goal of having two rooms ready for paying guests by the fall — with the support structure required of the rest of the Inn — wasn't realistic. And there were dozens of vital details we hadn't considered.

"Let's shoot for May of next year," said dad.

That gave us fifteen months to our opening, plenty of time to address those dozens of details. But it was fifteen months without income. Equipment bids were pouring in, and we'd just signed a $28,000 contract with Lucas Aluminum for windows and siding. This raised our budget to $122,000, toward which my parents had already invested thousands of dollars.

"Maybe it's time we got a loan," I suggested one night over the macaroni special at Yesterdays.

Dad nodded as he pried a piece of over-cooked macaroni from his fork. "I'll get an appointment with the bank."

Before the 54 new windows could go in, the old ones had to be removed, and the wall sills, headers, and studs repaired. We replaced rotted framing for days on end — redoing the damaged studs, shoring up door frames, nailing down loose sheathing beneath the clapboard. We went through a one-hundred-pound box of 10d common nails in a matter of days, slamming them into the iron-like oak studs. I changed hands every few minutes, the blows echoing like gunshots in the alley behind McCracken's, where Duke glared at me from the end of his leash.

The first day of spring I moved to the other side of the Inn, raking off the old shingles to expose the poplar siding, where rusted nail heads showed the location of the corner post. I started a nail and it sank in without resistance. I figured I'd hit a gap between the plate and the corner post and started another nail a bit higher, but it also went in too easily.

Damn, I thought.

I pried loose the board and found the corner post was as rotted as a honeycomb. Dad came to see how I was doing, and needed but a glance. "Ouch!"

"I can't see what's holding up this corner of the building!" I said.

We set up our scaffold and worked until dark removing the siding, and by next day discovered rotted framing reaching well into the second story. We dropped everything else and worked straight through the second day, me on the scaffold and dad on the ladder, pulling with crowbars at nails that whined like tormented souls. Dad strained at a particularly stubborn nail until it suddenly broke free, sending him toppling from the ladder. I ran over to him as he rubbed his shoulder and pulled himself up from the grass.

"Are you all right?"

"Yeah." He brushed himself off, got the crowbar and started back up the ladder. "Don't tell your mother. She'll have a fit."

"Don't worry about me!" said Mom, frowning from a second story window. "If you want to break your neck, that's your business!"

Rot had spread through the Inn like metastasized cancer, and the next day we found a badly decayed 12" x 12" plate that was a main support for the second story. We hurried inside to find sunlight peeping in from the outside.

Dad snapped, "Get upstairs and warn your mother!"

I ran up while dad collected 2 x 4s. Mom was safely elsewhere, and we wedged in the 2 x 4s below the ceiling beam. For the next ten days the Inn lay open like a body on an operating table as we replaced damaged wood. Wrens circled in search of their old nesting places, warning us that spring was on a forced march in our direction, and I wrote Jo Ann that the extensive rot had set us back another two weeks.

Although my parents urged me to withdraw what I needed to live on from our account as part of my salary, we had such a tight budget I decided to look into substitute teaching. I met with Mack Wallace, superintendent of the Augusta school, whose office was in the Farmers Liberty Bank building at the top of an absurdly long staircase that squeaked like an old saddle.

"The main thing about substituting is that the kids try to get you off the subject," said Wallace. He crossed his legs, showing a crescent of white calf above his sock, then surveyed me through black-framed glasses to see if his comment had struck home. "You can't let 'em get you off the subject!"

"I'll watch out for that," I said, and told Wallace I'd taken education courses as part of my bachelor's degree, and had been a teaching assistant at Ohio University for my MFA in theatre.

"What about art? Can you teach art?"

I pictured a roomful of children covered with finger paint.

"Our problem is we can't hold art teachers. They wanna be near the big cities. If we don't hold onto one pretty *soon* we may have trouble with our accreditation!"

"Well, I can certainly teach art."

But my first call as a substitute was for home economics and sex education.

8. Entangling Alliances

I'd seldom gone to church in New York, but now it seemed a good way to take my mind off the rubble of the Inn and meet people. I also wanted to hear good music, but the attendance at Trinity United Methodist Church had shrunken to a couple of dozen regulars, and the choir had shrunken to nothing. It was a Sunday in April that Ann Altherton, the pastor's wife, led the charge to revive the choir by waylaying mom at the church door. Mom considered a moment before joining Mrs. Altherton in the choir stall. Then Mrs. Altherton aimed her enthusiasm at me.

"We need some *men!*"

"I don't sing very well."

"Oh yes, you do! I sat in front of you last week and I *heard* you!"

My real reason was Wednesday choir practice. I was already substitute teaching at least once a week, and had become a SHARE member and had gone to several meetings. If I had to take more hours away from the Inn, I wanted to spend them writing. Five months since I'd left New York and I hadn't touched my novel. My revised radio play had gone to the agents, but nothing had come of it.

A few other women joined Mrs. Atherton in the choir stall, and when they burst into the first hymn mom's soprano voice stood out. After the service organist Sharon Carl pulled me aside.

"Would you be willing to take over a Sunday school class? We desperately need someone for the younger grades."

"Well, we've got such a tremendous amount of work to do at the hotel, I don't think I can."

Then at the top of the aisle I was ambushed by Mrs. Haley, a grandmotherly woman with a bun of gray hair who pressed my hand.

"What this church needs is *younger* people to take over. The board of trustees can't get anything done. All they do is argue!"

I wondered if there was a bull's-eye taped to my back. Dad held his tongue, but I knew he agreed with Mrs. Haley. In an attempt to get the church affairs rolling along he'd just accepted the board presidency. He'd also been appointed secretary for the city's Hydro-Electric Board, created to plan a water-power plant on the river with some of the revenues going to Augusta. But I doubted my own ability to do so many things at once.

"Maybe some day," I said to Mrs. Haley.

Jo Ann flew in from New York, and since her birthday had come in March, I baked a belated chocolate cake. Then I showed her our progress at the Inn. Her eyes widened as she climbed the new fire-escape stairs and ran her hand over the freshly varnished woodwork.

"I'm impressed!"

She kept busy by writing an article for *Dramatics* magazine, and baking muffins and lasagna. She came with me to the university library to research the nuts-and-bolts of hotel operation, and we explored second-hand furniture stores in Maysville, where we bought a china cupboard blackened by time and neglect. It was a 1930s waterfall pattern, with a cornice capped with a carved plume and feathers. We stripped off the old varnish, exposing yellow-green poplar, golden maple, and cream-colored butternut. We uncovered hardwood veneers with chevrons and Art Deco inlays.

"The first piece of furniture for our house," I said.

"As soon as summer stock's over I'll know what my fall schedule's gonna be," she said, as we discussed our wedding plans.

9. Del

May dispersed the last of the fog, then inundated us with rain and an increasing tide of bills. We finally got our meeting with Farmers Liberty Bank VP Nick Colvin to apply for a loan. Our proposal included an income-projection analysis prepared by the Small Business Center at the university, where we'd attended the seminar. Colvin studied it with raised eyebrows.

"Pretty impressive!" Smoke from his cigarette mingled with his gray hair as dad and I studied the framed prints of tobacco farming on the walls. After a minute or two Colvin pursed his lips. "I'd like to know your thoughts on Augusta. How important are the ferry and Clopay?"

"*Very* important," said dad. "The new owner of the ferry is talking about running cruises, which oughta draw more tourists to town."

Dad wore a tan suit and blue tie, reminding me how distinguished he looked all those years coming home from AT&T with his suit and attaché case. Nowadays he evoked a sea captain more than a business executive.

"And Clopay's vital to the town," he continued. "Certainly will be to the Inn!"

I jumped in. "We're putting in a conference room with slide projector and VCR. And our coffee shop will allow businesses to have lunch so Clopay engineers won't have to drive back and forth to Maysville."

Colvin stubbed out his cigarette. "We'll probably go for eleven percent interest."

As we walked home dad heaved a sigh. "I was hoping for *ten* percent!"

But a few days later our bank application slipped into the background. Augusta had a government-subsidized loan program to help new businesses, with $17,000 available. Although the loans had a short pay-back period of five years, the interest rate was only five percent.

And we needed the money desperately. We'd signed a $14,000 contract for furnace and air conditioning units to the same supplier whom we'd just paid $11,000 for heat pumps. This was added to the $28,000 obligation to Lucas Aluminum for windows and siding — plus what we were spending on building supplies and utilities. Lucas was set to put in the windows the end of May, and the siding the first week of June. So the clock was running and that night we reviewed our schedule.

We still had window frames to repair and heat pumps to install, but the big job was the coffee shop expansion — which had been delayed by rain, leaving us three weeks to finish. We'd already dug the foundation trench, but the pressure-treated wood to go into it hadn't arrived from Miller Lumber Company, a local supplier. I was substituting at school, making it hard to keep up with our work. Teaching paid $34 a day and I was trying to save enough during the final weeks of school to last me through the summer. Clouds continually darkened the valley and pounded us with rain and hail that turned the trench into a quagmire. As we bailed out the water a Miller Lumber truck brought all of the 2x4s and 2x12s we needed *except* the pressure-treated wood.

"I feel like a race horse who's stuck in the gate!" exclaimed dad.

When Miller Lumber finally brought the pressure-treated wood it was May 11 and we set about building the coffee shop with a fury. We erected foundations in the sodden trenches and laid down the main footing beam for the floor joists, stringing up work lights and going well past dark till we were too tired to go on. May was half gone and rain continued to inundate us. We installed the joists and subflooring between cloudbursts, and raised the studs like masts in an angry sea. We tacked up tarpaulins, but the water broke through like bursting damns.

We're not gonna make it! I thought.

Then my sister Del showed up, the baby of the family.

"What needs to be done?" she asked, slipping a tool belt around her denim shorts. Del was a little taller than mom, a slender and attractive young woman with the strength and agility of an athlete and the grace of a dancer.

"Door frame," said dad.

"Heat pumps," I added. "Windows. Insulation — everything!"

"Why don't you two go on with the framing," she said. "I'll tackle the insulation."

"It's a pain in the ass," I warned, pointing out that the joists had to be strung with wire at two-foot intervals to hold the insulation. "And there's only a *foot* to work in between the joists and concrete!"

Del slipped a hammer into her tool belt, and when we came back a few hours later she had the wire tacked up as neat as telephone lines and pink insulation floating like waves of cotton candy. She knelt to cut the last piece of insulation, her hair tied back and sweat dripping from her tanned arms. It was the same dead-earnest expression she'd had when knocking a ball into a corner pocket as Indiana University Women's Billiards Champion. She used to go to the local pool hall to clean up on the factory workers, until word spread that she couldn't be beaten and the men stopped playing for money. She came again the next day and helped nail up the sheathing for the walls, and by the end of the weekend the coffee shop was back on schedule.

"How about moving to Augusta?" I asked. "You could be co-innkeeper!"

"No way!" she laughed.

10. Ladders

The final job to prepare the way for Lucas Aluminum's window and siding crew was the coffee shop roof, and one evening dad and I nailed in the rafters as the waning sun rays warmed our backs and shouts wafted over from a tennis match in the park across the street. It was splendid weather, lazy spring weather, and during supper on my parents' front deck we'd watched a mallard float down the river. It luxuriated in the current, bobbing at insects until it was a brown speck in the vast expanse of green.

"We oughta get in a game," said dad. "Before the summer gets away from us."

We had played tennis during my visits to Augusta over the years, but hadn't gone to the courts that were a mere hop from the Inn's front door more than once or twice since I'd moved from New York.

The final sun rays departed as dad moved his ladder to put in the last rafter, and out of the corner of my eye I saw him reach out and brace himself on a 2x4. The nail holding the 2x4 popped loose and dad fell headfirst, throwing out an arm in a wild effort to catch himself. He struck the floor and cried out as I rushed down my ladder. His arm was twisted and the wrist bone poked at the skin.

"I'm afraid it's broken," he said, stooping in pain.

I helped him to his feet and let his tool belt fall to the ground as we hurried to the house.

"Don't worry," mom said as we went through the door.

She brushed the hair from dad's eyes and helped him to the car while Rolland, who was visiting, phoned the Maysville hospital. They told him Dr. Shouse was on call, their orthopedic surgeon. Thirty minutes later we got dad to the examination room, then mom and I went to the admissions desk to do the paperwork.

"Dr. Shouse is on vacation," said the nurse.

"But we phoned!" I protested.

The nurse straightened some papers. "Well. . . . whoever you spoke to was mistaken. Dr. Shouse is away."

Mom drew in a breath. Most people raise their voices when they're angry, but mom gets quieter. "Who else is available?"

"The nearest would be Lexington."

"That's eighty miles!" I said.

"I'll make some calls," the nurse finally offered.

A doctor took x-rays and came out an hour later. "Wrist bone's badly shattered."

Dad's face was marble white as he cradled his arm. He wasn't a stranger to pain, having had his tonsils removed without anesthesia on the Indiana farm when he was a boy, and there was that German machine-gun wound — suffered before spending some scary days in a lice-ridden prison camp. He could stand a measure of pain, but this wasn't World War II, for God's sake, much less a farm in the 1930s. The doctor gave him some pain killer, then another hour ticked by before the nurse appeared.

"They're expecting you at Saint Elizabeth South."

Saint Elizabeth at 70 miles was only slightly nearer than the Lexington hospitals, and I drove us across the Maysville bridge to Ohio, whose US 52 was smoother than Kentucky's Route 8. Another 90 minutes dragged by as I ran a gauntlet of small town stoplights scattered between the sad motels and isolated farms, and got stuck behind a succession of trucks. We slipped by Point Pleasant, birthplace of Ulysses S. Grant, and I regretted that we'd never taken time to go there. Oughta do a few things like that, I thought. Play some tennis and take a boat on the river, even if we didn't go all the way to Borneo.

11. Loans

"Dr. Schmitz has come in," said the nurse, assuring us dad was in good hands.

We'd reached the hospital at ten o'clock, four hours after dad broke his arm.

Schmitz performed surgery the next morning, and while dad was in the recovery room Schmitz showed us the x-ray. He was in his 30s, with rugged good looks and very much down to business as he snapped on the viewer.

"Not a perfect repair, but Charles should get ninety percent of the movement back in his arm." I saw the silhouette of the shattered ends of the radius and ulna, with a second break in the ulna and a bone chip wedged in like shrapnel. "Because Charles is so active, I'm taking a radical approach," said Schmitz.

When dad was wheeled back to his room we saw what Schmitz meant. Running along dad's arm from elbow to thumb was a graphite brace — the material used in Olympics-grade bicycles. The brace was secured to the hand and forearm with pins that penetrated the flesh, threaded like wood screws into the bone. It was disturbing to look at.

"It's got it all over a cast for freedom of movement," said Schmitz. "The pins will hold the wrist bones perfectly still so Charles can exercise his fingers and thumb."

The night of the accident mom and I had gotten home at two a.m. We'd been in such a rush to the hospital that I hadn't locked up the Inn, and as I went over to do it I found dad's tool belt where it had dropped on the path. It had gotten a heck of a beating over the years and the leather was patched with duct tape. I wiped off the dew and hung it over the saw table.

Three days after surgery dad walked to the Inn on legs wobbly from pain killer to see how things were going. He was struggling to master the art of sleeping flat on his back. The first night he'd rolled over in his sleep, jarring the pins embedded in the bones with a dagger-like jolt of pain.

"Take it easy on that ladder!" he said.

"I certainly will," I said, grinning at him.

The deadline for the new windows was hurtling at us, and I rushed the coffee shop roof — making the compound bird-mouth and plumb cuts on the rafters to form the angles for the hip joists, trying to remember high school geometry, but relying mostly on hammer-by-the-seat-of-my-pants carpentry. I botched up the cut on the first rafter, threw it aside and started another as Rolland arrived from Columbus to help.

"Am I glad to see you!" I said.

While his arm mended dad returned to his drafting board to refine his drawings, but he was restless and slipped over to monitor our work, his arm cradled in a sling.

"Looks good," he said.

Later on we found him in the shop, the tool belt strapped to his waist as he took measurements for another job. His birthday came a week later, and mom baked angel food cake, his favorite dessert. I debated giving dad a poem I was working on, about how he taught me and my brothers to use tools when we were kids, but I hadn't finished it and gave him a book instead. Someone else's writing.

May ended, and our increasing anxiety over our mounting expenses drove us back to the bank to find out what was happening with the loan. The paperwork was bogged down with Nick Colvin on vacation, so we hurried our application on the city loan, realizing it might be our only recourse.

We finished the coffee shop roof with 36 hours to spare, and Lucas Aluminum's four-man crew installed the windows — 54 energy-efficient units that changed the Inn as though it had put on glass slippers. A few days later Lucas' crew unloaded their trucks and nailed on the vinyl siding, starting with aluminum-coated Styrofoam insulation that blazed in the sun like a Zeppelin before fitting on the blue siding. The Inn was finished June 21, transformed from a patched and bedraggled nightmare to a glowing country hostelry.

Jerry Litzinger drove by in the grocery van and slammed on his brakes. "Whose place is this?" he shouted out the window.

"What do you think?" I asked.

"You guys can be proud," he said with a tremor. "I bet it never looked this good in the good old days!"

People who'd driven by the Inn for years without a glance slowed down and stared as if the Queen Mary had docked, and our phone rang with inquiries about our opening date.

"I've got family visiting this summer," a woman said. "Can y'all put `em up?"

People asked for jobs and showered us with résumés. Omer Johnson interviewed us for the *Kentucky Post*, a bearded, white-haired reporter who could pass for Colonel Sanders. The story was headed "Family Rehabbing Augusta Hotel." This spurred more phone calls and raised our spirits with the enthusiasm the community was showing in our project. But little did everyone know that *indoors* the Inn was still a shambles, and we were forced to put up a sign:

~ COMING ~

THE LAMPLIGHTER INN, BED & BREAKFAST

SPRING OF 1987

The day the windows went in Jo Ann came from New York. My parents asked us to lunch on their front deck, and after the meal I took Jo Ann's hand.

"We're *finally* getting married!"

Mom let out a cry and hugged Jo Ann.

"This'll be our big event of the year!" said dad, slapping me on the shoulder.

I'd neglected the cupboard Jo Ann and I had been refinishing, and vowed to spend an hour or two a week on it till it was done to hold her books and musical scores. She stayed three days, then flew to New York to work on *Last of the Red Hot Lovers* and *West Side Story* at the summer theatre.

"When you come back the Inn will be halfway finished," I promised.

When we filed our city loan application we learned that no one else had applied, and we were ecstatic at having a good shot at getting the full $17,000. But a week later city manager Judy Bonar stopped by in her car.

"Art Taylor rushed in an application just before the deadline. Something for that old bank of his. He musta talked real good, `cause the Board's recommending that he get half the money."

For a minute we couldn't speak.

"He wants the money for the *bank?*" said dad. "That amount of money wouldn't begin to save that monstrosity!"

Judy shrugged and drove off, then mom erupted. "Well, that does it. With the political cronies Taylor's got, he'll probably get the entire loan!"

"Maybe not," said dad. "The Board recommends who gets the loan, but the final decision rests with city council."

We knew that two of the six council members — Jerry Litzinger and SHARE president Lane Stephenson — were fed up with Taylor's intransigence over the crumbling bank, and would undoubtedly support our application. We were uncertain about the sympathies of two other council members, and feared the remaining two might champion Taylor's application.

The city council met the next day, and we went to learn the fate of our application, sitting among a few dozen onlookers, including an Augusta *Times* reporter. Taylor beamed at us from a seat across the aisle. In a newspaper interview he'd refuted the allegations about his ferry boat practices, and he brimmed with confidence. His tan face was bell-pepper red in contrast with his nattily trimmed white hair and cream-colored dress shirt. Taylor went by his middle name, Art, but his first name was Roy, and I saw that his shirt cuffs were monogrammed with all three initials. RAT.

Mayor Weldon sucked on a cigarette and gaveled the meeting to order with a guttural drawl that reminded me of the old character actor Eugene Pallette. An hour later Weldon got to the loan.

"If I remember my ABCs, Taylor comes before Tongret, so we'll listen to you first, Art."

Taylor's slacks had a razor-sharp crease and the light bounced from his highly buffed shoes. His shirt collar opened like the petals of a flower, and he exuded cologne as he handed copies of his proposal to the council. He thanked the council for letting him speak, and explained that his proposal didn't have the actual details of his plans. Not as such.

"What I'm really asking the city for is a chance to *stabilize* the bank building. My estimate of the situation is that, at this time, traffic patterns on Main Street don't warrant any renovation of the bank, because I can't be certain of earning enough rent to cover my costs. Most of you are business people and understand that." His words oozed out like tanning oil. "We have to face it; there's simply *no activity* on Main Street. Whatever investment is made in the old bank must come from the city loan fund."

Taylor sat down and council member Lane Stephenson raised his hand. "The main thing I'd like to know is, if you got the loan, would you be willing to match it with your own money to make the bank safe?"

Taylor smiled. "It depends on contingencies and patterns of growth. . . . My investment would take that into account."

Lane looked as if a bee had buzzed him. "I'm not sure I caught that. What I'm asking is, would you be willing to invest some of your *own* money if you got the loan?"

Taylor nodded. "I'd certainly look into it. We'll do our best to look over the levels of support from the city, as well as the degree of business activity in town to see if it continues to move favorably toward a closer inspection of that issue."

Lane plowed a hand through his hair. "I guess I'm not being clear. If you're given a loan from the revolving fund, would you — or would you not — be willing to invest your *own* money to repair the bank?"

Taylor's smile sharpened, and he repeated what he'd just said in different words. Lane flung himself back in his chair. "Forget it!"

Council member Mike Bach ignored Taylor and turned to Mayor Weldon. "Could you tell me why the condemnation suit against the bank was delayed?"

Weldon released a lung full of smoke. "'Cause Art promised to start making repairs on it. But so far it ain't happened."

Jerry Litzinger's gray eyes flashed. "This business of needing a taxpayer-supported loan before you begin work on the bank is nonsense. Here's Mr. Tongret, who's taken the bull by the horns, while you've let your building fall apart. Then you put up that sign last winter about Main Street dying, putting the blame on the town. That rubbed me the wrong way!"

Taylor's smile came unriveted, and Mayor Weldon conferred with Judy Bonar in Eugene Pallette undertones. It was our turn, and I got ready to hand out our meticulously typed proposal. The cover letter on our russet-colored stationery gave a breakdown of the $40,000 we'd already invested in the Inn, and summarized the income projections made by the Small Business Center. We offered our blueprints for the council's review, and explained how the Inn would aid the town's economic and cultural improvement. It looked very professional and my heart was slamming to get started.

"We can't really decide about Art's proposal till we look inside the bank to see what shape it's in," said Weldon. "We're gonna ask the Maysville Fire Department to look at it." Weldon peered at us through the tobacco haze. "We'll take up the Tongrets' proposal next week."

12. Hired Hands

We invited the council members to visit the Inn to see for themselves the improvements we'd made, then charged ahead with our work. There were still heaps of plaster and lath to remove, and as our lodger Leroy Raines was still unemployed from the factory, we decided to offer him a job. We'd given work to Ada Sue mowing the hotel lawn, but stopped because she insisted on going barefoot while mowing. Leroy's door was unlocked when I knocked, and I found him in bed with a sheet over his head. The AC and an electric fan were running full blast.

"You wanna job?" I asked.

"My back's gone out," he said, peering at me from under the sheet with his stocking cap pulled down to his eyes.

I glanced at the roaring AC unit and the fan, and left the apartment. I thought about hiring Sambo, who spent his summers like his winters at the pool hall, but learned he was in the county jail for God knows what. Then Dwight Atkins appeared, a nineteen-year-old National Guard member. He looked strong and healthy, with a neat appearance, intense blue eyes and sandy hair, evenly trimmed above the collar of his olive drab National Guard jacket.

"I'll have to start you at minimum wage," I said.

Dwight twisted the toe of his shoe in the sawdust. "I'll do the work. M'girlfriend's five months pregnant and I gotta get some money real fast."

I had him strip out plaster in one of our second-story rooms, and a couple of hours later went up to see how he was doing. "Looks like a coal mine in here," I laughed.

Dwight pulled off his respirator. "I've seen worse."

"You're pretty good with that crowbar."

Dwight grinned. "'Cause I play a lotta softball!"

"How's your team doing?"

He removed his goggles. "We clobbered 'em Friday night. I got two homers."

"This is coming along," I said. Then I noticed cigarette butts on the floor and a bulge in Dwight's T-shirt pocket. "I'd appreciate it if you didn't smoke indoors. This place is a tinder box."

He smiled sheepishly. "I know I oughta quit. But it's a habit."

Council members Jerry Litzinger, Lane Stephenson, and Jody Maloney accepted our invitation to see the work we'd done at the Lamplighter.

"Good heavens!" said Jerry at the lobby entrance. "You've wrought a miracle!"

Jody ran her hand over the mantelpiece. "I haven't been in here since I was a girl. What memories. . . !"

I paraded them through the rooms and explained what we planned to do, then led them back to the lobby. Jody held out her hand. "Thanks for the tour. I'm impressed!"

Lane stared out the window at a tree sprouting from the roof of Art Taylor's bank. "As far as the loan goes, you've got *my* support!"

"Ours, too!" said Jody and Jerry.

That put three of the six council members on our side. At worst, then, it would be a deadlock and Mayor Weldon would have to break the tie.

A few days later Dwight showed up an hour late. I was busy in the lobby, and he slipped in and shuffled his feet while waiting for me to speak.

"Where you been?"

"M'sister was supposed to wake me up, but she didn't do it."

He was late again the following week, and mumbled that he was toying with the thought of getting an alarm clock so he wouldn't have to depend on his sister.

"You can get one for five dollars at the drugstore," I said.

I gave him an advance on his pay and he bought one. We moved him downstairs to tear out an old ceiling, and he was whaling away at it from the top of a ladder when a *kaboom* brought me running. I found him sprawled on the floor with the crowbar at his feet.

"I slipped!" he said.

Mom rushed in. "Alan's father can tell you about nails that come loose from the top of a ladder!" Dwight smiled awkwardly, and mom laughed as she helped him up. "You'd better go home for the rest of the day." We gave him an ice pack, but he came back after lunch with only a slight swelling on his nose.

"Safety first!" I reminded him as he went back up the ladder.

But I failed to follow my own advice as I retreated to the cellar to smash up the ancient cast iron furnace and its octopus-like network of pipes with a sledge hammer. Dripping wet in the humid July heat and impatient to finish, I wiped the mist from my goggles and swung the sledge hammer with my full strength. A metallic ringing filled my ears as something sped toward me like a Major League fast ball that knocked me against one of the stone walls. Pain shot through my head and the cellar spun around. The goggles were unbroken, but blood dripped onto the dirt floor between my feet. A chunk of cast iron the size of my fist had struck the goggles with such force that their rim had cut into my face. The work light went blurry and I thought, Christ, no health insurance, and I'm gonna be blind!

Blood streamed down my face as I hurried to my apartment and looked at myself in the bathroom mirror. A deep gash hovered just above my right eyelid. I rinsed it in hydrogen peroxide and held a tissue to my eye as I walked to Dr. Brindley's office. It was closed and I remembered it was Brindley's day at the hospital. I went back to my apartment and phoned the clinic at Brooksville, the country seat, eight miles away.

"Come straight over!" said the nurse.

A half hour later Dr. Christiansen probed the wound, and I lay there trying to guess what life would be like without an eye. I'd read Sammy Davis, Jr.'s autobiography and knew it wasn't a picnic.

Dr. Christiansen put down his lens. "Quarter of an inch lower and we'd be cutting out a black patch for you."

He gave me six stitches and a tetanus shot, and when I got home I took some aspirin to quell a thunderous headache. I had some double vision — which Dr. Christiansen said was to be expected for a day or two — but I went to the closet and dug out the fencing mask I'd used when taking lessons at the Santelli School of Fencing in New York. I returned to the cellar and revenged myself on the furnace as I pummeled it into a pile of scrap.

Then Judy Bonar called from the city office with even better news.

"The Maysville fire chief looked at Art Taylor's bank and had a fit. Said if it was in Maysville it would be torn down *ee-mmediately*. That gave the city council the ammunition it needed to deny Taylor's loan request, and all six council members voted that the bank be condemned and torn down *ASAP.*"

"About time!" I said.

"There's more. The last thing council did was decide on your request. They voted *unanimously* to loan the full seventeen thousand dollars to the Lamplighter!"

13. An Unexpected Offer

The city loan infused us with a new fervor, but it was hard slogging in the weather. Summer brought 100-degree temperatures, humidity like paste, and a moon that glared at us like an ember. Sail boats were becalmed in the river and the purple martins made daring maneuvers outside my window to feed their nestlings. A pair of tardy wrens found a home in a cardboard box tucked in the firewood. But the possum seemed to have gone vacationing to a cooler climate. In July the rains were replaced by drought that baked the fields to a crust as the farmers whined over their coffee at Yesterdays about withered corn and anemic tobacco. The sun blistered the roofing on the Inn and roasted the attics, forcing us to live in front of electric fans.

Bonfield stopped by to pick up his newspaper and passed along the news. "Art Taylor's gonna defy the city. Dug in his heels and gonna fight the condemnation in court!"

"He has no money to make the bank safe," I exclaimed. "But plenty to keep it standing?"

Confident that the city would prevail, we immersed ourselves in our renovation. Our goal was to make the lobby a *showplace*, but there wasn't a square inch of wood, brick, plaster, tin, or glass that didn't have to be stripped, refinished, repaired, or replaced. We spliced in new floor boards, and I crawled on my stomach like a salamander around the cellar, leveling, shoring up stone columns, and reinforcing the sagging joists with new lumber. Silt from the river's innumerable floods clogged the passages, and as we hauled it away we found a 1923 Coke bottle and an 1837 penny the size of a modern quarter. We took the bottle as a good omen, since 1923 was the year the building had been transformed into the Parkview Hotel from a livery stable and tavern cum whorehouse.

"And the year your mom and I were born," dad pointed out.

I dragged along a hydraulic jack in my burrowings through the cellar to force up the joists, cranking them up a few centimeters at a time as Dwight watched the bubble in the level on the lobby floor above.

"She's on the mark!" he shouted.

The floor inched upward, twisting its way back to its 19th-century position. Iron pipe from the old gas and water lines filled the crawl spaces like metallic pythons and I sawed them out as I went, lying on my back or propped up on an elbow. By summer's end we'd stacked up a ton of pipe, barnacled with rust.

Leon came from California on another business trip and helped install a massive support beam for the lobby ceiling, then we added new flooring over the chasm where I'd nearly fallen into the cellar the year before. Leon smiled as he drove a nail into the last board.

"First time in decades that somebody can walk through here without vanishing like Jonah down the whale!"

Del stole time from her busy weekends, as did Rolland and Sid. We scraped off the rust from the curlicues in the lobby's pressed-tin ceiling, and dad sculpted reproductions of the missing panels with fresh plaster.

Mom fell and bruised her knee, and when she wrapped it in an elastic bandage she was a match for dad with his sling and me with my stitched-up eye. The working wounded. Then she was diagnosed with glaucoma. Her vision wasn't impaired, but she'd have to take eye drops twice a day — balanced with the medication she was taking for high blood pressure and cholesterol. Did she ever regret taking on the hotel? I wondered.

"Those are next!" she cried, turning her refinisher's eye on the lobby doors.

We wrestled them from their hinges and laid them on saw horses where mom peeled off the hides of old paint and patched the cracks with wood filler.

As summer baked its way across the landscape we framed in the office at the east end of the lobby, fashioning a nine-foot counter for the front desk and milling shelves and display cases. We laid out the coffee shop restrooms, utility closets, and furnace room. Miller Lumber delivered more 2x4s and drywall, and West Virginia Electric supplied more wiring. Dwight stayed busy day after day tearing out plaster and lath.

"I never seen so much plaster and lath!" he groaned.

At the same time we reclaimed the yard, which sloped into the Inn so rain and melting snow poured into the foundation. We ordered eleven dump-truck loads of top soil, grading the yard away from the Inn to dramatically improve its looks. We planted bulbs and shrubs, and weeks later the Inn burst out in a Claude Monet palette of color below the blue siding.

Dr. Schmitz removed the brace from dad's arm the end of July, and dad worked harder than ever. The cut above my eye healed so well I forgot which eye had been threatened. I exchanged long letters with Jo Ann at the theatre in upstate New York, where she said *Last of the Red Hot Lovers* had done well, *West Side Story* was generating brisk business, and rehearsals for *No, No Nanette* were going smoothly.

"How about a December wedding?" she asked over the phone one day. "The day after Christmas?"

"A great time to be in Arizona!" I said. I was still refinishing the cupboard whenever I could steal a few minutes from the Inn, and attacked it with renewed zeal.

Our $17,000 loan check came from the city, and we hired the woman at the local H & R Block office to do a monthly statement.

"We've got a hired hand, a loan, and a bookkeeper," I told Jo Ann. "If that's not being in business, I don't know what is!"

It was also in July that Mack Wallace saw me on the street and offered me a job teaching 10th, 11th, and 12th grade English at the Augusta school. "I know you're busy at the *ho*tel, but the principal's arranged the classes so they don't take but half a day. You'd be done teachin' every day by eleven o'clock."

"What's the pay?"

"Eight thousand, seven hundred and eighty-seven dollars. But that's for a *regular* teaching certificate. You've got only an *emergency* certificate, which pays sixty-seven hundred dollars."

When completing my bachelor's degree I'd taken education courses qualifying me to teach high school, but since I'd become an actor instead of a teacher my credits were obsolete.

Wallace adjusted his black-framed glasses. "You could get your regular certificate by taking some classes."

"Out of the question," I said. "I'm far too busy to take classes."

A week later Wallace asked me to his office at the top of the creaking stairway of Farmers Liberty Bank. "Alan, we'd like to work with you on this. Three classes ain't too much of a load, and I'll try gettin' you more money. You see, we really need help with the *dramatics*."

So that was it. In addition to teaching, the board of education wanted me to direct the senior play! I flopped back in the chair. "Directing's a lotta work!"

73

"Hold on," said Wallace. He called Frankfort to ask about my certification, but the man he needed was away and Wallace said he'd keep trying till he got an answer. A few days later Wallace waved to me in the street. "I'm putting together some new figures!"

He said he'd gotten the board to raise the $6,700 offer to $8,000. And he'd persuaded Frankfort to issue an "adjunct instructor" certificate — permitting me to teach without the classes.

I mulled it over as I crawled around the cellar on my stomach, wedging more stone columns beneath the joists. The weather was so sultry that river and sky were one, refracting the landscape like a rising wall of flames, and the pipes sweated thick drops into the mounds of dirt that ran in all directions through the cellar like the dunes of a subterranean desert. It was cool, quiet, and dark, a good place to think as I weighed my need for income versus our needs at the Inn. If I took the teaching job, how much would it jeopardize our renovation work?

But I also hated taking money out of our hard-pressed account. The $17,000 was going quickly, and two days earlier Rawley Tate had told me he was vacating the apartment. Unless we found a new tenant, we'd lose $200 a month. I spent a restless night dreaming I was teaching a grade school class made up entirely of identical quadruplets.

Next morning I talked things over with my parents. "Could be interesting," said dad. "But you should ask for more money!" mom insisted.

I took the job and went to the school for my textbooks, walking under the clock tower with its four dials turned to the compass points. The school building dated from 1900, a two-story affair plus basement with kindergarten through 12th grade, and a gymnasium that had been tacked on in the 1920s. Plans for a music building were underway, but music teacher Linda Kerns rehearsed the band wherever she could find space — on the stage or cafeteria, or in the basement corridor by the malodorous restrooms. The school stood out against the flaring sun, a creature of brick scales and flagstone walkways converging wing-like onto the white-framed entrance.

Inside was floor-to-ceiling trophies. A life-size bronzed basketball towered above smaller trophies of tarnished nickel- and brass-plated figures in gym trunks. But there were no new trophies on the horizon, as I remembered reading that the boys' varsity team had lost something like 30 or 40 games in a row.

I strolled into the building's main hallway over a waxed floor warped like a ship's deck, where the July heat brought out the odor of cleaning solvents and damp mops, and was suddenly aware of hundreds of eyes staring at me. I glanced around at graduation photos dating back to 1896 that covered every inch of wall space. Young men with strong jaws and broad ties knotted below pomaded hair; young women in full bloom with guileless smiles. Teachers frosting the air with wire-rimmed glasses, their skulls throbbing with Latin roots and Longfellow's poems. I'd stepped into a time machine, stuck in the past.

"Mr. Tongret?"

The principal, Walter Reinhart, beckoned from the top of a stairway.

After collecting my books, I asked Reinhart if we could set the dates for the senior play.

"The gym's awful busy," he said, stretching his long legs beneath his desk. "Varsity and junior varsity boys' and girls' basketball. Band and cheerleading. . . . It'd be best if you did the play *before* basketball season."

"How about mid October? That'll give us six weeks to rehearse."

Reinhart was thin as a hat rack and tugged at an equally thin mustache. "All right."

"I'd like to do most of the rehearsals right after school."

He frowned. "We'll hav'ta keep after-school practice to a minimum. The gym's pretty darn hectic even *before* basketball season, and the school board don't like the kids being in the building too many hours."

"It's gonna be difficult with only two or three hours' rehearsal a week. Even professional actors need more than that!"

Reinhart knew of my background in theatre and wasn't inclined to argue. "The teachers last year didn't know what the blazes they were doing, and I don't think they ever had a full rehearsal. Most of the kids never learned their parts and we had to cancel the play!"

"That won't happen this year," I said.

Reinhart stared at me. "I'm sure it won't. Anyway, Wallace was teed off about it. The senior play's the only dramatic event we've got, and one of the few ways the seniors earn money for their trip to Washington." He scrutinized the calendar. "Why doncha do the play as a class activity? You could rehearse during school hours."

"But class is only fifty-two minutes. About four and a half hours a week."

Reinhart bent his head. "Well, I'll see if I can get you some time after school."

I went to look at the stage, which had been constructed at one end of the gym. The curtain was open, revealing a confusion of black drapes and a plywood shell from the previous year's aborted production. One of the wings was taken up with a wire cage with band instruments and a room where Linda Kerns gave music lessons. The opposite wing housed the basketball coach's office. The fragments of remaining space were crammed with folding chairs, soiled gym mats, and barbells. Other than the shell there was no scenery, props, or other stage paraphernalia.

Where are the *lights?* I wondered as I squeezed through the things piled up in the twilight. All I found was a strip of household spotlights fixed to the ceiling.

As I walked home I was tempted to call Mack Wallace and shout, "I can't take this job!" Teaching three classes of different grade levels of English was a serious undertaking, and it would be tough getting enough rehearsal for the play. But where else could I get money to live on? I'd just sent a $3,000 check from our Inn account to Lucas Aluminum as final payment on the siding and windows, and $6,000 to our furnace man. Only $6,000 remained of the city loan.

I passed through the garden on the way to my apartment where the bench reminded me of Edward Albee's *The Zoo Story*, a play I'd done years earlier at a professional theatre in North Carolina. The play takes place around a bench in New York's Central Park, and one of the characters has a line about how it's sometimes necessary to go a long way out of the way in order to come back a short distance correctly. That's me, I thought. To get time for writing I had to open the Inn. But to open the Inn I needed to teach in order to have money to live on. And in order to teach I had to direct the senior play.

14. Off to School

Mack Wallace treated me and the new basketball coach, Steve Simpson, to dinner at the Rotary Club, held since 1492 at Gertrude Schweir's boarding house on the river where no two plates or cups matched, and where Gertrude entertained her guests with windup animals that gamboled around the table, knocking over the salt and pepper shakers and falling into people's laps. Simpson had been hired because even more dear to the board of education than the revival of the dramatic arts at the Augusta school was the need to restore the community's honor by reversing the varsity boys' embarrassing string of losses. Tobacco and basketball are Kentucky's legs, with the arts lost somewhere in between.

I searched my anthologies for a play, a tricky business because the senior class had 22 females and only *two* males. I got a haircut, bought an $80 Penny's suit in Maysville, and spent my nights absorbing grammar books and literature anthologies. I wrote lesson plans for the first six weeks of class, and during the sermon on Sunday mornings found myself jotting down ideas for teaching, while dad jotted down ideas for wiring. The third week of August I reported to school to fill out insurance forms and attend seminars on class discipline and aptitude test interpretation.

"I'll show ya how to use the thermofax machine," offered Wally Tibbs, a teacher built like a gone-to-seed sumo wrestler who taught retailing. He waddled down to his classroom in the basement, which looked like it belonged in Sing-Sing, where he ran the school's book store out of a metal cabinet.

"I'll take a ball point pen," I said. "With red ink."

"Better take a dozen of `em," said Wally.

The first day of school the students got their books, completed attendance sheets, and were drilled about proper behavior as mandated by the school handbook. Humidity was as thick as cold cream and I threw open the windows, admitting the *cha-chunk! cha-chunk!* of freight trains from the nearby tracks. Students squirmed in their desks and their skin squeaked on the wood. My seniors filled out a questionnaire I'd prepared about the play. Several volunteered to do lights, sound, scenery, or props, but only seven girls and one boy wanted to act.

I stewed this over as dad and I removed the hotel's tottering old stairway to the former porch and replaced it with a new and much grander stairway into the lobby. It was a complex piece of construction that dad had spent many hours laying out on his drafting board.

He flexed his wrist. "Still building up my strength. How's school?"

"I'm worried about getting enough rehearsal time." A chalk line on the floor indicated where our Lamplighter stage would go, and wires spilled from a panel in the wall for the sound system and lighting dimmers. I shook my head. "We're better equipped here than they are at school!"

In class next day I wrote my selection of play titles on the blackboard and the seniors voted their first, second, and third choices. Then I met with the other senior sponsors to make the final selection.

"These are pretty goofy!" chuckled Bill Case, who taught history.

"They're better than some I've seen," said Wilma Wallace — Mack's Wallace's wife and the home economics teacher.

Three of the plays on my list had some pretense to dramatic merit, including a dramatization of *Little Women*. But the seniors were thinking more along the lines of Steven King than Louisa May Alcott, and chose *The Calamityville Terror*, a "chiller-thriller with an unusual amount of comedy." I crossed my fingers that the comedy would save us. It was about a girls' school in a haunted house, with parts for seven females and five males, which meant I've have to double some of the parts and rope in more male actors.

It was my first day of teaching and I went home hoarse from talking above the screech of the fan and the chatter of freight trains. The sultry air enveloped me and a bedraggled robin and her fledgling stood atop the purple martin house waiting for a vacancy.

"There's room at the Inn," I said.

15. First Reading

The play scripts arrived and I brainstormed what to do about the male roles. Troy — the only senior boy who wanted to act in the play — could do the lead, but that left four male parts begging. What about making the caretaker of the haunted house a female? I wondered, and I decided to do it that way. Another part was a murdered man's ghost who had no lines and came in at the end of the play, and I asked Coach Simpson to play it.

"Sure thing!" he said, rolling his grizzly bear shoulders. "Long as I don't hav'ta come to practice too often."

That left the parts of two teenage boys who dated the girls in the school. They couldn't be re-written as females, and I had no choice but to have girls play them.

"They're gonna get the giggles!" warned Bill Case.

"Just so they don't have to *kiss!*" said Wilma Wallace.

We had auditions, but three girls were absent and I assigned their parts without hearing them read. On my way home Lacey stopped me — one of the girls whom I'd cast as a boy. She was the smallest girl in class with the flat chest, freckled face, and boyish grin of Tom Sawyer.

"You were absent, Lacey. I had to cast the parts!"

"That's all right, Mr. Tongret. I just wondered, how short should I wear my hair?"

Casting was over and I went home exhilarated. I found dad toiling in the Inn's bowels in the gaping rent carved out for the new stairway where he was cutting 20-foot stringers for the treads. I helped him wrestle a stringer into place, then went to work installing the conference room floor, and moved so quickly that I smashed my thumb with the hammer. I was still swearing when a booming sound shook the Inn.

"Come look!" said dad.

We ran to the river where the booming continued like approaching thunder. Although the source of the sound was a few miles upstream it dwarfed the woods on the Ohio shore, and we could have spotted it at ten times the distance — the largest sternwheeler riverboat I'd ever seen, firing cannons for publicity. Its five decks towered above the water and it stretched out like a Manhattan block, a shimmering white palace with twin ebony smokestacks large enough to swallow a pair of Volkswagons. Red, white, and blue bunting brightened the boat's upper decks and the music of a Dixieland band rode the river's surface. The boat moved at a ferocious clip, as if several acres of landscape had been dislodged, and in a few minutes it was abreast of us. Passengers waved from the railings and the radar arm inscribed circles above the broad windows of the pilothouse. *MISSISSIPPI QUEEN* blazed in tall letters near the stern, and the mammoth red paddle kicked up a silver mist and thrashed the water into a roiling wake.

Well! I thought. I can put up with smashed thumbs and a lot of nonsense at school if I can see a sight like this once in a while!

At our first read-through the assistant stage manager and one of the cast were absent. "This is a bad start," I said, taking a firm hand. "Now somebody's gotta read the part for her."

"I'll do it!" said Anthony.

Anthony was boys' varsity basketball equipment manager, a beanpole of a kid with a pimply face who'd signed up to work backstage. Kathy Wilson, our stage manager, gave him a script, and we gathered in a circle on stage beneath the ghastly household spotlights.

"I don't want anyone straining for a performance tonight. Let's take it easy, get all the words in, see what your *characters* are like."

Cathy read the opening stage directions and we began. When Lacey started to read the male character she was playing, everyone laughed and she covered her face with the script.

I smiled at her. "They're jealous."

Everyone settled down and the seniors forgot the sweat streaking their faces. I forgot my mashed thumb and remembered my own senior play 21 years earlier, when I played George Gibbs in *Our Town*. Some of the seniors gave good readings. Lana, a slender blonde who read *Beowulf* with less understanding than a French poodle, came to life like a butterfly transformed from a caterpillar. Her eyes filled with animation and her voice swelled. I could tell that Abbey was going to be good as a demented schoolgirl, and Lucia — the class cutup — turned her instinctual timing to splendid advantage as the grizzled caretaker.

"I think this guy *drinks*," Lucia suggested. "What if I have a bottle of Old Grand Dad in my back pocket?"

Even Anthony, reading in for the absent girl, enjoyed himself. The seniors hooted at one of his lines and he reddened with pleasure.

Next day I gathered Walter Reinhart, Mack Wallace, and school custodian "Pike" Ingram on stage to discuss the set, and warned them that I needed help if the play were to succeed. "For one thing, we've gotta have more *room*."

We climbed among the folding chairs and barbells as Pike rubbed a hand over the stubble of his chin. "I'll try to git some of this stuff removed."

"We also need scenery," I said. "Since we have no flats, we'll have to repair this plywood shell. It's gotta look like a Victorian living room. We need drapes, a chandelier, and plenty of paint."

Pike looked the other way, then Wallace charged forward and tripped on a gym mat. "I'll provide the paint," he said, picking himself up. He had building materials from some apartments he owned, and seemed relieved that we wouldn't be spending school funds to finance our set. "Just lemme me know the colors y'want."

"My main concern's these spotlights," I said. "There's no way to *dim* them."

Wallace peered through his black-frame glasses. "We had a dimmer apparatus, but nobody was using it, and to my recollection it was put in storage. Maybe Pike can dig it up."

Pike muttered in my ear. "That dimmer was junked. Wallace *told* us to!"

Reinhart tugged at his mustache. "I'll see what I can do for you."

I was jubilant with this small victory, and jogged home to take Jo Ann's mother and aunt to dinner, who were visiting Augusta. The first play reading had gone well, and although it was by no means a great play, it had some good moments, and I felt the kids could do a fine job with it. We took Jo Ann's folks to dinner at Brodrick's Tavern in historic Old Washington outside Maysville, which had provided Harriet Beecher Stowe with the setting for the slave auction scene in *Uncle Tom's Cabin*. We tramped through the antique shops, and strolled by the home of Albert Sidney Johnson, one of the Confederacy's great generals.

"Do you suppose we can find a house like that?" Jo Ann asked.

It had three stories to ramble around in and write books, and plenty of lawn for a dog. A shady porch for iced tea and conversation.

"Why not?" I said, putting my arm around her.

My teaching had begun well, and if I could make it to May the Lamplighter would be open and we'd start looking for that house.

Tina, the girl who'd missed the first read-through, told me she also had to miss the first blocking rehearsal. She had a child and was getting divorced, and showed no interest in the play. I was muddling over what to do when Anthony's beanpole frame approached my desk after class had let out.

"You did a good job last night," I said.

"It was *fun*." He watched a moment as I erased *Beowulf* notes from the blackboard. "Need me to do it again tonight?"

"As a matter of fact, I'm gonna replace Tina. You want the part?"

"Hell, yes!"

When we got on stage I saw that Pike had removed the barbells and chairs, but the black curtains were still in the way. I went to the furnace room and found him with his feet up on the workbench.

"We need those curtains down as soon as possible."

Pike took a leisurely drag on his cigarette and released a huge mushroom of smoke. "I ain't forgot."

The seniors pushed the curtains as far to the side as they could, then following the floor plan I'd made for my stage manager, Cathy, we cleared the music stands and arranged folding chairs to serve as furniture. Everyone was punctual and we started rehearsal.

"Use pencils," I warned. "We'll be making changes as we get this monster on its feet!"

The cast pitched in with their full attention, and in an hour we blocked the first scene when Gwen, the head prop girl, slipped over to me. "Mr. Tongret, I gotta go home."

"But there's an hour to go!"

"I got things to do!"

"But who's gonna make the prop list?"

Gwen's eyebrows rose to a peak. "I have to fix grandpa's supper!"

"*You* have to fix it? There's nobody else?" She shook her head. "Well, next time get together with Diane and make sure one of you is always here."

The final hour we got well into scene two before stopping, and I congratulated the seniors. "Great job. See you Monday!"

Friday night, and the seniors glowed as they ran off to dates or to jobs at the video store or Carota's Pizza that had just opened. Jo Ann and I showed her mother and aunt around Cincinnati, and I put down more flooring in our conference room while dad poured the foundation for a walkway outside the coffee shop.

"Take a rest once in a while," said Jo Ann. "You're gonna burn out!"

"Everything's going good!" I said.

Monday we rehearsed during class — an "official class activity," as Reinhart had suggested. It was decent weather and Coach Simpson took his PE class outdoors, giving us the gym to ourselves. Blocking was slower than on Friday, and we got only halfway through the play when the bell rang.

"We won't get back to this scene for awhile, so review your blocking. And *start learning those lines*!"

Lucia waved. "See ya tomorrow!"

"So long, Mr. Tongret," said Anthony.

"Keep up the good work," I said. Anthony reddened and hurried off.

I went to the classroom for my books, where the fluorescent fixtures created a milky effulgence. The hardwood floor was darkened with years of wax and the yellow walls glared between the blackboards. A copy of the Ten Commandments hung from the wall, next to Gilbert Stuart's unfinished portrait of Washington and photographs of World War I battle scenes. The American flag stood at attention in the corner.

How in God's name can I make this work? I wondered. It was a large room, but most of it was packed with desks and bookcases, radiators, and a platoon of lockers. A supply cabinet hogged even more space. Our next rehearsal was two days off, and unless the weather was good and Simpson took his PE class outdoors, we'd be rehearsing *here*.

The attic, I suddenly realized.

I got a key from school secretary Mary Alice at the office and climbed the stairway. As I unlocked the door, a pall of dust alighted and a blade of light fell from a huge dormer window, and when I flipped a switch, a few naked bulbs twinkled below the timbers that trussed up the immense slate roof. Bird droppings caked the uneven floor boards and cobwebs stretched in all directions. Halloween, Christmas, and prom decorations hid in the shadows amid retired textbooks and broken desks. A padlocked door led even higher to the clock tower, and beyond it was another section of attic that looked less crowded. I stepped over dead pigeons to reach it, and found it to be nearly the same size as the stage.

I hurried back to the office. "Any reason we can't rehearse upstairs?"

Mary Alice blinked. "In the *attic?*" She blinked again. "Well . . . not as long as Mr. Reinhart don't mind."

"Good. On days when Coach Simpson needs the gym, we'll rehearse up there!"

It was 85 degrees and wet as a haddock, and I loosened my tie on the way home. I had a long night ahead of me. In addition to planning the blocking for act two, I had six-weeks' tests to prepare and 80 student journals to read and comment on. Jo Ann had returned to Arizona with her mother and aunt, and I'd accomplished less than I'd hoped over the last several days. But it was finally cooling off, and next day was the beginning of autumn. I glanced up and saw cirrus clouds with the refreshing appearance of vanilla ice cream tumble onto the horizon.

16. Acting Up the Rafters

Jo Ann returned to New York to continue her theatre career — while working out our wedding arrangements by long distance. "It's so beautiful by the river!" she wrote in her next letter. "So *peaceful*. I'm looking forward to doing some writing down there myself!"

My parents and I took advantage of the crisp, dry days of late September to landscape more of the yard — but when I had after-school rehearsal there was little time for the Inn. The seniors helped me prepare the attic, attacking it with brooms and clearing away the desks and prom decorations. Stage manager Cathy Wilson scooped up the dead pigeons as Troy and Anthony batted away cobwebs, although some of the girls were squeamish.

"This place is *creepy*," said Lana.

"Perfect for a mystery play!" I reminded her.

We started rehearsal, but minutes later an ominous sound came from behind the padlocked door.

"Holy bejesus!" said Cathy, her eyes widening above the prompt book.

We stared at the padlocked door as the sound grew ominous — a metallic scraping — and I wondered if one of the seniors had gotten the key from Mary Alice and slipped behind the door to play a joke.

"Jeez!" said Elinor. "I'm getting outta here!"

Then Anthony chuckled. "Oh, for God's sake. It's the *clock!*"

Pike had showed me the clockworks a few days earlier — an impressive mass of hardware made by the Howard Manufacturing Company in Boston in 1900 when the schoolhouse was built. It was a seven-day clock with an escapement mechanism powered by weights on long cables, regulated by a pendulum in a shaft in the ceiling of the library. Edgar Allen Poe's "The Pit and the Pendulum" couldn't have had a more spine-tingling setting.

"We oughta make a recording of it for the play!" said Lucia.

Next day we rehearsed on stage, where it was hot enough to bake meat loaf. The seniors shouted their lines above the rattle of the electric fan, and were impatient to finish. The first flush of excitement over the play had faded, and discontentment also spilled over from the classroom. The seniors were due for their six-weeks' test the next day and were apprehensive. Four sophomores and seven juniors had flunked their tests, and that afternoon retail teacher Wally Tibbs had paused in his sumo wrestler strut down the hallway and smiled impishly at me.

"There's a lotta grumbling about your classes. One of my girls said, 'I thought we were gonna have fun in English. But Mr. Tongret's *hard!*' You oughta do what I do, Alan. If my kids do bad on a test, I draw a bull's-eye on the black board and let `em shoot spit wads at it. I give `em extra points and they love it!"

Spit Wads 101.

I told Wally I'd give it serious thought and went on my way. I was requiring my students to keep a daily journal and think critically about the literature we were reading. But some seniors had told me the previous English teacher had given nothing but multiple-choice tests. "He was a great teacher," exclaimed Lucia. "He didn't make us do journals or essays or nothing. And if we didn't know any of the test answers he *gave* `em to us!"

Knowing Lucia's knack for fooling around, I took these comments with a grain of salt, but wondered if I was asking too much of my students. In addition to *Beowulf* the seniors were studying Caedmon's "Hymn," portions of *The Canterbury Tales*, and the opening chapters in the grammar book. All of my students were keeping journals and watching Robert McNeil's *The Story of English* on PBS, and some of the seniors were falling behind. Troy, the school basketball star who averaged 20 points a game, wasn't learning his lines.

"You're holding everyone up," I said.

"Got things to do!" he quipped.

"Learning your lines is one of them!" I turned to the rest of the cast. "I know it's hot. But we need to keep our minds on our work!"

Doreen was absent because of her aunt's death, and the prop girl was out for a doctor's appointment. No props had been collected and the cast was working around imaginary tables and armchairs. Doreen also missed rehearsal the next day because of a mess-up in her family's schedule. I'd read somewhere that Kentucky had the nation's highest rate of teen pregnancy among unmarried white girls, and I could well believe it. Like several of my students, Doreen was an unwed mother with a small baby, and she explained that there was no one else to look after the child.

"If it happens again, bring the baby *with* you!" I said, trying to control my exasperation.

Lacey was also absent to watch her younger brother while her parents went shopping, and next day I asked her up to my desk.

"Remind your parents that the play's a class activity. Attendance is mandatory."

"It don't matter. Dad says *one* rehearsal after school a week is enough."

"Maybe if I talk to him?"

Lacey shrugged her Tom Sawyer shoulders. "They don't support me in *anything* I wanna do!"

We'll see about that, I muttered.

It took an hour driving around the tangled back roads of Bracken County to find the one-story frame house Lacey's parents rented. It sat off from the blacktop road, stark amid fields of withering grass. Lacey's father — Eldon Combs — opened the door and gave me a tenuous handshake.

"C'mon in, Mr. Tonkurt."

Eldon was a small but powerfully built man with several days' beard growth, and as sunburnt as mahogany. The room was dimly-lit and heated with a wood-burning stove made from an oil drum that reeked of soot. Despite the fire there was a chill, and Lacey's mother came in leading a boy of eight or nine by the hand.

"I wanna talk to you about Lacey," I said.

Eldon motioned for me to sit, and he joined his wife on a tattered sofa as Lacey's brother bounced up and down between them. Eldon explained that the boy was retarded.

"And Lacey's the only one he'll mind."

"I was wondering about Lacey's absence at play practice. . . ?"

"We had a yard to mow and it was gettin' late. Needed Lacey to watch the kid."

Eldon spoke politely, but without apology. He'd been a ferry pilot, but had quit over a dispute and ever since had worked as a casual laborer. Most days he and his wife drove around Augusta in their pickup truck, making endless excursions of the streets with their son bouncing up and down on the seat between them. How on earth did they afford the gas? I wondered.

"We hav'ta take Lacey along when we go to the doctor," Mrs. Combs added, holding her son's hand as he moaned and yanked at her.

She was short and heavy-set, with hair pinched into a bun and skin burned nut brown. "Lacey's the only one who can manage him!"

Appeal to their pride, I thought. "Lacey's doing a good job. She's playing the part of a boy, which isn't easy."

Eldon rubbed his hands over his thighs. "I know she's excited about the play. We're gonna come see it, for sure!"

I jumped at this opening. "That's why we need to rehearse after school. There's a lot to learn and we've only got three weeks left." I gave Eldon a copy of the schedule. "After-school rehearsals are marked in red. There aren't that many, but we need the kids at all of them if the play's gonna work. It's a team effort, and if someone's missing it's hard on the others."

"This don't look too bad," said Eldon, furrowing his brow.

Their son wailed, and Lacey's mother pulled him to her. "Hush!" She related some of the troubles they'd encountered in seeking help from the government. "They can't do anything with him, neither!"

I felt strange all of a sudden, and wondered if I weren't overstepping my bounds. Who the hell was I to butt into things that touched on this family's financial survival? Maybe Eldon had used poor judgment in quitting the piloting job, but he wasn't a sponge. He took jobs rather than ask for handouts.

At the same time, Lacey would have only one shot at high school. College was unlikely, and she'd have few opportunities for the kind of discipline demanded of the senior play, and the joy it could give in return. She'd claimed that her parents didn't support her activities, and I wondered if they shouldn't be nudged into doing a little more. Maybe the question was too complex for me, her English teacher, to sort out. Surely it should have been a social worker talking to her family rather than me. I wanted to get out of there.

Eldon handed back the schedule. "I don't think we'll have much problem with Lacey showin' up. But if somethin' comes along. . . ." His eyes flashed.

I was relieved to get home and help dad pour another section of concrete walkway outside our coffee shop. As difficult as it was at times, the Inn suddenly seemed easier than directing the play, where there were too many shifting sands. I ran the cement mixer, shoveling gravel in the fresh air and exhilarating in the chance to work my muscles as dad leveled the wet concrete with his screed. A silent V of geese streaked the sky. It was the weekend, and as the concrete cured we demolished the final wall that had served as a partition for the sewing factory. After nine months of steady work the Inn's wounds were healing.

17. Heat — Or Histrionics

Late September, normally mild and dry in Kentucky, brought more rain and pushed the humidity to 96% as temperatures flirted with the 90s. The air clung to the skin like wet newspaper, and my red-faced students glared at the sluggish clock and argued over where I should place the fan. I shuffled it from one side of the room to the other, supplying each half of the students with 26 minutes of blustery oxygen. There was no fan at my desk and the sweat puddled beneath my shirt.

At Monday's rehearsal the attic broiled below the slate roof as the seniors struggled through the play. Most of them were learning their lines, an actor's most vulnerable point. Then something darted out of the shadows and several girls screamed. It darted by again, and I realized it was a bird trying to escape. The seniors covered their heads and ran down the stairway.

"It's a vampire bat!" said Lucia.

"That does it!" said Cathy. "I'm not going back in *there!*"

We finished rehearsal in the classroom, and never returned to the attic. All of our cleaning and preparation were wasted, and from then on we had to sacrifice ten minutes of every rehearsal to clear away desks and return them when we were finished.

Tuesday night we returned to the gym, and the undercurrent of nerves I'd sensed the previous week broke through to the surface. Pike was setting up chairs on the gym floor, and Lucia — always early — explained that the academic team had a competition.

"They're gonna practice as soon as we get our butts outta here!"

"Then we'd better get our butts moving!" I said as the seniors dribbled in. "Top of act one, everybody! Music plays as Mrs. Stowe stares at the portrait!"

Elinor took her place as Mrs. Stowe and Lucia entered as the crotchety caretaker. Stage manager Cathy Wilson was out sick, and her assistant had dropped out entirely, leaving me to split my attention between directing and prompting. Elinor forgot a line, stared at the floor as if it were carved on the boards, then raised her lashes at me. I gave her the line and she went on until she forgot another line.

"You've gotta learn these, Elinor!"

"I know my lines, Mr. Tongret. I just can't remember the words!"

Lucia already knew her lines and started a speech that kicked the scene into high gear just as Mr. Reinhart ambled on stage with a microphone with Pike trailing behind. Reinhart bent his head toward me. "Gotta set up for the academic competition. Be outta your way in a jiffy."

I stared at Reinhart in disbelief, then turned to Elinor. "Go on."

She and Lucia continued as Pike uncoiled the microphone cable into the wings and shouted, "All right! See watcha got!" Reinhart tapped on the microphone. "Testing! . . . Testing!" Nothing happened, and Pike came back to check the cable connections before going off again. "Maybe the problem's back here!"

Some chairs crashed to the floor and Lucia shot me a glance. "Just do your best," I said, losing my place in the script. She rolled her eyes and continued until Reinhart waved his thanks and left the gym. Troy and Shirley Mae — the play's villain and his girlfriend — came on for their scene with Elinor, and for a page or two they labored through their lines before Troy took out his script.

"We've only got two weeks, Troy. You won't be able to read your lines when there's an audience!"

"I know!" he scowled. "I know!"

He closed the script and paraphrased the next speech as Reinhart and Pike reappeared and set up a ladder in the middle of the stage. Shirley Mae stared in exasperation.

"Just work around it," I pleaded.

Then a few minutes later Elinor stopped mid-speech. "I have to cross to the hallway. How am I supposed to get there with a stupid ladder in the way?!"

"Go down stage and around. We'll sort it out later."

Elinor thrust a hand on her hip. "This is the pits!"

She spat out her line and exited, then Troy and Lucia did their scene as Reinhart blew on the microphone, now hanging from overhead. Voices came from behind me and I spun around to find Ms. Wynn and Mrs. Lockhart — academic team sponsors — whispering like deflating truck tires at the rear of the gym. I turned back to the stage as Lucia threatened to "Git the sheriff," then she scuffled with Troy before he grabbed the hammer from her tool belt and raised it over her head.

"Black out!" I called.

Doreen and Sonya strolled on for their scene while Ms. Wynn and Mrs. Lockhart hissed their way to the front of the gym. I watched in utter fascination, thinking they'd explain how they "only planned to be a moment," but they were oblivious to the rehearsal going on a few feet away from them, and I turned back to the stage.

"Transition music. Lights up!"

Then the shrill notes of a flute spilled through the door of Linda Kerns' music room. What next? I wondered. The scene hobbled on till Doreen stopped, and I checked my script.

"There's supposed to be a knock at the door!" I shouted.

Anthony shoved his head in from backstage. "I *did* knock!"

"Knock louder."

He battered the door frame — since Pike still hadn't hung the door — shaking the set. "You don't have to knock the place down!" said Sonya.

Doreen pretended to open the nonexistent door for Anthony and Lacey, then Lana and Dawn entered from the hall. The action was supposed to occur where Pike and Reinhart were tinkering with the microphone, and the actors arranged themselves wherever they could. Dawn said her line, and Sonya slapped her leg across the stage.

"I can't hear a thing you're saying!"

Dawn reddened.

"Try to speak up," I said. "Good practice if we get a noisy audience."

"We'll never get an audience at this rate!" said Anthony.

The flute squawked off stage while Ms. Wynn and Mrs. Lockhart prattled on. A few minutes later Reinhart and Pike took away the ladder, leaving the microphone dangling at mid-stage like someone on the gallows.

"It's like a dead body hanging there!" said Elinor.

I wiped the sweat from my face. "Keep going!"

The scene limped on while Ms. Wynn and Mrs. Lockhart wheeled their whispering caravan to the edge of the stage. Sonya watched them in amazement. The girls screwed up their blocking and I stopped to straighten it out. Lucia entered, dazed by Troy's hammer blow, and there was sudden quiet as the flute player switched exercises. Abbey entered and started a speech, stumbled once or twice, then threw up her hands.

"What's the use with all this crap!"

Only two minutes left, and I called everyone on stage.

"Thank God it's over!" said Troy, throwing down his script. Anthony shoved through the doorway. "Let's get outta here!" "Not fast enough for me!" echoed Elinor.

"Notes first," I said. The seniors groaned as I sized up their weary faces. "One thing nearly all of you must do before next rehearsal is review your *blocking*."

"What good'll it do?" Abbey snapped. "You keep changing it!"

"I've changed nothing. You weren't following what I'd already given you."

"You said we were supposed to do act *one* again!" said Shirley Mae.

"There wasn't time because half of you were late, including you!"

"You won't listen to our suggestions!" said Abbey.

"That's right!" said Shirley Mae, pointing at the portrait of the murdered man. "We think it should be in the middle of the stage, not all the way over by the fireplace!"

"When I asked for suggestions I meant about your parts. We can't have eighteen people designing the set!"

"This isn't fun anymore!" said Troy. "Heck, why do we need blocking anyway? In plays here in the past they just followed the movements in the book!"

"Yeah, and you see where that got 'em last year!" said Lucia.

"The directions printed in the script aren't meant to be followed slavishly," I said.

"You're treating us like Broadway actors!" said Abbey. "It's only a senior play!"

I blew up. "Don't ever say that! There's no such thing as 'only a senior play!' I've done many school productions and the actors always give a hundred percent. And don't forget that all of you voted for this play!" I shoved the script into my briefcase. "Your job is to learn your lines and blocking. There *will* be changes as we develop the scenes. That's why I asked you to use pencils. Now scram!"

They scattered, and I went home feeling as if I'd been kicked in the stomach. It was too late to work at the Inn, and I was too upset for school work. The thoughtless interruptions for the academic team had played a part, but I was obviously doing something wrong.

In the small hours of the night I sloshed about in the waterbed as I remembered the previous Friday, when we reviewed the six-weeks' test. Thirteen seniors had failed the exam — half the class — and report cards were due out the next morning. Only two seniors had earned A's, even though I'd graded "on the curve" by piling 26 points onto everyone's average. A number of seniors would find their names missing from the honor roll for the first time in their high school career. Some of the rehearsal mutiny had obviously stemmed from the low grades: When the actors were arguing with me I'd noticed Dawn Maloney — who'd earned an A+ in class — sitting quietly in the background. She already knew her lines, and like Lucia, had no need to join the mutiny.

18. Breaking a Leg

Octber brought battalions of black clouds that bombarded us with rain. It flooded fields where tomatoes and onions rotted, and delayed our completion of the cafe walkway. With report cards out, I had a breathing space to catch up at the Inn, and sawed up the last of our 2x4s to frame a hallway to connect the lobby with the back of the building. We'd consumed $800 worth of lumber in August and $900 in September, and I went to Miller Lumber for more.

But the cooler days failed to cool the tensions in the play. One rehearsal began with both Anthony and Troy arriving after we started.

"You're late!" said Cathy.

Anthony shrugged. "Had to put stuff away!"

He was equipment manager for the boys' basketball team. Practice had started earlier than promised for the season and had been scheduled right before our rehearsal. Then Troy came in, his hair wet from the shower.

"Isn't basketball over at four thirty?" I asked.

"Yeah, but the coach talks to us afterward. And I gotta get changed."

Simpson had practiced right up to the last minute — as was his prerogative — and gave his locker room chat as the boys changed. As the star player, Troy had to stick around for this talk, and I certainly couldn't expect him to attend play practice without showering.

Basketball and rehearsal shouldn't have been scheduled back-to-back, but it couldn't be helped now. Simpson had done me a favor two or three times earlier in the year by turning the gym over to me, and I knew that if I wanted him to play the ghost, I'd have to live with Troy dragging in late after basketball.

"Get ready for your first scene," I said, barely disguising my displeasure.

Later that week we prepared our sound effects. The school's reel-to-reel recorder had fizzled — a suitcase-size contraption with 1940s technology — and I badgered Reinhart into borrowing one from another school. One of the seniors dug up a recording of creaking doors, thunder, and discordant violins that we dubbed onto our tape.

"What a hoot!" said Lucia.

The students had fun and we all seemed to be pulling together again. Pike hung the doors on the set, and we patched the holes and painted the walls. Wilma Wallace and Bill Case lent a hand, and in three hours we transformed the shell into a sinister piece of Victoriana. Our dimmer board for the lights still hadn't materialized, and I ran by Reinhart's office to ask about it.

He wrinkled his mustache. "I passed that one along to Mr. Wallace. It's *his* problem now!"

Absenteeism continued to dog us, beginning with Shirley Mae, who told me next day that her grandmother was dying. "So I'll hav'ta miss practice."

"I'm terribly sorry," I said. "See you in class tomorrow."

At rehearsal I asked Lucia and Lana to take turns reading Shirley Mae's part. Our sound effects were ready, and Marilou set up the tape recorder offstage with a flashlight.

"All the cues marked?" I asked.

Marilou flattened the script against her knee. "I think so."

Cathy shouted, "Lights fade out for scene one — that's your cue, Marilou!"

The screeching violins tumbled out the speakers, as if demons had invaded the gym.

"That's *too* scary!" said Lana.

Dawn entered and froze in front of the fireplace. "There's no candles. I hav'ta practice lighting them!" Doreen joined her. "The matches aren't here either!" Abbey sprang out of the closet. "I can't find my knife!"

Cathy slammed down the prompt book. "*Props!*"

There was no answer and I rushed to the stage. "Gwen? . . . Diane?"

Lana poked her head in. "They're not here, Mr. Tongret."

I turned to Dawn and Doreen. "You'll have to mime your props. Abbey, use a ruler or whatever you can find for the knife."

After rehearsal I was about to go home when I saw Gwen. "I thought it was clear that we need you or Diane at each rehearsal. We had no one to set up today!"

"The actors know where to get things."

"That's not how it works, Gwen. The actors are busy with their parts, and can't be expected to track down props. Besides, there are props you still haven't brought in. I need you here every time."

"I'll come in when I damn well want!" She ran out of the gym.

Next day Reinhart called me to his office. Gwen was already there, and her eyes reddened as he hovered over her. "I want you to tell Mr. Tongret what you said to me."

Her eyes welled up. "I'm sorry about what I said yesterday. I've gotta lot going on at home, and I'm falling behind in my school work."

After Gwen left, Reinhart shook his head. "It's her family. Her parents are dead and she lives with her aunt and uncle. But her grandfather lives there too, and he's the one who calls the shots. He wants Gwen to cut back after-school activities. He doesn't mind her playing basketball, but doesn't want her staying after school for play practice."

The arts win again, I thought. "What if I talk with him? I had some luck with Lacey's parents."

Reinhart sucked in his cheeks. "I don't think you'd get very far. Her grandfather's an old fart who'd rather skin someone than talk to them!"

We hashed it over and decided my only recourse was to replace Gwen. But at rehearsal other matters came to the fore. Marilou was absent, leaving no one to run the tape recorder.

"And Lacey's not here!" said Anthony.

"Where the blazes is she?" I asked Cathy.

"Beats me!"

Eldon Combs had probably gotten a job and had Lacey watching her retarded brother. I ground my teeth, and asked Anthony to read her part. Rehearsal stopped a few minutes later when Troy failed to make his entrance. Then Pam popped in from the wings, suppressing a giggle.

"When I came in tonight I saw him chasing some cows down the road!"

Troy lived on a farm, and thanks to his truant livestock he missed the entire rehearsal. The evening was wasted, and our opening was only a week away.

I racked my brains for ways to catch up while squeezing in a few hours at the Inn. The rain had stopped and I patched new holes in the roof, wondering if we'd ever see the end of them. Knowing there'd be times when I'd have to stay late at the front desk, I began constructing a loft bed in my office. Aunt Margie and Uncle Ray returned from

Illinois to help wire and insulate the coffee shop. Two construction workers had taken Rawley Tate's room, but they suddenly skipped town, and another one took their place, supplying us with the much-needed rental income. I was up till midnight preparing the September figures for our bookkeeper — staring at the bills stacked on my desk and wondering how on earth we'd hold out till May.

FIVE DAYS TO OUR PLAY'S OPENING and things moved like a boulder plunging off a cliff. I dug up Pike at the furnace room, rousing him from a sleep sounder than Rip Van Winkle halfway through his 28-year nap.

"Would you mind taking another look at the closet door? You hung it upside down, and the doorknob's shoulder high!"

Pike rubbed his eyes. "Hm."

Then I called Mack Wallace to remind him that time was running out for getting a dimmer board. I couldn't find anyone to take over props, so I divided the chore among the cast.

"Bring whatever you can find. Chandelier, rugs, armchair, and a sideboard."

MONDAY NIGHT REHEARSAL WAS A MIRACLE in that for the first time the whole cast was present at once, although several were late. The tardiness prevented us from doing more than two scenes, and the actors continually begged for lines. A few of them walked through their roles like marionettes, especially Doreen — who was supposed to jump when frightened from behind by another girl.

"Oo!" she squeaked, hopping like a cuckoo clock bird popping out of its door.

"Try it again," I said. "Keep in mind that people are being *murdered* in this house, and the killer might be behind you."

"Oo!" she said, with another dainty hop.

Lucia stifled a laugh from the wings as I went on stage to Doreen. "The problem is you're anticipating. Think about what Dawn's saying!"

"Oo!"

I realized that Steven Spielberg and Kenneth Branagh combined couldn't get a performance out of Doreen and let it go. The seniors kept asking for lines, like nestlings demanding worms, and we ran out of time after getting only part way into the third scene.

I threw down my script. "Seniors, you've gotta learn them! Paste them over your bed or in front of the toilet if you must, but learn them! If you get stuck in front of the audience you'll have to get unstuck by yourselves!"

"Won't Cathy be prompting?" asked Elinor, widening her eyes.

"No, she will not. You will learn your lines like actors!"

ON TUESDAY SHIRLEY MAE'S GRANDMOTHER DIED, and she told me she'd have to miss one of our three performances to attend the funeral. In addition to the Friday and Saturday night shows, we'd scheduled a Friday morning preview for the grade school.

"I'll let you know as soon as the arrangements are made," Shirley Mae sniffled.

I unloaded the news on Reinhart. "I won't have someone walking through her part with a script — even if had I someone halfway reliable to do it. Whenever the funeral is, we'll have to cancel that performance."

Reinhart phoned Wallace before giving me an answer. "Wallace agrees that we'll have to cancel one of the shows, but says let's wait and see what happens. Maybe Shirley Mae will realize it's more important to fulfill her obligation to her classmates than go to the funeral. She's already missed a lot, hasn't she?"

"Are you kidding? She doesn't even know what play she's in!"

At the next rehearsal two other seniors were absent in addition to Shirley Mae — one for a hair appointment and the other to see her orthodontist. I was resigned to losing the girl to the orthodontist, since the appointment had been made weeks earlier, but I was furious about the hair appointment. It was especially painful because it was Dawn — one of my most reliable seniors.

"Mom says I *gotta* go," said Dawn.

She was clearly embarrassed to be placed in this position, and I let it go. Gretchen, who was doing lights and needed the rehearsal to check her cue sheet, was also absent. We muddled through, and afterward I stormed to Reinhart's office. It was breaking into my skull that the source of most of our problems was the same one we were facing at the Inn and with the neglected buildings on Main Street: So many people in town just didn't give a damn.

"If these absences continue I'll have to cancel the play altogether. Very few of my students' parents are supporting them!"

Reinhart's face darkened. "Same damn problem as last year!"

I recalled my promise to Reinhart six weeks earlier that the play wouldn't be canceled while *I* was director, and I burned with humiliation. I returned to the stage where I'd arranged to meet Bob Snapp. Snapp was on the school board and also worked for the power company. He listened to my plea, then put a hand on my shoulder.

"Listen, Alan. Person you wanna see is my boss, Hook Spradlin."

I felt like an idiot for not having thought of it myself. Spradlin was head of the local power company office and *Lana Spradlin's father* — one of my leading players. He was certain to want his daughter to look good on stage, so our dimmer board was assured.

WEDNESDAY BROUGHT MILD, BREEZY WEATHER, and I ran to the Inn to see how my folks were faring. Dad was balanced on a ladder to secure a piece of siding that had loosened in the heavy rains. He couldn't keep away from ladders, and climbed around as if the broken arm had never happened.

"How's the play?" he asked.

"I'll be glad when it's over!" I said.

Mom's hair was done up in a handkerchief and her fingers stained. "Come look!" She showed me a side table she was refinishing, then frowned at me. "Are you getting enough to eat? Come over for some tomatoes. I've got oodles, and there's tuna casserole. Jo Ann doesn't want a skinny husband!"

The murdered man's voice had to come from beyond the grave, which meant using an offstage microphone with an electronic filter. Pike fiddled with the amplifier as I tried the microphone that had been used for the academic competition, but we couldn't get it to work, so I scavenged the microphone from my portable tape recorder. Pike started to leave and I asked him to take another look at the closet door.

"What about it? I got it right side up, didn't I?"

"But you used nails instead of screws." I opened the door and it scraped against the floor. "They're coming loose!"

Pike squinted. "Hm."

That night the cast was in costume for the first time, brought from home or borrowed, and we practiced opening and closing the curtain.

"Godalmighty!" said Cathy as she strained at the rope. "There's gotta be a corpse on the other end of this thing!"

Gretchen waved her cue sheet from the bank of switches. "What do I do?"

There was no sign of a dimmer board from Hook Spradlin, but I knew he wouldn't let Lana down. "Just flip them on and off."

The cast got in place for the first scene and I called to Marilou. "Play the pre-show music so everyone can hear it."

We waited as nothing happened, then I went backstage and watched as she pressed buttons on the borrowed tape recorder. The power indicator was lighted, but no sound came out. I removed the back panel and found a blackened tube. The last spare had probably been used in 1939.

THURSDAY WE REHEARSED WITHOUT SOUND EFFECTS, and the dilemma with Shirley Mae came to a head.

"My grandma's funeral is Friday afternoon," she said with weepy eyes. That meant the Friday show for the grade school would have to be scrapped. "I also hav'ta go to the viewing tonight."

"Tonight? You're gonna miss rehearsal *tonight* as well?"

I wanted to shake her like a rag doll and tell her to stop mooning around. She gave me a red-eyed nod and went home.

More urgent than Shirley Mae's absence were the sound effects, because we had them recorded on a reel-to-reel tape with no machine to play it. We sacrificed an hour to make a new recording on cassette with my own recorder. Then I spent a couple of hours rigging a chair to creep across the floor as if propelled by the ghost as required in the script. As I worked, Mary Alice asked me to the office to take a call from Gretchen's mom.

"Gretchen's running a temperature, and I'm sure it's the flu!"

I hung up and shook my head at Mary Alice. "If I ever agree to do another play at this school, set me on fire."

Gretchen was doing lights, and I had no idea if her partner — Hilda Jane — could manage alone. All they had to do was throw switches, but there were lots of them to throw, and it had to be done quickly and at the right moments if the blackouts were to have any effect. But the question was moot, because Hilda Jane failed to come to rehearsal, and no one knew where she was. Maybe enjoying one of Augusta's fourteen tanning booths. Anyway, the seniors gathered on stage in costume and makeup.

"We'll be experimenting with sound effects, so keep on your toes. And sorry about the lights. Mr. Spradlin's working on a dimmer for us."

Things went badly all night. Troy and Elinor forgot a ton of lines. Lacey was daydreaming and missed an entrance, and there was more giggling backstage than tires screeching at the Indianapolis 500.

"Folks, you don't seem to realize that tomorrow this gym's gonna be filled with people watching this play! They'll hear every bit of nonsense going on back there!"

Cathy yanked at the curtains, which even with the oil I'd squirted on the pulleys inched into place like sloths, making it impossible to create the brisk ending the scenes demanded.

We went on to the next act, and Doreen suddenly stopped in the middle of her line by the mantelpiece. "The flashlight's not here!"

"Did you check it between scenes?" She shook her head. "If this happens tomorrow night, *fake it.*"

We got to the creeping chair bit, but it took several tries to get it properly timed. I'd also rigged a portrait to spin around as if charmed by the ghost, but it flopped. We hadn't gotten beyond the first act and were out of time. I walked home exhausted and dispirited, and found a note taped to my door.

Doing laundry, so bring whatever you have.

Mom

FRIDAY MORNING OF OPENING DAY we ran all of Shirley Mae's scenes. She surprised me by retaining most of her lines, but was upset about her grandmother's death and screwed up a good deal of blocking. I simplified things where I could and crossed my fingers that she'd get through the show without smashing into too many walls. During lunch break I made another attempt at the trick portrait and got it spinning properly, then the seniors assembled for our final rehearsal. We'd never once had a full run-through, and this was our last chance before facing the audience. The dimmer board hadn't come, and I left a frantic message with Hook Spradlin.

Cathy called "Places!" and as Marilou hit the first sound cue the music came out loud and clear, then went scratchy and stopped. My little recorder was eighteen years old and had simply given up the ghost.

"This play's jinxed!" said Cathy, with massive understatement.

"*I've* got a recorder!" said Sonya.

She ran home for a boom box, but despite our best efforts the rehearsal was as doomed as the Hindenburg's final flight to New Jersey. The curtains begrudged the fact that they'd been roused from a long slumber, and expressed it by moving slower than jam through a soda straw. Marilou got erratic results because the boom box had no pause button, and the spotlights took the Victorian set from total black to blinding daylight. The school band traipsed through the gym in act one, and kept things symmetrical by traipsing back again in act two. Construction on the new music building outside sounded as if a bulldozer was about to smash into the wings.

Then word came that Mr. Bach, the barber, had died of a massive stroke. Lana was dating Mr. Bach's son and broke into tears. Hilda Jane — who'd found her way back from the tanning booth — was a close relation of Mr. Bach, and she walked away from the light switches without a word, and we never saw her again.

"See you at seven sharp!" I said to the seniors.

I went home to shower and found a letter from Jo Ann. She needed my help with our wedding invitation list, and described the cake she'd ordered. Honey-almond frosting and Amaretto filling. I wished I was in Phoenix with her and the cake.

FRIDAY NIGHT THE GYM WAS SILENT WHEN I ARRIVED and the folding chairs threw orderly shadows across the floor. I went backstage and found no dimmer board, but I'd ceased thinking there would be. We had no gels for the ugly little spotlights, and there'd be no twilight effects, no dimmed lamps or spooky shadows. The ushers arrived with the programs they'd cranked out on the mimeograph machine, and I gave them a quick lesson in house management.

"Seat the audience as close to the front as possible so they can *hear* and *see*."

Then Gretchen appeared, pale and haggard after her bout with the flu. "You don't look so good," I said.

She didn't even try to smile. "There's a dead possum in my head."

"I don't think Hilda Jane will be here. You and the possum are on your own."

At 7:00 the cast showed up to dress and make up in the restrooms, and we commandeered Coach Simpson's office for a green room. The alarm sounded at the volunteer fire department, but the siren headed out of town and we forgot about it.

"Everybody's here but Anthony," said Cathy.

Anthony lived close by, so I wasn't worried, and I gathered the cast to set the curtain call.

"This is what we've all worked for, and I think you're gonna do fine. Just do what we've rehearsed and be prepared for laughs. They might surprise you. The tradition in theatre is that it's bad luck to say 'good luck'; so instead you tell someone to 'break a leg.' I want all of you to break a leg."

"You, too!" said Lucia.

The seniors dispersed to finish their makeup. A few minutes later the ushers began seating the audience, and nervousness spread through the wings as the seniors realized the chattering people beyond the curtain had come to see *them*.

Cathy glided through with her prompt book. "Fifteen minutes!"

Marilou pushed a button on the boom box and the evening took on a festive air as scraping violins flooded the gym. Then one of the ushers rushed back and said the fire was at the old Chatham Apartments outside town.

"The whole place has gone up! That's where Anthony is!"

I pushed my heart back into my chest. At the start of school I'd received a list of the students who were in the fire department so I'd know whom to excuse when the sirens sounded. Anthony was on the list, but it hadn't occurred to me that he'd be involved in a fire when he was supposed to be in a play. By 8:00 he hadn't come, and I tried to ignore the pounding in my chest. The audience had grown to 80 or so and more were coming in every minute. I went to Marilou at the boom box.

"Have more music ready. We may have to hold a few minutes."

I hated it when plays started late, and went to the foyer to watch for Anthony as Reinhart rushed over.

"What the hell ya gonna do?"

"There's no one to replace him. *I* can't even do it. I have too much to do backstage!"

Reinhart's eyes receded in his head like the muzzle of a twin-barrel shotgun. "If he doesn't get here I'm gonna wring his neck. He don't have to be at that fire. He's just dicking off!"

Cathy had already called "Places!" and the actors paced in the shadows, muttering their lines and blowing out their cheeks. Gretchen braced herself against the switch panel, and I double-checked the microphone connections. Being short of male voices, I'd be doing the ghost's offstage lines myself. Elinor touched up her makeup in the spill from Cathy's work light. Lucia, countrified in her caretaker's overalls, made wisecracks.

"Hey, Mr. Tongret! Is this how they do plays in New York?"

"You betcha!"

Shirley Mae was subdued from her grandmother's funeral, and Troy fidgeted with his tie. Lana was primed with cherry lipstick and ready to go. Dawn sat in our makeshift greenroom, reading a novel. Doreen tiptoed on stage to check the candles and flashlight, then went back again to check the matches. Hair spray fogged the wings and the cloying odor of pancake makeup aggravated the churning in my stomach.

Cathy tapped me on the shoulder. "Ten after!"

Damn, I thought. Why'd this have to happen? A few seniors had screwed around, but four or five had given their all. In six months they'd be leaving school. A few would go to college, but most would take a close-to-minimum-wage job at Clopay or one of the Maysville factories. Others would be slinging fast food or living on government assistance. They'd have few chances to create magical memories. Marriage and children, showing up at work for 30 years. All of that was harder than putting on a play.

But I also wanted the play to succeed for my parents, who were out front after another of their endless days at the Inn. They'd seen me many times as an actor — at the New York Shakespeare Festival, at Ford's Theatre in Washington, D.C., and a dozen regional theatres. This time I wouldn't be acting, but I wanted it to be good.

I went to the foyer where the ushers stood in a clump. "If there's latecomers, seat them as quietly as possible."

I'd planned a curtain speech to invite the audience to the cafeteria at intermission for homemade cookies and fudge to help pay the seniors' way to Washington, but now I'd have to apologize for our late start. I looked at Pam in the ticket window, who waved a handful of dollars at me.

"Over a hundred people!"

I went outside, where country music drifted over from McCracken's Bar. There was no sign of Anthony, and the river's black surface threw my dark thoughts back at me. I swore, then went in to give my speech, having no idea what to say, but vowing that if and when Anthony showed up I'd hang him from the basketball hoop. Then he ran in, his face perspiring from the fire and a two-way radio strapped to his belt above his fireman's boots.

"Sorry!" he gasped. His radio crackled with static as he started backstage.

"Just concentrate on the play. And Anthony —" He turned back to me. "— take off the radio before you go on stage."

SUNDAY I SLEPT LATE. There was a heavy mist that soon burned off to reveal an incandescent sky. After church dad and I repaired some damaged tiles on the cafe roof, while Del and mom planted daffodil bulbs below the bay window. *The Calamityville Terror* was over. Both performances were ragged, but I was amazed that the show had gone on at all. Line problems dogged us, and at one spot the play stopped for what seemed a month before Elinor got herself going. Come on! I wanted to scream. It was probably only a few seconds, but my heart ached offstage. Lacey broke up once, her small, boyish shoulders shaking with giggles, and I scolded her. I may have been too rough on her, because later she was in tears. In any case, her parents never came to see her in the play.

Whenever Anthony came offstage he monitored the progress at the fire on his radio. Troy spent his offstage moments trying to soak up the words of his shakier scenes, and made it through without too many blunders. I got my own words out over the microphone without mishap, and Gretchen pulled us through on the grotesque spotlights. Her flu was over by Saturday and the dead possum had presumably gone away, and she smiled once or twice as she flipped switches. Dawn went confidently about her performance, and was plenty loud enough. Lucia swaggered as the crusty old caretaker and got a ton of laughs. Lana sparkled, belting out her lines as her confidence grew. Smeared with fake blood, Coach Simpson brought shrieks from the audience. They loved him. After the final scene the actors whooped and hugged, then the curtain opened for the last time.

The actors went down to meet the applause, and their eyes misted with delight.

19. Autumn Leaves

With the play over my life shifted to high gear at the Inn. After eating my 85-cent lunch in the school cafeteria each day I hurried home and labored at our renovation, then dragged myself to the apartment to eat dinner, create lesson plans, and pay bills till midnight. Jo Ann wrote that she'd selected a wedding dress of water taffeta with puffed sleeves and a lace collar, and said, "I might wear flowers in my hair — if it doesn't make me look like Ophelia in her mad scene!"

Fall disrobed the trees, expanding my view of the iron-gray river and sending the purple martins on their migration. Halloween brought ragged faces looming and pumpkins leering. The more dilapidated the house in Augusta's streets and alleys, the more likely it was beset with witches and goblins lashed to trees or sprawling in the yard. October also brought more rain that battered the Inn as new leaks sprouted up around the windows and gutters.

"Do you think there's a curse on the Inn?" I asked my parents, going to the roof for the umpteenth time. "Maybe someone was murdered in the attic!"

We kept our day laborer Dwight busy, who spent beyond his means on his pregnant girlfriend's doctor bills — and on cigarettes and pool games. He asked for more advances on his pay, and finally left to find a better job before coming back a month later to beg for his job back.

He'd sprouted a mustache, as if preparing for the role of father. We gave him a 50 cent an hour raise, and one day he came in grinning.

"M'girlfriend had a baby boy!"

Taking advantage of a mild November, my parents planted a row of saplings, then transplanted two evergreen shrubs from their own garden to a spot by the bay window, arraying the yard like a forest glade. Our heating contractor delivered the husky Whirlpool gas furnaces and air conditioners, and set up his oily pipe-threading rig in our lobby.

"This means the first half of his fee is due," dad reminded me.

"We've only got a thousand dollars left from the loan!" I cautioned.

And other bills were pouring in.

As the Inn blossomed the rest of the street looked grimmer in comparison, and we worried that it would turn away lodgers. The condemnation suit against Art Taylor's moribund bank building still hadn't gone to court, so the huge eyesore would continue shadowing the corner of Second and Main for months to come. At night I dreamed about shelling it with a howitzer.

Despite our careful spending November drained the last of our city loan money. My parents pumped more of their own money in our account so we could pay $6,440 to the furnace contractor, then we returned to Farmers Liberty Bank to hurry along our loan application, which was finally approved.

"We'll need another sixty thousand to finish," said dad, as we once again reworked our budget. "But let's ask for a ninety-thousand line of credit — in case of unforeseen problems."

"And there will be!" I mumbled.

The Inn grew heavy with the odor of threading oil and hot solder as we fired up the first of our three Whirlpool furnaces. Warm air padded through the lobby and up the stairs, and we tore out the ancient gas heater Bonfield had repaired and traded it to a local shop for an antique chair. It had a built-in writing surface, similar to the one Dickens used to write his novels that I'd seen on a trip to London. It reminded me of my goal to *get writing by May.*

We built a wheel-chair ramp to the coffee shop restrooms, and put in a skylight that chased the despair from the upper hallway that for years had been lit by only by the gloomy pair of naked bulbs. As insulation was finished in the guest rooms we shimmed the studs and nailed in drywall by the tons — giving me plenty of opportunity to learn how to apply mud without slopping it onto my shoes.

"The battle scars are disappearing!" said dad, as we carted off another load of plaster and lath to the dumpster.

Truck loads of new lumber, drywall, 100-pound boxes of nails, insulation, wiring, and paint flowed in, making it a daily metamorphosis. The riverfront was also undergoing a metamorphosis as the Beehive restaurant opened after six years' effort. We ate there the first day and it was jammed. Service was slow and the waitresses untutored, but chef Luciano Moral's food was tantalizing.

I called Jo Ann in New York, who was heading off that evening to see a play. "Wish you could join me!" she said.

She was crowding in as much as possible before moving to a town where the chief cultural attraction was a one-lane bowling alley that still employed a pin boy. I worried that she'd have second thoughts about leaving New York, but in late November she gave up her apartment and flew to Phoenix to help her mother prepare for the wedding.

"Got an offer to direct a play here in January," she wrote. "But I'm turning it down. I don't want anything to interrupt our first months together!"

20. Unwelcome Guests

Dad was best man, and my parents went sightseeing around Arizona for a well-earned one-week vacation. Jo Ann and I went rock-climbing on Camelback Mountain and toured the ancient Indian ruins at the Tuzigoot National Monument. We enjoyed the art galleries in Sedona and Jerome, and picnicked beneath jade-colored paloverde trees before returning to Augusta to bare trees and snowbanked sidewalks. We unloaded the microwave oven and other wedding gifts in the apartment and put the cash we'd received into an account to buy a house.

"I'll add something from each paycheck," I promised, as we lined up Jo Ann's books and sheet music into the refinished cupboard.

Warmed by our new Whirlpool furnaces, we worked long hours at the Inn as dad wired the coffee shop and I stuffed in batts of insulation. Mom and Jo Ann refined plans for guest-room decor and selected names: Victorian, Shaker, Bluegrass, and Starboard Berth.

"We need something theatrical," said mom. "With show posters and copies of *Playbill.*"

"Why not the *Actors'* room?" said dad.

It was five months to our opening and the economy was thriving. Financial wizard Louis Rukeyser announced on *Wall Street Week* that the Dow had broken 2,000. After school one day I discovered something else had been broken when I found the city police cruiser outside our door, as Sergeant Greg Cummins questioned my parents in the lobby.

"Somebody kicked in the doors last night," said dad. "They took all of our electric drills!"

"You're the third place that's been hit this week," said Cummins, 30s and clean-cut with a spotless uniform. "They got Kelsch's market, and several thousand dollars' worth of tools from Mike Buckley's workshop."

"Did you see that?" I pointed at the imprint of gym shoes in the plaster dust.

Cummins nodded. "A kid of ten or twelve, I'd say. But I'd guess there's more than one person involved. Word gets around when a place has tools in it. You mind if I talk with your tenants?"

Lem was at work, but Dotty told us she'd noticed the lobby doors open when she took her garbage down the night before.

"Why didn't you tell the Tongrets?" Cummins asked.

Dotty leaned her head to one side. "I dunno . . . I didn't *see* nobody!"

Cummins asked what time she took down the garbage. "Eleven thirty." Cummins turned to us. "She mighta frightened them away. Otherwise they'd have taken a lot more than your drills."

Cummins grilled the construction workers who rented our other apartments, who claimed to have heard nothing. "But we've got an idea who mighta done it," Cummins concluded.

Dad wired in a burglar alarm, and three weeks later there was another break-in. One of our lodgers told us he'd been awakened at five o'clock in the morning by the alarm. Someone had jimmied the lock in the alley door, but left empty-handed. Cummins questioned a number of suspects, and set up a sting operation in an abandoned house that he filled with tools and kept under surveillance for several nights. Neither the sting nor the interrogations led anywhere — but the break-ins around town mysteriously stopped.

21. Wince

Jo Ann pitched into Augusta like Annie Oakley taking on the Wild West Show. She was hired to teach exercise classes at the local Catholic school, St. Augustine, and volunteered for the Sternwheeler Regatta committee. She substituted at school, and for a few days we worked down the hall from each other. She coached the varsity cheerleading squad and wrote a training manual for them. She published an article about the Coast Guard cutter when it made another trip down the river, and reviewed a benefit concert given by Israeli jazz pianist Liz Magnes for the *Ledger Independent.*

"You're the one who oughta slow down!" I said at dinner one night.

"I like staying busy!" she laughed, serving homemade vegetable soup and a carrot cake she'd baked.

Then she spent two weeks on the scaffold in our lobby, painting a variety of colors on the pressed-tin ceiling. Michelangelo in sweatshirt and jeans. The end of February she accepted another production of *Guys and Dolls*, at the Musical Theatre of Arizona in Tempe — allowing her to earn some money while staying with her mother. It was our first separation as newlyweds, and before going she bought an aspidistra plant for the window overlooking the Inn.

"Keep it flying!" she said.

By March it was clear we couldn't possibly finish the Inn by May, and we pushed the opening to September — a year behind our original start date.

"But we need to start finding a chef," said dad, to cheer us up from this new delay. "And I think Leon's right that we need one who'll *lease* the coffee shop."

Del arranged the interviews through her office in Cincinnati, but the first candidate we interviewed — who'd served as the personal chef for the president of Toyota — said he had no interest in owning anything and didn't want to invest money in our cafe. The next candidate managed a Skyline Chili and was so keen on the Inn that he brought his wife and daughter along, but admitted he wasn't in a position to pay for equipment. Several other chefs interviewed, but they abhorred the idea of investing, and none of them set us on fire as the kind of person we really wanted. Until we met Wince Faulkner.

Wince entered the scene on a balmy Sunday in March when Augusta was bursting into an Eden of flowers. Tourists swarmed over from Ohio on the ferry and crowded into the Piedmont Gallery, the two antique shops, and a weaving studio that had just opened, and to taste samples at a potato chip factory that had recently started. It was Wince's day off as executive chef at a restaurant in Cincinnati, and he utterly thrilled us.

"What a charming town!" he said, snatching a hearty handshake with each of us.

He was large with rounded shoulders — as if he'd spent all of his 57 years bent over a stove with the ferocious concentration of Stokowski at the podium. He was infectiously genial with fine white hair that set off puckish features, and had he worn a beard he'd have filled anyone's bill as Santa Claus. We settled in my parents' living room with coffee and Wince handed us his résumé.

"I see you teach at the Cincinnati Technical College," I said.

Wince laughed. "I never went to culinary school myself. But I've taken lots of seminars and training programs, and I like to pass along what I've learned. A lotta chefs around the city are people I trained."

"How'd you get started?" dad asked.

"Scrubbing pots in a chili parlor when I was a kid."

But his résumé made it clear that he'd become one of the most accomplished chefs in the region. He made his reputation at the Windjammer, Cincinnati's most popular restaurant, where he'd served 14 years — first as cook and eventually as executive chef.

"I see you've been head chef a lot," I said. "And consulted on several places."

Wince nodded. "Quite a few places, and I was at the country club several years."

He'd won the Bonappetit Award for special recipes, *Hospitality* magazine's Top Food Gourmet award, the Epicurean Award, and Top Executive Chef Award for the Best Dining Place in Cincinnati.

"Any family?" mom asked.

"Married with three grown children. I live mostly for cooking."

"Why would you wanna take on an untried coffee shop so far from Cincinnati?" dad asked.

Wince threw his round shoulders back in his chair. "For one thing, I'd like to get away from the city, to a smaller place where I can concentrate on the patron. The *patron's* what counts." He raised his eyebrows. "And I'm not too happy with my present job. I make a good salary, but the owners don't understand that things have to be done in a certain way, and that you can't skimp on quality. Sometimes I go in on my day off to see how my cooks are doing, and I find the owners messing about with the ingredients, or cutting back on the portions. You can't do that! It cheats the patron, and compromises my reputation!"

I got to my feet. "We'd better show you the Inn."

Wince fell in love with the place and fortified us with his energy and ideas.

"We could do wine and cheese tastings!" he said, striding through the skeleton of 2x4s that was to become our conference room. He thrust his hands against his ample waist. "And you oughta use this for overflow dining. *Banquets*. You can seat thirty-six in the dining room and this'll bring it up to seventy-five or eighty."

Dad asked Wince if he would invest in the cafe, and Wince smiled bitterly.

"I had my own place for a year, the Chef Faulkner Supper Club, with a couple of partners." He said they'd pumped in considerable money and sweat to make the Club successful, but the property owner refused to renew the lease, and the restaurant folded. "I'd prefer to work as an employee. If I do well, you can give me a bonus. Your place can do very well, and I know lots of people who'll be overjoyed to drive down here for dinner!"

Wince's visit threw us into a quandary. It was now clear that we were unlikely to find a chef willing to invest money, so we began getting used to the idea that we'd have to buy the equipment before we could lease the coffee shop. This would saddle us with more expense, but if someone of Wince's caliber was excited about our Inn's potential, it was worth it.

Wince climbed back into his customized Cadillac. "I'll be happy to advise you on the setup and equipment. And I don't wanna fee. It's not often someone gets a chance to be in on the beginning of a place like this. Just gimme a call!" He waved and drove back to Cincinnati.

"My Lord," said mom. "He really likes the place!"

We had an interview with another chef set for the next day, but in our minds we'd already hired Wince, and we began to expand our plans.

Dad revised the drawings to provide more room for the kitchen and make space for a chef's office. We wanted a kitchen where Wince would feel at home, realizing that instead of a mere appendage to the Lamplighter, food service would be the centerpiece, the quickest means to financial stability.

"To heck with the coffee shop," said dad. "We're gonna have a *restaurant!*"

School ended, and as a senior sponsor I went to the prom, with the gym a wonderland of tissue paper transformed into carnations and roses. Jo Ann came with me to see the king and queen crowned, as Marilou, a member of the court, strolled down the aisle with her seven-months' pregnancy abundantly evident. I couldn't take time away from the Inn to go with the seniors to Washington, but I rode the bus on the school outing to the Museum of Natural History in Cincinnati. I gave final exams and conducted my last class while the seniors autographed every bit of their classmates' property they could lay hands on, as if they were about to depart for Mars. I went to the faculty picnic at the city boat dock, and copied final grades into the bank vault records where other teachers' handwriting — most of them long dead — had been entombed for a century.

Commencement was held on the school lawn by the railroad tracks on a sweltering Sunday. Linda Kerns banged out "Pomp and Circumstance" on the piano, and my throat tightened with pride as Dawn Maloney received two scholarships — plus the French award, Beta Club award, and English award. A breeze scattered the certificates from the podium, and the speaker joked about it as Walter Reinhart and Mack Wallace hustled after them. The seniors' names were called and they filed down for their diplomas. The girls walked with bird-like steps in their high heels to keep from tripping in the grass; dads applauded and moms dabbed their eyes with tissues.

What had I taught them? Anything? I'd saved a few thousand dollars of my pay, but we'd had to push back the Inn's opening date. Benediction and recessional. My students wore a rogues' gallery of expressions as they marched out. Anthony and Troy laughed and swaggered. Elinor was deeply sober while Lana cried. I wished Troy well at Eastern Kentucky University, and he sheepishly accepted my handshake. Anthony, who'd lined up a job at the potato chip factory, chuckled. "I bet you thought I'd never make it, Mr. Tongret!"

Lacey wept, looking 12 years old in her gown, and I hugged her. Lucia-the-clown was also headed to Eastern Kentucky University — where, of all things, she intended to major in English and become a teacher. She punched me in the arm as her eyes moistened.

"I'm gonna miss you, Mr. Tongret! Even if you did work our butts off!"

Then came Dawn Maloney, who put out her hand. I knew that the two scholarships were not large and she'd be working her way through the community college in Maysville before going to a university.

"Let me know how it goes."

"I will," she said, in that voice that so delicately carried her lines in the senior play.

I let her hand go and walked away from the schoolhouse for the last time.

22. Trees

To brighten up our restaurant Sid made a stained-glass window of a peacock with brilliantly colored tail feathers, crafted between classes at law school, and his wife, Karen, gave us a stained-glass window of an old-fashioned gaslight she'd made for our lobby.

"Wait'll Wince sees these!" said dad.

The tulips planted the previous fall made a rainbow around the bay window, and Jo Ann and I set out 30 arbor vitae trees. Jerry Litzinger, who'd left Kelsch's grocery to open his own produce store on Main Street, complimented us on their appearance.

"It's a shame the rest of the street looks so *bad!*" he said.

It was a year since the city had condemned the bank. Dad had written the Augusta *Times* criticizing the delay, pointing out that in another Kentucky town a man had been killed by a brick falling from a condemned building.

Jerry fumed. "Most of the town agrees with that letter!"

Dwight left us for good, and we replaced him with Tony Taylor — no relation to Art Taylor — whom we knew from church. He was early 40s and had been everything from brawling bartender to auto worker.

"I had to drive way north of Cincinnati every day," he said, telling us about his job. "And they kept pressuring us to work overtime! Just gimme a job in Augusta and I'm happy. I *like* Augusta!"

Tony thrived on telling stories, and we gave him a variety of jobs — tarring the roof, assembling a file cabinet, stripping paint from furniture. "This reminds me of something," he'd say as he charged into the story. I also learned something else about him, beginning in April when he went out to mow the lawn. After one turn around the yard he came inside, a handkerchief tied around his forehead.

"You know, Alan, this would go a lot faster if I borrowed Tom Appleman's *riding* mower!"

"Well, if Appleman doesn't mind — "

Tony was out the door and came back a half hour later on the riding mower, but twenty feet into the yard it died. He cranked away a few minutes, then poked his head inside.

"Dead battery!"

He jogged home for his car to jump-start the mower, but it died again as soon as Tony made another go at the grass.

"Be right back!" he said.

Twenty minutes later he returned with a battery charger. "Gotta get that blankety-blank thing charged up so I can get it back to Tom Appleman!"

Two hours since he'd begun, and the lawn was virtually untouched.

"This reminds me," he said, slipping off the handkerchief and folding it into a neat square. "There's something that always puzzles me about grammar. You're an English teacher; is it supposed to be 'mowed the lawn,' or 'mowed the grass'?"

Another dry spell shriveled Augusta's lawns and alarmed us about the new trees, and we watched them closely. Jo Ann and I grew fond of caring for them, feeling that we were preparing for our own property. A bag worm appeared on one of my parents' evergreens, and we searched the trees at the Inn to make sure they weren't infested. We found some brown spots, but the nursery told us it was normal. In early

July Jo Ann's mother got a bronchial infection that threatened to become pneumonia, and Jo Ann went to stay with her.

"Don't know when I'll be back!" she said as we drove Route 8's roller-coaster hills to the airport.

I checked the trees daily and found a Japanese beetle tucked like a concealed microphone beneath a frond. Other beetles appeared among the 30 trees and we attacked them with the hose, pulling all of them off we could find. Over the next few days more brown patches formed, and I worried that the trees were dying.

Part II

1. Red Tape

An actor friend from New York, Bob Donahoe, came to visit. I showed him around Augusta, Maysville, and Old Washington, then we retraced Daniel Boone's footsteps at Blue Licks State Park — where in a late Revolutionary War skirmish Boone barely escaped with his hide from a detachment of British and Indian fighters. We canoed up Bracken Creek, which feeds into the Ohio River upstream of Augusta, after undulating for miles through jungle-like undergrowth along low-lying corn and tobacco fields. The creek's meandering secludes it from the outside world, and the sun hypnotizes with a tropical drowsiness as turtles slumber on rocks and water moccasins skim the sluggish, brown current. As we reached one of the creek's broad pools we drew in our paddles and let the canoe slip over the water's skin, murmuring against the stump of a tree.

Something materialized and swept by us, a creature four feet long from dagger-like bill to tail, its Olympian wingspan stretched to mythical proportions. A great blue heron, gliding in primeval silence a few feet above the water, gaining an inch or two in altitude for every 100 feet forward, moving magisterially down the length of the creek until it disappeared over the treetops.

Bob watched in awe. "If I ever decide to leave New York, it'll be for a place like Augusta!"

Jo Ann's stay in Phoenix lengthened to a month as her mother teetered on the edge of pneumonia. The expense of her trip was gobbling down our savings until she got a TV commercial, but the check was lost somewhere between Hollywood and Augusta.

"My final teaching check has come," I said on the phone. "And I'm determined to stretch it out till we open."

The canoe trip with Bob was one of the rare respites from our work, yet despite all we'd done, it was obvious that we were unlikely to have the Lamplighter ready by September. We were now more than a year behind our original schedule, and I vowed to redouble my efforts to speed things up. I gave written notice to Lem, Dotty, and the construction workers that they'd have to vacate the apartments in a month, and we placed a $3,660 order for fire-resistant doors for our guest rooms.

The major hurtle now was to get approval from the Department of Housing, and dad pushed himself preparing finished drawings of the work we'd done. Our library had swollen to include the *Kentucky Hotel Law and Code* and *Kentucky State Plumbing Law, Regulations and Code, The BOAC Basic National Mechanical Code, McGraw-Hill's National Electrical Code Handbook*, the *Kentucky Building Code*, Bianchina's *Illustrated Dictionary of Building Materials and Techniques*, and dad's well-worn copy of William P. Spence's *Architecture: Design, Engineering, and Drawing*.

If anything, this Mt. McKinley of ink created as many puzzles as it solved. For one thing, the building inspector told us that the 5/8" inch drywall on the halls and main stairway had to be increased to one inch. Yet the code book merely said that stairways and halls had to resist fire for a "minimum period" of time. Whatever that meant. Architect Robert Lape, whom we'd contacted a year earlier, finally had room in his schedule to take us on. Dad's meticulous drawings were blueprinted and passed on to Lape's draftsman, who re-drew them over Lape's signature in preparation for submission to Frankfort.

"I'll negotiate these through the Department of Housing for you," Lape promised. "It can be a nightmare down there!"

Plumbing was another nightmare. As early as May dad had hustled to complete the drawings while I hacked out the old pipe, but it wasn't until August — 18 months after our renovation began — that Frankfort approved the plans and dad was able to meet with regional plumbing inspector Jim Perry at his Brooksville office.

"These are about the best drawings I've seen," said Perry. "But you don't mention who your plumber is."

"*I'm* the plumber," said dad.

Perry swiveled his chair. "Not unless you got a license!"

When I got the news I exploded. Dad was a superb plumber. He'd plumbed his own house, as well as the two apartments next door to it on the river that he and mom rented. He'd also done the plumbing for a small commercial building he and mom had renovated in Maysville, and a cabin Del had built. He had considerable experience, and we'd certainly do the work according to code and have it inspected. So why on earth did we need a licensed plumber, other than to line someone's pocket?

Dad shrugged. "Because it's the law."

The news sent us reeling, and after I absorbed it I scoured the Yellow Pages for phone numbers, but it was mid-September before we found a plumber who'd drive down to Augusta. He looked at the Inn and bid $9,200 for the job.

"That's twice as high as I thought it would be!" dad exclaimed, but the next plumber bid $15,500.

"I can't believe it!" I cried. "Maybe we should forget the Inn and take up plumbing!"

Dad did his best to laugh. "Well, at least it can't go any higher. The next guy's gotta be more reasonable!"

Another plumber inspected the Inn, then went home to prepare his bid before calling us. "Tell you what I'll do," he said on the phone a few days later. "Although the building's falling apart and will give unexpected problems, I'll take it on for twenty-eight thousand dollars."

That did it. We put a note in John Bonfield's newspaper, and a few days later he came by in his T-shirt and the .22 Derringer pistol clamped to his belt buckle, his crimson hair glowing with tonic. He poked around at the changes we'd made since he'd repaired the gas heater a year earlier as dad pointed out what we needed: Plumbing for eleven bathrooms, prep sink, ice maker and laundry area, a commercial-size sink and dishwasher in the kitchen — probably larger than any job Bonfield had ever tackled.

"Bless me," he muttered, pushing his red-tinted glasses to his face and squinting at the holes and crevices where hot and cold water pipes, drain lines, and vent pipes would somehow have to go. He crept down to the cellar to inspect the ancient pipe that brought water in from the city, and stared into the attics from the top of a ladder. "Well, it won't be *boring*."

He took off his glasses and wiped them on his T-shirt. "I'll take on the job for a flat fifteen dollars an hour. If you aren't satisfied, you won't be stuck with me." He put his glasses back on and looked at me with a glimmer. "And I'll depend on *you* to crawl around the attics and cellar!"

While her mother recovered from the bronchial infection Jo Ann found work in a production at a Phoenix resort, and she began planning cabarets for the Inn.

"Can't wait to see the stage in action!" she said on the phone. "I've got loads of ideas!"

Her check for the TV commercial came, and I mailed it to her. She continued trading decorating ideas with mom and Del, who finished the first of our guest rooms and named it the "Parkview." It was decorated as it might have been when the hotel opened in 1923, with an original iron bed, rocking chair, and early 20th-century pattern wallpaper.

We at last had a room ready for guests, although its bathroom wasn't finished, and there were still eight other rooms to complete. And after being hit with the requirement for a plumber, we were struck by another hurricane when our architect met with State Fire Marshal Jack Rhody in Frankfort.

"Rhody's demanding that we install a *fire sprinkler system*," said Lape.

Architect. Plumber. And now a sprinkler system! Our renovation was becoming gargantuan.

"Is there nothing we can do to avoid this?" I asked. "It's gonna murder our budget!"

We were having lunch, and mom raised an eyebrow at dad over the apple pie she'd made. "How much will it cost?"

Dad shook his head. "Our only hope is that Lape can persuade Rhody to permit a *limited* sprinkler system. Heck, we've got the guest rooms protected with steel doors, extra layers of plaster — and we'll have state-of-the-art smoke detectors."

I stewed it over the rest of the day, panicked that we wouldn't find the money. Thousands of dollars going out and nothing coming in! And lurking at the back of my thoughts was the fear that this could cripple us enough to prevent the Inn from opening at all.

Then we learned about Kenny Bratton. Kenny was a Bracken County native who'd built a thriving business near Dayton, Ohio, and spent his weekends at a cozy vacation home he'd constructed on the river to indulge his hobbies of boating, water skiing, and horsing around. Kenny's business was Hydro Security Systems — an installer of industrial fire sprinklers. We stopped by Kenny's house — where he was about to hop in a Jacuzzi with a bird's-eye view of the river.

"I got some great old memories of that hotel!" he said. "Used to get into all kinds of trouble running around there as a kid!" He scratched his substantial belly, looking very much like a kid in his swimming trunks and Beatle's haircut. "Soon as you get 'er open, I'm gonna come for breakfast!"

"The state fire marshal's got us by the throat," said dad. "There won't be any breakfast if we don't get a sprinkler system."

Kenny looked back and forth between dad and me. "Hell, most of my work is factories and office buildings. I don't do places like the hotel. Too damn much trouble!" He sloshed around in the Jacuzzi, biting his lip at the warmth. "God, that's good!" His Buddha-like figure submerged in the steamy water. "Tell you what. I'll come by for a look tomorrow."

Kenny went through the Inn top to bottom, shaking his mop of hair. "How the hell would I get my fat gut into all these toad holes! I knew it'd be a lotta trouble!" He peered into one of the attics. "Hell, I'll just send my *sons* into the tight places!"

The plumbing and sprinkler systems had to be coordinated through Frankfort's Department of Housing, and the field inspector assigned to Bracken County — Herb Nagy — came in June. Nagy was mid-20s with a ruddy complexion and retreating hairline. We took him through the building, then dad unrolled the blueprints.

"Everything seems in order, Mr. Tongret," said Nagy, as he zipped up his jacket. "You've done a good job on these. But of course, I can't make any official comments. You gotta have your architect get these to *Frankfort*."

2. Shopping

It rained harder than the previous year, laying the humidity on with a steamroller, with stretches in June when we felt the sun had abandoned us for good. I crawled through our five attics in search of leaks, and brushed more tar on the roof. By July our spirits were as sodden as the riverbank, and when August drifted in we sought release at the annual church picnic at the boat dock. Beforehand I stopped by Jerry Litzinger's produce store where the dog days ravaged his fruit and vegetables. Jerry's hair had thinned and his shoes were scuffed from endless trips down the aisles of his market, but he conjured a smile as he rang up my strawberries.

"I'm not doing so well," he said. "How 'bout the hotel?"

"*Pain*fully slow."

Our church had a new pastor whom I met at the picnic, a man in his 50s with wire-framed glasses and the improbable name of Livingood. I mentioned a few experiences I'd had teaching as he eyed me with Norman Vincent Peale optimism.

"Our youth simply don't get enough leadership at home!" he proclaimed.

I got the impression he wanted me to organize a youth group, but pretended to miss the hint. After a year of teaching I had no more energy for guiding teenagers. Yet the glint in Reverend Livingood's eye warned me he'd try again.

A producer offered Jo Ann the role of Mary Magdalene in *Jesus Christ Superstar* for the fall in Tucson. Her mother was improving, but her aunt was suffering from what appeared to be Alzheimer's disease, and Jo Ann went about getting an appointment for her at the Mayo Clinic in Scottsdale.

"God, I'm depressed!" she wrote. "I don't know when I'll get back to Augusta!" She ended up turning down the role in *Superstar* to have time to look after her aunt.

To take my mind off things I rummaged through the closet in search of my novel with the conviction that if I could start writing I'd have at least some sense of accomplishment. Instead I found my trumpet, which I hadn't played since high school. The valves were sluggish as I blew a note that was as dull as an old penny. I ran a scale, cracking the top note. I went to the low register and back again, then played a few phrases of "Whispering," a piece I'd learned in third grade, remembering the good times I'd had in high school dance and concert bands. I oiled the valves, took out my old methods book, and limped through the opening exercise as the setting sun peeped between rain clouds beyond the river.

Sid graduated from law school, and between bouts of studying for the bar exam he helped us redo Lem's apartment.

"What's going on with that?" Sid asked, glaring at the old bank.

"Art Taylor's appealed the demolition order. And it's taking forever!"

Sid shook his head. "If someone doesn't mind paying legal fees, he can muddle things up a long time!"

"I constantly think about taking dynamite to it!"

That afternoon Reverend Livingood stopped by, and said he was astonished at the quality of work we were doing.

"You Tongrets have more energy than anyone I've met down here!"

"I just hope the community appreciates it," I said.

"Appreciate it heck," Sid weighed in. "I hope they come here to eat!"

"They will," said Livingood, fixing his eyes on me. "Say, I wonder if you'd do the children's sermon on Sunday?"

Some days earlier the church secretary had resigned and the board begged me to replace her. I turned them down because I was already serving as secretary for our family corporation and for the SHARE organization at the museum, and keeping three sets of minutes was more than I wanted to take on. But the children's sermon was only a few minutes a week.

"Sure," I said.

Livingood pumped my hand. "That's fine! Just fine!"

Sunday morning I went to the front of the church with a potted geranium. "What's this?" I asked the kids, pointing to a small plant beside the geranium.

"A weed," declared a boy.

"It's a wild flower," I said, giving the common and Latin name. "Just reminds us that we need to value all living things, despite appearances."

The kids smiled, and after the service Livingood patted my shoulder. "That was swell! And you notice how the kids paid attention?"

"I enjoyed it."

"Then how about doing it the next few weeks?"

"Well, given our schedule at the Inn, I'm never sure I'll be here. Why don't we take it one week at a time?"

"Then you'll do it next week!"

What a clever guy, I thought. The following Sunday I was back at the altar, talking about Aesop's fable of the miser, and after the service Livingood showered me with praise. Perhaps the coals of my ego had been fanned, or maybe I felt I owed the church more than just sitting in the congregation, but I agreed to do the children's sermons on a steady basis.

But Livingood wasn't finished. "Alan, some time I'd like to get your ideas about starting a choir!"

We were investing heavily in restaurant equipment, but still lacked the hood assembly to vent smoke and fumes from the range and deep fryer. Hoods are custom-made of heavy-gauge steel and must be approved by the fire marshal. Architect. Plumber. Sprinklers. Kitchen hood. Our renovation was threatening to turn into Frankenstein.

We scrambled around in search of a licensed firm to design and build the hood, and in October got our best bid of $3,400 from Oscar Pell in Lexington. We gave his engineer the go-ahead to begin drawings, but this delayed our opening even more, which we pushed back yet again — to the spring of the next year. We were a year and a half behind our original target and wanted to make sure we held onto our chef, so mom and dad stopped by Wince's restaurant in Cincinnati.

"I want you to try my new puffed-pastry dessert!" he said, darting out of the kitchen when he'd gotten word they were there.

Mom surveyed the crowded dining room. "Looks like you're doing well."

"We're doing great, but I'm anxious to start at your place. I've got so many plans!"

We contacted a restaurant equipment supplier in Cincinnati, who sent a man to propose a layout for our kitchen. Wince came to listen in, and shook his head in bemusement after the salesman left.

"He's a nice kid, but hasn't thought out his plan carefully enough. I get the feeling he's never really *cooked*." Wince settled into a chair with the plan on his knee and sketched in some changes. "If we move the cooler here, it'll save a lotta steps. And the salad counter needs to be closer to the servers. On a busy night that's important." The light from the window in the chef's office caught Wince's fine white hair. "And keep in mind that this guy's proposal's built around selling you new equipment. You can get plenty of *used* stuff in good condition. Lemme give you some suppliers to call. If you want, I'll go along with you." The laugh lines deepened around his eyes as he got into his Cadillac. "I've dealt with these people. They know they can't pull any shenanigans with me!"

A week later we went to a restaurant auction in Cincinnati, and Wince advised us on how much to bid. We spent $2,500 on 40 bentwood chairs, baking pans, a double-wide commercial refrigerator, stainless steel serving tables, and a 20-quart Hobart mixer as solid as a cement mixer. It seemed like a lot of money, but we found out that a new mixer alone would run over $2,500. We were discovering that the difference between domestic and commercial kitchenware was like comparing a Caribbean cruiser with a battleship.

We collected our purchases with a large rental truck, dollies, and our hired hand, Tony. The Falstaffian refrigerator we'd bought had to come down a winding marble stairway and was so heavy that, even with the doors and shelves removed, it crushed both dollies.

"There's gotta be an easier way to earn a living!" Tony said a few days later. He'd been sending out résumés for weeks, hoping for a job in electronics or management, but settled for a machine-operator job at Clopay. "It's a new start," he said, feinting some jabs. "And it reminds me of another job I had. . . !"

Later in the summer Wince escorted us to Thomas-Sysco, Cincinnati's largest restaurant supplier, in a building spread out like a city. A saleswoman led us past test kitchens spilling forth exotic aromas and display rooms gleaming with equipment, then up an elevator to a lounge. She served coffee and loaded us down with catalogs.

"We're mostly interested in table settings," said Wince. "Something durable to hold up for breakfast and lunch, but nice enough for banquets."

The woman opened a chinaware catalog. "Something with a country motif?"

Wince regarded us. "I think we wanna keep it simple. I don't like a strong pattern, because it won't go with a lotta things. I tell you what. If our plates were cream-colored or off-white, with just an accent of black."

"That would look nice in candlelight," said mom.

The woman hurried to her office and returned with a slip of paper.

"How about a set of bone-white china with a narrow black trim? Service for a hundred and eight. It's a discontinued design that was ordered by a restaurant that changed its color scheme. I can make you a *very* good deal on it!"

We spent the next two hours ferreting through more catalogs for things to accompany the china — salad plates from France, matte black salt and pepper shakers from Syracuse China in New York, bud vases and sugar caddies, water tumblers and wine glasses, heavy-duty beer mugs, and 108 sets of flatware.

The saleswoman snapped her order book shut. "I'll have the prices to you in three days."

Practicing the trumpet became a release from our mounting pressures. On the nights when I played half decently, simple things like Bohm's "Calm is the Night," I forgot the splinters and mashed thumbs, the leaks that had returned to our roofs, and the frightening sums we were spending. I started the classic Arban-Clarke *Method for Cornet and*

Trumpet, working on range and attack as my control and vibrato improved. Some nights I practiced at the Inn among the heaps of furniture, with no other sound but the settling of the building.

Jo Ann returned in September, and we made love for three hours straight. Her mother had fully recovered from the bronchial infection, and Jo Ann had gotten an appointment for her aunt at the Mayo Clinic for December. Jo Ann joined the Maysville Community Choir, auditioned for a film in Cincinnati, and ran a three-day cheerleading clinic at the school. She fed me roast chicken, stuffed manicotti, and cherry cobbler, and conspired with mom on room decorations. One night I played a couple of pieces for her on trumpet.

"Not bad!" she said.

"Sunday you'll get to hear me sing."

"Sing? *You?*"

In addition to doing the children's sermons, I'd joined the board as Worship Committee chair — with oversight for the choir. Our next door neighbor Kathy Riebel volunteered to direct, but other than her husband, Jerry, the only male in church whom I could talk into singing was Tony, or former helper.

"I will if *you* will!" he said, faking some punches.

On Sunday we got through the hymns without embarrassment, and won some nice comments from the congregation.

"Very good!" said Jo Ann with a hug.

I started looking forward to Wednesday night strolls to church with mom, and Jo Ann came along as our substitute pianist. But now I was committed to Wednesday choir practice, and monthly board meetings in addition to the SHARE meetings, and wondered if I'd lost my senses. And there was the annual "work day" at church, when Dad and I climbed the cavernous attic above the sanctuary to assess the aging wiring, then ascended the belfry with Reverend Livingood to clean up from the pigeons and oil the bell wheel. I pulled at the rope, ringing a peal that echoed up Fourth Street, making me feel like Quasimodo. Hotel, senior play, SHARE, church. Everything I touched needed fixing.

When the prices came from Thomas-Sysco, Wince negotiated a ten-percent discount, then led us on a safari through Cincinnati in search of stock pots, pans, and serving platters. He zipped through the aisles like a kid in toy land, but was all business the instant I held up what looked like an excellent pot. He shook his head and pointed at the handle.

"These little rivets won't hold up. There's no welding! Water will get in and loosen it over time." He patted me on the shoulder and tossed the pot back.

We thundered off to another store where we found oak dining tables with glass tops.

"Easy to clean," said Wince.

We bought nine tables and 36 chairs, and added two ice cream parlor tables for seating on our stage when the cabaret wouldn't be performing. Our unfinished conference room was now a warehouse groaning at the seams with equipment and furniture.

"*The Old Curiosity Shop*," said Jo Ann.

"And I'm Little Nell!"

As Christmas neared Wince was deluged with banquets at his restaurant, and several weeks passed before we saw him. To show our thanks my parents sent him the largest sugar-cured Kentucky ham they could find with a note that read, "For your *private* enjoyment!"

3. Floods

Dad and Bonfield went to the Bracken County court house at Brooksville for the plumbing permit, paying five dollars per water "opening" for a total of $290.

"I'll get started first of the week," Bonfield grunted.

Monday came and he didn't show up, the first sign of what several people had whispered to us — that Bonfield did good work, but had so many jobs going he was hard to hold onto. It was November, when he was servicing furnaces all over Bracken County. Tuesday went by, then late Wednesday his panel truck appeared. It was 40 degrees and he wore his habitual T-shirt under his flame-colored hair.

"I'm looking forward to learning a lot from you," I said, helping Bonfield lug his equipment into our shop. He muttered something and disappeared till Saturday.

He finally launched things by checking the existing waste water lines, accomplished by stopping up all of the openings with inflatable rubber "plugs" and subjecting the lines to enormous pressure by having me fill them with hundreds of gallons of water with a garden hose on the Inn roof. If the water level dropped it indicated a leak somewhere. After several minutes the water failed to rise in the pipe, and Bonfield yelled out the door.

"There's gotta be 'nother line!"

The other line had to be under the 40x60 foot concrete slab, but where exactly?

"We'll hav'ta trace back from the city line behind the building," said Bonfield.

Dad and I started digging and ran into an old sidewalk that had to be broken out with a sledgehammer — and I went for my fencing mask before taking it on. We dug our way around boulders and rusted pipe, bricks, pottery shards, and an old patent medicine bottle. By evening the trench was four feet deep, but there was no sign of the city line.

"Let's start again tomorrow," said dad, his face glistening from the work.

Next day we deepened the trench and by afternoon my shovel struck cast iron — the city line. As we straightened up to relax our backs, mom dashed over from the house.

"The mayor just called and said it's all over with the bank. The jury *rejected* Taylor's appeal!"

Dad and I threw our shovels in the air. "Hallelujah!"

The city began demolishing the bank and by mid-December all that remained was the vault — standing defiantly amid the shattered brick like an artillery bunker.

Building inspector Herb Nagy visited again, and stared aghast at the changes we'd made since his first visit in June. "Frankfort hasn't gotten your plans yet! Why hasn't your architect sent them in?"

"We thought he sent them weeks ago!" said dad.

Nagy stormed around the lobby, glowering at the new staircase, the leveled flooring, the refinished doors and new paneling. "The work you're doing is *illegal!* You're not supposed to be doing *any* of this till the plans are approved!"

"It's all done according to code," said dad, raising his voice. "Our architect met with Jack Rhody last summer. Check anything you want!"

I boiled over. "It would've been approved months ago if Frankfort wasn't filled with morons!"

Nagy stepped back. He let out a breath and softened his expression. "Well, I can see that you're doing things properly. This is very good work. But it's gotta come through Orrin Lutner's office!" He sighed and went to the door. "Make sure your architect mails the plans as soon as possible."

We got in touch with Lape, who made an excuse about having gotten behind on things. He mailed the plans to Frankfort the following week.

Bonfield disappeared to put in a furnace for another antique shop. We were glad to see more shops opening, but wanted him to ourselves for a few weeks. He drove by and frowned through his tinted glasses at the trench and muddy pipe, then jumped into his truck after muttering he'd be back. Two weeks passed before we saw him again, during which we kept busy on other chores. Jo Ann taught a second series of dance classes at St. Augustine and we shopped for pianos for our cabaret, finding one an octave shorter than standard models.

"I'll be darned," said dad. "I saw pianos like that in the war, on the back of Jeeps when they entertained us from the USO!"

It was the right size for our small stage, and we renewed it with black enamel.

Bonfield caught up on furnaces and came back to run a pressure test on the sewer line we'd uncovered. As I filled the line with water on the roof, one of the plugs popped loose like a rifle shot and water flooded the Inn. Dad and I ran for mops, but it was too late to refill the lines for another test and Bonfield vanished again. Then he returned and supervised more pressure tests which indicated additional hemorrhages in the lines buried below the mammoth concrete slab.

Dad winced. "It'll take forever to break up all that concrete!"

"Not worth it," muttered Bonfield. "Better to lay new pipe."

It meant tearing out some of the new flooring we'd just installed in the men's restroom, and I swore as I ripped apart the work we'd done with such care only weeks earlier.

Bonfield studied dad's blueprints, then planned the course, angle of rise, and connectors he wanted while I cut PVC on the table saw. The challenge was to find the most efficient route around the obstacles that were too detailed to appear on the blueprints. Bonfield worked thoughtfully, his T-shirt staying spotlessly white as he set each pipe. He never rushed or worked up a sweat, and was the most warm-blooded man I'd ever seen. His rose-tinted glasses shone and his red hair glistened with tonic beneath the work light. He went long periods without saying a word, then would suddenly mutter as if he'd forgotten me.

"Gonna be hot tomorrow. S'posea hit fifty degrees!"

"Torrid," I'd say.

Del and my brothers helped with the trenching, and we removed boulders to the back yard to make a garden wall. I rented a jackhammer to lay the new lines in the concrete slab, and after twelve hours of continuous pounding the floor was mounded up with rubble and sand.

"You'd think we were demolishing the place!" said Rolland.

By early December the trenching was complete and gleaming white PVC lay everywhere. There were so many Y-joints, T-joints, elbows, connectors, and reducers that it looked like an Erector Set gone mad. We laid new lines in the outdoor trenches, shoring up the earthen walls collapsed by rain and snow.

"Good work!" said plumbing inspector Jim Perry, approving one of the lines.

With the main sewer lines in place, the days became more tedious as we ran the central waste stacks to the second floor with branches of smaller PVC for the bathroom drains and vent pipes. Bonfield laid out the paths while I bushwhacked ahead — cutting holes through flooring, studs, and joists. Some holes demanded a saber saw; others a reciprocating saw to muscle through the iron-like oak. The blades heated up and threw sparks as I ran into nails, and blades continually broke. Some areas were too confined for anything but a keyhole saw, and once or twice the space was so tight I used a naked blade wrapped with tape for a handle.

"Plumbing surgery," Leon observed.

I rigged work lights and set up ladders for Bonfield, made countless trips to the storage bins to fetch cans of glue, fittings, or elbows, and cut endless lengths of PVC with the radial arm saw. More than once I misinterpreted Bonfield's muttering.

"Naw," he'd chuckle. "That's naw whadda meant!"

I learned to bring two or three kinds of joints at once. By mid December we'd replaced one of the two old drain systems, and Jim Perry observed another water-pressure test. I filled the labyrinth of pipe with water from the roof as Perry run his flashlight over the PVC joints.

"Looks OK!"

He pasted a certificate on one of the pipes when Bonfield noticed that a temporary cap was crooked on one of the toilet flanges. He tapped it inquisitively with his wrench, and the cap exploded into the air on a fountain of water, soaking Bonfield and flooding the Inn. His face reddened as he wrung water from his T-shirt.

"Guessa forgot that `un!"

Jim Perry laughed, while dad and I rounded up the mops.

For a time Bonfield was working steadily and the upheaval overwhelmed the building. Trenches cut through the floor amid heaps of broken concrete, sand, and soil, and we battled to keep our tools free of dust. Mom grabbed a broom every time she passed through the shop. By Christmas the waste lines had been completed to half of the guest rooms, and to mark the occasion Bonfield surprised us with a buttermilk pie.

"Christmas present," he said, putting it on the saw table where we divided it up on the spot.

"Be sure to thank your wife," I said.

Bonfield's eyebrows shot up. "My wife! *I* baked it!"

Jo Ann went to Phoenix to take her aunt to the Mayo Clinic. It was my third Christmas in Augusta, and I sought consolation in Fournier's *The Wanderer*. The year ended with mixed signals for the Inn and the town on which it depended. A new deli called the Lunch Basket opened, but Yesterdays closed from incompetence and exhaustion. The potato chip factory also failed. My proposal to the community library to read Christmas stories for children was accepted after a long meeting with the board, but when I showed up the library was dark and the woman responsible for opening the doors never came. I put a notice on the door and moved the readings to the Three Bears Day Care Center, where a half dozen children and their parents clung to my words.

"We so much enjoyed it," said the woman in charge. "Thank you!"

A small but cheerful victory over television.

Our evergreen trees prospered — having survived the bag worms and brown fungus — and by the first snowfall their spiny tops stood a foot higher than in the spring. I plowed through the *Arban* trumpet book and got good enough that I was no longer ashamed if someone overheard me. It was two years since I'd left New York, 24 months' grappling to open the Inn. My hands were callused and my knees ached from the endless keeling required of our renovation. I'd completely abandoned my novel for the time being, and had written nothing other than my journal. With all of this haunting me I made a New Year's vow that we'd have the Inn open by April. It was unlikely that we'd hold out much beyond that, because sooner or later there'd be a failure of finances, if not of will.

"Sometimes I feel like we're carnival jugglers!" said dad.

4. The Carnival

Jugglers indeed, and the trickiest juggling was with the Department of Housing. Soon after Herb Nagy's November visit our architect sent the drawings to Frankfort, but a day before Christmas we got a letter from Orrin Lutner, the Plan Reviewer assigned to the Lamplighter, asking us to stop construction.

"What a mess!" said dad, handing me the letter.

Lutner demanded that we provide more details — about doors and hardware, fire suppression and water-flow, kitchen hood duct work, exhaust fan and extinguishing system, on and on.

"My God!" I said.

Absorbing the letter was like a minnow choking down a whale. It took us a full day to compile the information on the doors — three typed pages of fire-test ratings, materials, hinge types, and descriptions of the lock assemblies, right down to the serial numbers. The other points mentioned in Lutner's letter were being arranged through our licensed contractors, and would have to await their drawings.

"We have to ignore the warning to halt construction," I said, and dad nodded.

We had thousands of dollars going out each month with no income, and had no reason to trust the state's capacity to act in a timely manner on our application. Even Lutner admitted in the letter that because of "time constraints placed on the review process" some of the information he was demanding might already have been "contained in the drawings or specifications" sitting on his desk!

"If Lutner's too pressed for time to study the drawings we've already sent," I exclaimed, "where will he find time to study *additional* drawings?"

Herb Nagy came in January for his monthly visit. Although he didn't say as much, we had the impression that his superiors were pressuring him to make dead sure our project was halted. But instead of looking around, Nagy chatted a few minutes in the lobby before going on his way.

"Mild winter," he said, looking out at the vault of Art Taylor's bank.

It was clear he was doing his best to give us some breathing room.

Another bit of delicate juggling was Wince, whom we feared losing because of our repeated delays. I phoned him in February, and he was groggy with a cold.

"We're doing good business," he said. "But the owners are interfering too much. I can't really do the kind of work I want . . ."

"We're pushing ahead down here," I said, hoping to cheer him up.

Bonfield required less subtle juggling. In early January when Jim Perry tested another set of drain lines, fountains of water shot out several places and presented us another flood to mop up. Bonfield's method when working on a complex area was to lay out the pieces of PVC like parts of a model airplane to see that they fitted properly, which meant he occasionally had so many pieces that he'd miss gluing a few connections, which we never discovered until they gushed like Old Faithful in front of Jim Perry. Despite the over-looked connections, Perry was satisfied.

"You guys are getting this thing licked!"

He pasted up the certification on the lines, allowing us to cover the trenches with concrete and cart away the mounds of soil that had littered our lives for so many months. In the meantime our water heater arrived — a $2,000, 400-pound behemoth which we wrestled into place like a bear in a straitjacket. It rested on a skid which dad steadied as I removed the bolts. The last bolt slipped free and I tugged at the water heater to clear it from the skid; but I tugged too hard and the water heater toppled and smashed onto the concrete ramp inside the kitchen, badly denting one side.

"God," I said, glancing miserably at dad. "I've done it now!"

Bonfield straightened the dent and soldered the copper pipe to connect it. "That's as far's I go right now. Hav'ta run more lines 'fore I can get water to it."

Having no idea if our costly water heater still worked, we moved on to our next pressure test, and I returned to the frost-covered roof with the hose to fill the system with water. Jim Perry hiked from room to room shining his flashlight. "Looking good! Looking good!"

There was a roar in the cellar and we ran down to find dad soaked from head to toe, gasping for breath as the last of the chilled water gushed out a six-inch pipe. The seal had broken on the pipe, and Perry found another leak elsewhere.

"I'll have to see another test!" he said.

Choir director Cathy Riebel phoned one night to ask why I hadn't said anything about playing trumpet.

"Because I don't play very well," I said.

"I've *heard* you." Cathy lived next door to my parents. "It sounds splendid, and I want you to play Sunday. Add some pizzazz to the service! Come early on Wednesday and we'll go over the piece before the others get there."

Wednesday night I was a wad of nerves as Cathy clapped for attention. "Alan's gonna join us, but on the third verse I want everyone to drop out so he can take it as a solo."

I made a mistake or two, but we got through the hymn without difficulty.

"Amazing how much sound comes outta that thing," exclaimed Tony. He had a fine voice, a light but resonant tenor. "Sure don't need an amplifier!"

Sunday morning I was more jittery than when I'd played "Home on the Range" at a Cub Scout assembly in the third grade, and kept the mouthpiece in my pocket to keep it warm. As Reverend Livingood made the announcements I crouched in the choir stall blowing into the trumpet and working the valves. The first valve suddenly stuck. I unscrewed it and found that the felt had deteriorated from age. I removed it, but now the valve sat a quarter inch higher and made a distracting *thunk.*

The offering came, and as the ushers went up the aisles to the clinking of coins I tried figuring out what to do. Whisper to Cathy that I couldn't play? I blew softly into the trumpet and discovered that the offending valve didn't harm the sound. But could I get the right fingerings with the valve out of alignment?

"A highlight of our worship is the music our choir works so hard to prepare!" Livingood announced.

Cathy raised her arms and the choir stood up. The piano sounded the introduction — and I was startled to hear myself playing much better than at Wednesday night practice.

February chilled us to the marrow of our bones. Jo Ann went to Arizona to take her aunt to a neurologist, and my sister Del scouted out furnishings. Antique gold-framed prints of Lincoln and Washington for the Presidential suite, a red-plush theatre seat for the Actors' Room, a five-piece parlor suite upholstered in French Gobelin fabric for the lobby. We had endless water tests with floods to mop up and fittings overlooked by Bonfield to glue. Dad and I spent weeks framing in the new bathrooms as Bonfield ran in plumbing. Rain continued leaking around the heat pumps and windows, and my letters to Lucas Aluminum to get them repaired went unanswered. April came and the Augusta *Times* ran a picture of mom painting from the top of a ladder. The townspeople were convinced that the Tongrets were born and raised on ladders.

5. Rain

In the middle of the April deluge I had a painful discussion with Jo Ann. It was Easter Sunday evening and I was feeling rotten from having played the trumpet poorly with the choir. In addition to the two Sunday services the choir had also overtaxed itself singing for the community Good Friday service. Rain had pounded Augusta most of the day, leaking afresh into the Inn, and I was working late clearing up paperwork I'd pushed aside for days.

"I hate seeing you work such long hours," said Jo Ann.

"Gotta get things done," I said. "You work pretty hard when you're doing a show, don't you?"

"Yeah, but it ends in a few weeks. This has been going forever!"

I looked up from the desk. "A few more months. . . ."

She busied herself about the kitchenette. "I just hate to see you bury yourself down here. It's beginning to seem like such a dead end."

I looked at her in surprise. "But as soon as the Inn gets running I'll get on with my writing, and we can do some things. Maybe travel in a year or two."

She folded her arms. "I don't know if you'll have time after the opening. There'll be other problems. And it hurts me to see you using your talents like this. It's such a waste!"

"Hell, I wasn't doing much with my talents in New York. And it's cheaper down here." I went to the window in frustration. Rain fell in torrents, and I knew it would be streaking down the walls and staining the paint in two or three guest rooms, as it had done countless times before. I turned back to Jo Ann. "We're doing the best we can. We had no idea we'd run into all this crap with Frankfort."

"That's what I mean. All of you are working so hard, I just wonder if it's gonna be worth it. Is it really what you want?"

"Sure. It *will* be!"

"And what about us? I think we need to decide what *we* really want. What we'll be doing in five years. The more I see of this town the less convinced I am that we'll be happy here. It seems that so few people down here *care* about what you're doing. At the Inn, at church, or at school. Most of them want the town left as it is. Improve it and they won't thank you. You couldn't even get the library to open so you could read Christmas stories to their kids!" The rain was deafening and I went for my umbrella. "I just don't want you to shortchange yourself. You've got too much to offer!"

The path was a sea of mud, and I was more weary than angry thinking about what horrors I'd find at the Inn. I knew that Jo Ann was caught in an impossible position. Her ailing mother and aunt were in Arizona and she was married to a man who was indentured to a building that had become a bottomless pit of costly and unpleasant surprises. And what had become of our dream to buy a house? My savings from teaching had run out and I was waiting for my $470 tax return to live on.

The mud sucked at my feet as I approached the Inn, barely discernible in the wall of rain.

6. Frankfort

Herb Nagy returned in February and threw a fit. "Why hasn't Frankfort gotten the sprinkler drawings? They can't move ahead with the approval until they see them!"

Our fire-suppression man, Kenny Bratton, had sent us preliminary drawings in January, but had proposed putting sprinkler heads below the ornate ceiling in the lobby, which we thought would mar its appearance. At our architect's suggestion we'd asked Kenny to simplify the drawings, and had written Jack Rhody contesting the 100% system, arguing that we were meeting or exceeding the fire safety requirements applicable to the Inn, and citing the precedent of special consideration normally accorded historic structures.

"We're still waiting on a reply," said dad, turning the tables on Nagy.

Nagy phoned Frankfort and learned that Orrin Lutner had indeed received our letter three weeks before, but hadn't informed Nagy of it, who was clearly embarrassed. "It's still on the boss's desk. Either Lutner or Rhody will reply in a few days."

"All we want is flexibility," I said. "You don't walk into historic buildings in Lexington or Louisville and find sprinkler heads sticking out everywhere." I drew his attention to the lobby ceiling, which had taken weeks to restore, and on which Jo Ann had spent so many days painting from the top of the scaffold. "I thought the idea was to save lives — not to turn buildings into shower stalls."

Nagy studied the ceiling and his eyes lit up. "What about putting in a dropped ceiling!"

A few days later Rhody sent a letter denying our appeal. He brushed aside the points we'd raised and insisted that sprinklers *could* be placed in ornate ceilings such as ours without marring their appearance. Of course, Rhody had never actually seen our ceiling. I was so angry that I handed the letter to dad without comment and went upstairs to the Shaker Room, where I'd been nailing in flooring. The hammer blows grew heavier as I bent one of the nails, wishing it was the fire marshal.

In mid March, Kenny finished the revisions of the sprinkler drawings and sent them to us for review. Based on this information, dad met with Lutner in Frankfort to see how close we were to their demands. Lutner spoke first.

"As Jack Rhody explained, you've gotta have a one hundred percent system. There's no way around that, considering it's a wooden structure and is gonna be used for overnight accommodations."

Dad chewed his lip. "If that's what we have to do. . . ."

"But there's some things that'll make it easier without compromising safety." Lutner pointed his mechanical pencil at the blueprint. "The sprinklers in the guest rooms can go through the *walls* instead of the ceilings. And we *don't* think it's necessary to sprinkle the attic."

Dad felt immensely lighter. Putting sprinklers in the walls would save considerable expense, and the elimination of the attic sprinklers might save $25,000. Dad met with Kenny to make certain his new drawings would reflect precisely what Lutner had decreed. Kenny made additional measurements, then sent the drawings to Frankfort.

But early May Lutner rejected Kenny's drawings. The letter was accompanied with two pages of complaints and demands, and the linchpin was Lutner's assertion that Kenny's drawings didn't propose a 100% system. Kenny hurried to Augusta to discuss it with us.

"The drawings *do* have a one hundred percent system. We did everything Lutner asked!" He shook his head. "Shit! The only thing I can guess is that Lutner's going back on his word, and will force you to put sprinklers in the *attic*. Maybe he wants them in the closets and dead air spaces too. He's sure as shit changing the rules on us!"

Our architect, Lape, hadn't gotten a copy of the letter, but he was stunned when dad told him the news. "As soon as the letter comes I'll go to bat for you," Lape promised. "Find out what's going on in Frankfort!"

Then Nagy came by with his supervisor, Kelder. It was obvious that we'd made considerable progress on the Inn since his last visit — more "illegal" construction — but Nagy said nothing as Kelder strolled around the Inn admiring the work. At last Kelder shook his head.

"It's a shame this place is over seventy-two hundred square feet. If it was a shade smaller you wouldn't be subject to a lot of the restrictions. You wouldn't need a full sprinkler system, for one thing. But from the looks of things, you'll have to have a one hundred percent *dry* system."

Kelder explained that dry systems were unaffected by freezing and would be required in our attic.

Dad's jaw tightened. "That's not what Lutner said at our meeting!"

Kelder raised a hand. "Just between us, Lutner can be a little . . . *puzzling*." Nagy grinned and Kelder went on. "A dry system for this place might run forty or fifty thousand dollars."

After Nagy and Kelder left I turned to dad. "That's interesting about the seventy-two hundred square-foot figure."

Dad pulled out the blueprints and measured the rooms. "Sixty-nine hundred square feet! Including the cellar!"

We were *under* the minimum size for a sprinkler system! In a frenzy we dug through the code books, but found no mention of the 7,200 square-foot regulation Kelder had referred to. We phoned Lape, but he said he'd never heard of it either. We tossed aside the code book in disgust and went back to work. Another bit of wishful thinking gone up in smoke.

Jo Ann outlined three cabarets for our stage, Broadway songs, Hollywood musicals, and music by Stephen Foster, George M. Cohan, and Irving Berlin, using sheet music from her own collection. We sent fliers advertising for a pianist and music director to the colleges and universities. Then she was hired to choreograph a series of musicals for the University of Cincinnati College Conservatory of Music's summer theatre operation that kept her on the go for the next eight weeks.

May vanished without progress on the sprinkler problem, then in June our architect fulfilled his promise to go to bat for us by arranging another meeting with Lutner and dad.

"I'm insisting that Jack Rhody sit in on this," said Lape.

Rhody was Lutner's boss, the highest code enforcement official in Kentucky and the court of last resort. His presence proved critical, because he overruled Lutner on several key points. Rhody returned to the understanding that had been agreed on in the prior meeting between dad and Lutner, that sprinklers weren't necessary in the attics or bathrooms, and permitted us to place the dining room sprinklers in the walls, rather than the ceilings as Lutner had insisted.

Now that we had a clear idea where to head — witnessed by the fire marshal and our architect — Kenny proceeded with a final set of drawings at his Ohio plant. He came by in June to determine the exact locations for the 69 sprinkler heads.

"I've done my estimates on what this'll cost you," he said. "An even fifteen thousand."

We didn't know whether to be grateful or horrified. It was certainly cheaper than installing a dry system in the attic — but a whale of a lot more than the $3,000 we'd originally budgeted. In some ways we'd been incredibly, if charmingly, uniformed.

7. The Hood

Juggling the kitchen hood was like tossing around handfuls of explosive gelatin. We gave Oscar Pell at the Lexington firm a $1,600 deposit in January, and his engineer — Carl Swain — got his drawings to Lutner in mid-February, which Lutner rejected for failure to "include enough information" and "meet specific requirements of the codes. . . ."

Oscar Pell thundered at us on the phone. "My engineer's *never* had drawings rejected!"

He tore down to Augusta with Carl Swain to take additional measurements, and Swain told us that the key to the rejection was Lutner's requirement for *tempered* air in the kitchen.

"When it's cold outside you gotta heat the incoming air to match the indoor temperature, using a make-up system."

Pell nodded. "We've gotta include plans for the system in the new drawings. And I'm gonna warn you that they can be very expensive."

I glanced at dad, who was doing a good job of reining in his reaction to this latest shipload of bad news. "Guess you better get some estimates."

Pell and Swain left and I went back to the Victorian Room where I'd been repairing the floor. It had been an awful week, culminating in the sudden death of Jerry Litzinger from a rare heart disorder. He was only 37 and left behind his wife and the little produce store. My mood was grim as dad came in to get a tool.

"Maybe we oughta find out what's going on in Frankfort," I said. "Call our state representative or somebody. If they keep laying stuff on us like this we'll never make it."

Dad looked at me in surprise. "I think we should wait till we open. If we do something now, Frankfort's likely to make things harder."

"But how can we open with all the crap they keep throwing at us? First it's one thing, then it's something else. We're already spending four thousand dollars on the hood, and this nonsense about make-up air is gonna push it a lot higher. We'll have to get half the people in the state staying in these rooms to pay for it!"

We'd revised our income projections and estimated from the amount of debt we were carrying it would take a 33% occupancy rate to break even — up from our first estimate of 25% suggested by Leon and confirmed in the projection prepared by the university months earlier.

"I can't see being forced to pay for costly equipment that might be unnecessary. Once it's installed we won't be able to remove it and get our money back!"

Dad's eyes darkened. "We'll just have to bite the bullet. Frankfort's got us. Afterward we can poke around and find out who's been sticking it to us."

I threw down the hammer. "But we may not be able to *pay* for the damn stuff! At the rate we're going they may even push us into bankruptcy!"

Dad blinked. "Your mom and I still have some money, Alan. We're certainly not gonna consider bankruptcy. We've got too much invested!"

I stormed out of the room, and that night returned to my apartment thoroughly drained. Too tired to pick up the trumpet, I sank in front of the TV with a PBS documentary about the China Ballet. Lights blazed in a Neo-Italianate theatre which seemed vaguely familiar as someone came on the screen whom I recognized. In fact, he looked like *me*, and he was calling instructions to ushers while urging the audience to take their seats. He wore a blue blazer like mine, but he was younger. Then I remembered the documentary that had been filmed when I was a theatre manager at the Brooklyn Academy of Music. I recalled the cameras dodging around as we dealt with the performance, but I'd never seen the documentary and had put the whole episode out of my mind. I was staring at a stranger.

"A make-up air system will cost you nine thousand dollars," said Carl Swain over the phone a few days later.

Dad made some calculations based on Swain's figures, and because of the amount of current make-up systems would draw, estimated that the system would consume $24,000 worth of electricity a year.

"It's a nightmare!" I said.

Dad walked away, leaving the note pad with the estimates by the phone. As usual he'd been doodling, and over the last year his sketches had gotten starker, with faces composed of angry, sharply incised features. One of the faces he'd just drawn stared out with the spiral eyes and jagged teeth of an Inca carving, and two more faces had the anguished, hatchet-like profiles of Picasso's *Guernica*.

I loved my father more than I could say and hated what was happening to him. To all of us. But I felt powerless, and for a few days we all went around in a stupor as dad reviewed the blueprints and made calculations. Then a few days later he laughed out loud.

"I think I've got it!"

I followed him to the kitchen where he pointed at the wall.

"All we have to do is put a vent *directly outside*. Fresh air will be drawn in by the hood fan, and will be warmed up almost immediately by the stove and other kitchen equipment. We don't need a separate make-up system!"

It was so simple it didn't seem possible that Frankfort would go for it, but we checked the code book and were convinced that the vent would satisfy the fresh-air requirement. A solution of perhaps $20 versus $9,000 of the unit Oscar Pell had quoted.

"Why in blazes didn't Carl Swain think of this?" I asked.

"Good question," said dad. He phoned Alpha Supply, the Cincinnati firm Wince had shown us, where we were buying a lot of equipment. Dad explained our problem, and next day Alpha's engineer measured our kitchen and said a simple vent to the outside would do the trick.

"Would you prepare an estimate for a hood?" dad asked.

"I sure will," said the engineer.

Armed with this backup we called Oscar Pell, who said he was as perplexed as we as to why Carl Swain hadn't thought of a wall vent.

"I want you to tell Swain to work a vent into his drawings and get them to Frankfort *ASAP*," said dad, "Or we'll have to accept the other bid."

"You can't do that!" said Pell. "We've got an agreement!" He argued that the contract we'd signed merely obligated him to get Frankfort's approval of the drawings "as far as they went," regardless of whether the system was permitted to operate.

"That's sheer idiocy!" I shouted into the phone.

Dad jumped in on the extension. "Listen, the only reason for *having* the drawings is to get the hood approved for operation! What do you think we're doing down here!"

Pell blustered. "Well, I'll see that Carl gets moving on this."

It didn't escape us that it was April first. Pell and Swain sped to Frankfort to iron out the problems with Lutner, and Swain called to report. "Lutner himself proposed a solution to take care of the make-up air. That we put a *vent through the kitchen wall!*"

Exactly what dad had suggested.

In mid June Swain phoned that the drawings had been approved. "I did the same as your architect," he confided. "Went over Lutner's head and met directly with the fire marshal, Jack Rhody."

"Good for you!"

"But this does it," said Swain. "They're getting screwy down there. This is the last damn hood I'll design!"

Two weeks later the approval letter came from Frankfort, stamped RELEASED FOR CONSTRUCTION in black ink. Swain surrendered the plans to the fabricators, and at the end of July a truck pulled up with our dearly won hood.

The Inn was beginning to gel so quickly that I asked Wince to come for a look and discovered that he'd taken a new job as executive chef of the Excelsior restaurant in Latonia, Kentucky. Latonia was a fast-growing city near the Cincinnati International Airport known for its thoroughbred race track. We had no contract with Wince and feared we'd lost him, but Wince put me at ease.

"I've been brainstorming some Lamplighter recipes," he exclaimed. "Wait'll you see what I've got!"

A week later his Cadillac rolled up at our door. We rescheduled our opening for the third week in August, and he bubbled with enthusiasm when he saw the improvements.

"The next seven weeks will go by in a flash!" he said.

8. Bob

When Tony left we replaced him with Dick Bach. Dick was just out of the Air Force and loved working with machinery, making him a good fit for keeping the lawn mower in top condition and servicing the host of kitchen equipment we were buying. But we had so much going on that we hired a second employee in May, Bob Donahoe. Bob was my friend from New York who'd visited the previous summer, an actor I'd met in summer theatre, and a classical guitarist who adored the Spanish romantic composers.

"It's time I left New York," he gushed on the phone. "I wanna smell some fresh air and go walking in the woods once in a while!"

"There's plenty of woods down here," I reminded him. Bob was an experienced actor whose prominent nose and deadpan delivery reminded me of film veteran Louis Calhern. "We'll do some plays, and your guitar's just what we need for our little cabaret."

After serving in the Navy, Bob had worked his way through Florida State University with a front desk job at Howard Johnson's, then in the banquet department at New York's Plaza Hotel between acting jobs. He had the front desk experience I lacked.

Over the winter I updated Bob on the tribulations of our renovation, and told him we'd probably be ready for him in June. But because of the delays I asked him not to give notice at his job till we were closer. Then he suddenly wrote that he'd quit his job and would leave New York in mid May.

I phoned him that night. "We still haven't got the sprinklers approved."

Bob's voice crackled at the thought that he was finally coming to the country.

"Doesn't matter. I plan to visit the family in Pittsburgh. I'll stay a bit longer and come to Augusta the beginning of June." June was six weeks off and I decided to gamble that the ice jam at Frankfort would thaw by then. He went on. "Maybe I can speed things along with all the construction and painting you're doing!"

He arrived in an aging Chevette loaded with guitar, sheet music, and books. He threw his arms around Jo Ann, with whom he'd also worked in summer stock. "If we get any more performers down here we'll have to open a branch of Actors' Equity!"

That evening Bob took out his guitar that he'd had custom-made in Spain and played in our dining room while I practiced the trumpet in the conference room. I'd heard him give a recital in New York and was reminded how good he was. He smiled when I came in to listen.

"You sound pretty hot on that horn. Maybe we can find something to play together."

Bob loved working outdoors, so I had him mulch the shrubs and arbor vitae trees, but he got poison ivy seriously enough to need an injection from Dr. Brindley, and I moved him inside to create the forms and procedures for guest registration, banquet reservations, and credit cards. He exhausted these chores in a few days and begged to help with the renovation.

"We need some painting in the bathrooms," I said, and Bob rubbed his hands with anticipation.

His long, carefully manicured fingernails — so vital to plucking guitar strings — caught the light like opals. I got him started, but when I went back later I saw that he'd forgotten a dropcloth.

"Don't really need one," said Bob, slapping paint on a bathroom ceiling from a ladder.

I pointed at some dribbles on the floor. "What about those?"

Bob squinted. "Well, it's water base, isn't it? Easy to clean up."

In a few days we finished the ceilings and I began putting down vinyl floor tiles.

"Why don't *I* do the tiles in one of the other bathrooms?" said Bob. "Get things moving along!"

"Vinyl's tricky," I said. "Why don't you watch me do a few?" I put down more tiles to show him how, spreading a cloth to ease my aching knees, then let him take over. He peeled the paper backing from a tile and pressed it down by the chalk line on the subflooring. "Make sure it's right on the line," I cautioned.

"It's perfect!"

He laid down three more tiles, then I knelt for a closer look and found that each tile was off-center from its neighbor, throwing the final tile off by a quarter inch.

"Better pull these up," I said.

Two of the tiles had to be discarded, and I repositioned the others. Bob's face reddened. "Guess it takes practice."

I shuttled him back to the office where he spent the next days laying out inventory forms and compiling a list of businesses to contact about our conference facilities. Then he searched me out in the upstairs hall where I was laying mud on drywall.

"Why doncha let me do this? Free you up for more important stuff!"

I saw from the look in his eyes he thought it was a pushover job. I'd been mudding for two and a half years and could finally handle a trowel. "It's pretty messy."

"Naw," he intoned in his actor's baritone. He scooped a trowel full of the stuff, but before he got the mud to the wall it spattered to the floor and surprise spread over his face. "Christ, it's slippery!"

Fourth of July weekend we nailed up drywall where the hall ceiling had collapsed from incessant leaks. It was 104 degrees and we squeezed inside the coffin-like space, mopping the sweat and brushing away bits of insulation that fell like ashes into our eyes. Bob was cutting drywall with a carpet knife and let out a yell as blood spurted from his index finger. The cut forced a two-week layoff from the guitar, and in sympathy I mashed my thumb with a hammer the same day, although trumpet players don't need thumbs all that much. The pressure to open the Inn was making me more careless by the day, and later in the week I smashed a finger with the hammer.

I dug around for more paperwork Bob could do when a saleswoman knocked at our door. "I want you to sit in on this, Bob, since you'll be doing a lot of the ordering." He rubbed his hands and joined the woman and me in the lobby.

She gave us a catalog as thick as the Manhattan phone book. "Most hotels use the individual size packets of facial tissue. Your overnight guests will end up taking the tissues with them, and this'll save you in the long run."

Bob turned to me. "Great idea!"

"Let's try the standard size," I said. "See how it goes."

The saleswoman turned the page with a marvelously manicured, pink-polished fingernail. "Bathroom tissue comes forty-eight rolls to the carton, and you'll want two-roll dispenser units for your restrooms in the restaurant. And of course, state code requires the sanitary disposal units for the women's room."

Bob put a dog ear in the page. "Yeah. We had those at the Howard Johnsons. Guess we should order them."

"We'll want to discuss the style with mom," I intervened.

"Oh. Right."

The woman explained their soap dispenser system, and Bob pushed up his glasses for a closer look. "This looks fabulous! Maybe we oughta put these in all the bathrooms!"

I closed the catalog. "I think we'll start with a carton of bathroom tissue and a gallon of all-purpose cleanser."

When Bob had been with us two weeks I knew I'd goofed really big hiring him as soon as I had. He was doing his best, but simply wasn't suited for construction work. And I was pulling out my hair in a losing battle to make our dwindling dollars go where they were most needed. I sat down with Bob in my office by the bunk bed.

"I'll have to put you on half salary till we open." Bob's eyes glazed over, and I felt as if I'd stuck a knife in his back. I cleared my throat. "I certainly won't expect you to put in forty hours a week. Just come in half time. It's only till we open."

He studied his bandaged finger. "The hours don't matter. But I have rent to pay, and meals. . . ." He was renting a room from Mayor Weldon for $50 a week.

"Well, your pay will certainly cover that, with quite a bit to spare."

He put his glasses back on. "Well, if that's what we have to do."

I left the Inn feeling ill, and wanted to get completely away from the place.

Our friendship was strained for a day or two, then it was as if the question of his salary had never arisen. He insisted on working a full week, plugging away at whatever I gave him to do. To soften the blow of his reduced salary I usually gave him lunch at my apartment. With Jo Ann gone again to Texas to do *Oliver*, there were only the two of us to cook for, and I made meat loaf in the slow cooker, French onion soup or omelets, spaghetti, or a chef salad. We had lots of melted-cheese sandwiches, or turkey franks heated in our wedding-gift microwave. But there were days when I was too hot and tired to do more than open a can of soup and slap peanut butter onto celery. We swallowed tall glasses of iced tea and discussed music and books. Bob didn't know one end of a saucepan from the other and raved about whatever I served.

"Hey, this is *good*," he'd say, tucking into a tuna fish sandwich. "How do you figure this out?"

"I read the label," I said.

But I longed to eat an elegant lunch cooked by Wince Faulkner.

9. Tremors

My parents had parceled out jobs and responsibilities according to interest and ability, but we often overlapped things. While finishing the lobby staircase dad sculpted a plaster bas-relief of a tulip. He'd devised smaller tulips as the cover panels for light switches, and the staircase tulip repeated this motif. He didn't mention his plans to do the tulip until it was underway, and I'd almost talked myself into liking it until dad added rose accent colors, which in my view detracted from the tulip's clean lines.

"Looks awfully bright," I said.

"Something to catch the eye," he replied.

Then he experimented in plaster with overlapping rings, using the rim of a large tin can to make the patterns. After painting the rings cream-white to match the rest of the staircase he brushed on a pastel green. The effect bordered on the abstract and was markedly different from the other walls. I felt it was a bad choice, and was miffed that dad had plunged ahead without sounding out the rest of us. Then things came to a head when he proposed using some wrought-iron fence we had to separate the dining area from the rest of the lobby.

"We can bolt it down here," he said, indicating the arch at one end of the lobby. Rolland was with us, and watched as dad continued. "We'll leave a three- or four-foot gap for a passageway."

"What if we have to expand our dining area?" I said. "Maybe add a third table? Won't the railing get in the way?"

"That's something to consider," said Rolland.

"Once we decide where our dining area's gonna be, we oughta stick with it," said dad.

"It seems to me that those railings are too large for the lobby," I countered.

Dad shook his head. "They're only four feet high."

I studied the arch from the far side of the lobby. "What about something more delicate, like wood lattice? We could hang plants from it and shift it around as needed."

Dad frowned. "I don't think lattice would look good in here. That's more appropriate for a garden."

The discussion went back and forth as dad and I pressed our views, becoming more entrenched while Rolland tried to mediate. We argued about who had the best aesthetic sensibility, and dad glared at me.

"Alan, I've had thirty-five years in management with a large corporation. I've been remodeling and renovating for years. I know how things oughta be done!"

"What about my years in theatre?" I shot back. "I know something about design and color!"

"Maybe we can settle this later," Rolland suggested.

I threw up my hands. "Well, before we start bolting down iron railings we oughta consult the decorating committee. That's what you appointed them for. Mom may have some ideas of her own!"

Dad raised his voice. "When it comes to choosing the railing, *I'll* make the decision!"

Mom and Rolland's wife, Jane, came in and our debate stopped. The lobby was hot with resentment, and I was stung by dad's insinuation that he was more capable than I to make aesthetic choices. After all, wasn't I the *artist* in the family? That night I poured out my resentment in my journal, and after exhausting several pages realized that all of us were badly on edge. What kind of dream were we building?

Underlying the rigors of hood and sprinkler systems, plumbing and leaking roofs, and managing our two employees was the issue of money. Nineteen eighty-eight had begun ominously when the bank notified me that our account was $300 overdrawn. My parents covered it with enough extra to carry us till a third loan was approved, while I ransacked the check register to find out where I'd screwed up.

Damn, I thought, discovering a couple of math errors, but the bigger discovery was that we needed to revise our budget. After a long meeting with my parents we estimated it would take another $54,000 to get us through, bringing our debt to $174,000 — two and a half times the original $73,500. My parents prepared to invest another $10,000 of their own, and we saw that the Small Business Center projection of break-even at 33% room occupancy was no longer valid.

"I think we'll have to delay blacktopping our parking area and getting the new roof till after we open," I told dad. "That'll lower our requirement to forty-nine thousand."

This amount would see us through to September 15 — our new opening target. Armed with our figures, dad went to the bank to request the new loan, and the Small Business Center revised our income projections, preparing two scenarios. The first pictured a harsh winter where we could expect few lodgers and slow business in our restaurant, burying us beneath a $20,000 loss for the year. The second scenario was more optimistic, projecting break-even during the first month's operation and a modest profit by year end, based on an average of five room rentals per night and 100 meals per day from breakfast, lunch, and dinner.

"We've just gotta pray for a mild winter," said dad.

By the first of September we ran into more trouble. I'd neglected to balance the checkbook for several days and pulled myself away from other chores to catch up. We were $400 in the red. While making an entry some days before, I'd hit the plus key on a $200 entry instead of the minus key.

I'm not worth a damn, I thought. My concentration was getting worse and the bills on my desk made me ill. That very day I'd made our $650 loan payment, and had just paid the final $1,600 on the kitchen hood, another $1,600 for the Ansul system, $5,600 to the bank for an interim note, $640 to John Bonfield, $1,600 down payment on mattresses, $500 to Miller Lumber, $1,500 for hotel insurance, $334 for stage lights, and $100 to the city for our business license. Paychecks were due Bob and Dick, and in a few days the quarterly federal tax payments had to be paid. Rolland's wife Jane had ordered our drapes for the dining room and lobby, which would come to another $2,000. I wanted to scream.

Then the apartment shook for several seconds. It was late at night and I called my parents. "What in God's name was that?"

"Had to be an earthquake," said dad. "We had one a few years ago that did some damage in Maysville."

I turned on the news and found that the earthquake had hit Mount Sterling, 50 miles south of Augusta, measuring 4.5 on the Richter Scale. It felt like a divine comment on the woeful state of our finances. Then Jo Ann called.

"*Oliver's* going well. Strong cast and a snappy orchestra. Wish you could hear them. . . . How are *you* doing?"

I filled her in on the latest news of our struggles with Frankfort.

"Tell your folks I said hi," she said. "And stop hitting your fingers with the hammer!"

10. Stalemate

The letter approving the hood drawings came from Frankfort in early July. The hood was trucked in on the 20th, and that same day we cut open the ceiling and roof above the kitchen and began constructing the chase where the hood would pass. Made of double layers of fire-resistant 5/8" drywall, the chase was supported with 14-foot aluminum studs that ran through the second floor and attic. Fastening the drywall to the studs was a tricky matter as I drove screws from an extension ladder with dad, Bob, and Dick holding the drywall. Always the ladders.

Next morning B&W from Old Washington installed the hood. It was heavy-gauge galvanized steel, four-feet by ten-feet with a 16-foot vent duct. The duct came in two sections. One section was threaded into the chase and welded on top of the other section before we raised both of them and welded them to the hood. Then we lifted the whole contraption to the kitchen ceiling. A young man with a round face whom we nicknamed "Hoss" headed the crew, a 6'6" 260-pound giant, but despite his muscle it took eight of us to hoist the assembly in place and steady it while one of the crew secured the bolts to the ceiling joists.

"I'm glad you got a small kitchen," said Hoss.

"This is small?" gasped Bob.

Hoss rolled his shoulders. "Hell. I've put in vents *twice* this size!"

Hoss went to the roof to make sure the vent was evenly centered in the chase before the bolts were tightened, and came back with a long face. "Damn thing's too short!"

Dad and I hurried up and saw the duct penetrating the hipped roof above the kitchen, but falling short of the adjoining roof at the front of the Inn.

"Heck," said dad. "All it needs is a one-foot piece welded to the top. It's Oscar Pell's mistake, and he'll have to pay for it!"

Relief flowed through my veins, and we walked around the roof, talking over what had to be done next to cope with the leaks while enjoying the fresh air. Across the alley a man was attacking Art Taylor's bank vault with an industrial grade air hammer that kicked up dust like a Mediterranean mistral. Two days later the vault was a pile of twisted rebar and concrete.

"At long last," said dad.

In early August Hoss installed the Ansul unit — the kitchen fire suppression system — and Herb Nagy inspected it. He lighted the six burners on our stove, then set off a smoke bomb as dad flipped on the fan. The vent went *swoosh* as the wall louvers snapped open to admit air from the outside. The draft rushed up the hood with such force that it yanked open the dining room doors and swallowed all trace of the smoke from the bomb.

Nagy reeled. "That's the best test I've ever seen!"

I handed him the authorization letter, and he signed it: "Smoke test OK."

Yet the sprinkler system remained. After his successful meeting with the state fire marshal in June, Kenny Bratton took a month to complete the final drawings. He delivered them to us in early July, and as a precaution we took them to Lape to make certain Frankfort would have no excuse to reject them a second time. In mid July Lape told us he was having his draftsman redo the drawings.

"Kenny's included too many notes pointing out the obvious — where he's *not* installing sprinklers. We wanna keep them precisely to the point. No less and no more."

The drawings went to Frankfort the end of July, but it was August before Lutner left word that he couldn't process the drawings till he had Kenny's signature on them. Kenny hadn't signed them because the drawings had gone directly from Lape to Frankfort. We couldn't reach Kenny at his plant in Ohio, but saw him in Augusta on Sunday, joy riding in his Jeep with his wife and some friends.

"Have you spoken with Frankfort?" dad asked.

"Yes, but I'm not gonna sign those drawings."

A moment's silence.

"What do you mean?" dad asked.

"I'm worried about those points where Rhody overruled Lutner, allowing less than a one hundred percent system. The liability for any injuries if there's a fire falls on *my* head. I'm not going along with that. Either Lape can sign them, or the state can sign them. That'll let me off the hook."

Dad leaned into the Jeep. "Hell, Kenny, we're losing a couple of thousand bucks a month over there! We've gotta get this thing resolved!"

Kenny brushed the hair from his eyes. "Frankfort's just trying to give us the shaft. If the drawings are OK, they oughta accept the architect's signature. I'm not gonna sign the things just to let the pressure off Frankfort. If something goes wrong, they'll come back at *me* as the guy who put in the sprinklers. If there's a problem ten years from now my name will still be on the damn certificate!"

Kenny released the brake and drove off.

11. Installation

Our worsening situation made it hard for me to sleep at night, regardless of how tired I was. And a few days later I was in a kind of physiological miasma while sanding a stack of trim boards behind the Inn. Dad came out and I shut off the sander.

"The sprinkler system's been approved." I stared at him. "Kenny called Lutner and persuaded him to sign a letter listing the variances that Rhody approved. Kenny says that letter will cover him, and he's now willing to sign the drawings."

I dropped my eyes to the mounds of sawdust. I'd expected this moment to come with a bolt of lightening. But I felt nothing.

"That's great. Really great."

The end of August Kenny and his two sons drove up in a truck loaded with hundreds of feet of pipe. Coated with oil to protect it from rust, the pipe had been pre-cut at Kenny's plant in 10- or 15-foot lengths and was marked with colored chalk to denote their intended location. They unloaded the pipe while dad and I tried to keep the newly decorated rooms from getting banged up. Kenny began the installation Saturday morning with a crew of six while Bob, dad, and I helped wherever we could. We cut openings in walls and ceilings, sawed 2x4 braces, and held pipe while it was threaded. Kenny's crew put in another 12 hours on Sunday but was far from finished.

"This is tougher than I thought!" Kenny said, shaking his boyish mop of hair as he dragged himself back to his truck "We'll finish next weekend."

It meant ratcheting our opening back another week, but we filled the days with a hundred other jobs. Del installed special-order window blinds in the Pullman Room — which was a dead ringer for a train car sleeper — and we picked out carpet for the Inn. Bonfield put in faucet handles and other fittings on the sinks and tubs, while mom and dad continued painting. I ordered soap dispensers and more mattresses, printed up reservation forms, finished the logo I was designing for our brochure, and dealt with a burgeoning stream of hopefuls who'd sniffed out the chance of a job at the Lamplighter. The massive, dolly-crushing refrigerator we'd bought at the auction wasn't staying cold and I searched the Yellow Pages for a repairman. And I somehow remembered to order roses for Jo Ann's opening of *Oliver* in Texas. I ached to have her with me, but the Inn was in such chaos I was glad she didn't have to see it.

The following Saturday Kenny didn't show up, and I went by his house. No one was around except a man working in the field, who told me Kenny was on the river.

"You won't see any more of *him* this weekend!"

I hiked down the bank and saw Kenny's power boat in the distance, pulling someone on skis. Another week shot, and Kenny called on Sunday to say he was sorry.

"I couldn't get the crew together. But we'll be out Thursday and will work straight through Sunday to get her done. Don't worry about it!"

Easy for him to say. He wasn't carrying our debt. We swallowed our chagrin and sallied forth on other jobs. We bought more lumber and chamfered it for trim, installed towel bars in the bathrooms, and painted door frames. There was always more painting. But Kenny didn't show on Thursday, and we wondered if he was infected with the same virus that sometimes afflicted Bonfield. Then Friday Kenny and his crew burst into the Inn for a 12-hour day, but still didn't finish.

"We won't be in tomorrow," said Kenny. "All the guys got plans for the weekend."

It was Labor Day and Augusta was immersed in the annual Heritage Days celebration, with antiques booths, food stalls, and flea market hucksters lining the streets. Another week that we were stymied in giving Wince a firm opening date, and the frustration tormented my sleep. I dreamed we were embroiled in a debate about finances and dad asked if the Inn could borrow $100 from me. I remembered the $100 Jo Ann and I still had in our house-purchase account, and with a feeling of acute regret I handed it over.

Then Wince enlivened us with a surprise visit. In July we'd asked him to hold off giving notice to the Excelsior, and on this trip he studied the improvements we'd made and discussed our impending operation. The Inn was hugely transformed from his visit in June. The kitchen was immaculate with white walls and ceiling, a gleaming gray floor, and appliances sparkling in every corner.

"Oughta put the steam table here," he said, thrusting out his arms. "All I'll have to do is turn around, and there it'll be."

We'd invested $4,000 in an automatic dishwasher, which gleamed like a newly minted coin of outlandish proportions beside the three-bin sink. A salad cooler, wet bar, and drinks dispenser fitted out the servers' station, and shelves packed every inch of wall space. A repairman had serviced the elephantine refrigerator, which hummed quietly. Fresh paint brightened the chef's office above a maple desk and shelves for cookbooks. Snowy white paint glowed in the prep room to match the kitchen.

"The ice maker oughta go by the door," said Wince, eyeing the room with satisfaction.

In the prep room at the back of the Inn dad had installed a commercial-size wash sink and stainless steel prep table with counter space for baking, and Dick had scrubbed and oiled the Hobart mixer. The stock room was set up for canned and dry goods, with floor-to-ceiling shelves and cabinets. There was a walk-in box the size of a garage.

"You've done wonderful!" Wince laughed as we led him to the dining room.

The lime-green decor blended with the oak mantelpiece with its antique mirror, and Del had hung a framed print of Renoir's *Luncheon of the Boating Party* by the bay window. Light streamed in from Sid's stained-glass peacock, and the piano shone with an ebony gleam on our stage. The spotlights had arrived from New York and were ready to hang. We showed Wince up the wheelchair ramp to the restrooms, inlaid with plum-colored ceramic floor tiles from Thailand, and dad's oak-trimmed wash sinks.

"Here's what the carpet will look like," said mom, showing Wince the samples. His eyes brightened. "You've got the best place around!"

"How are things at the Excelsior?" I asked.

Wince put his hand to his head. "Lord, we're busy! We've got all the Christmas and New Year's banquets we can handle. The owners know what they're doing. They stay out of my way!"

We discussed the training of cooks and servers, uniforms and work shifts. "Who'll be in charge of the restaurant when you're off?" I asked.

Wince leveled a finger at me, and I laughed nervously. "Then I've got a lot to learn!"

Wince smiled. "You won't have to know how to cook, but you'll have to know when the dishes are *right*, and when the place is running properly. You'll learn."

We still hadn't settled on a name for the restaurant, and Wince turned his eyes on dad. "How about the *St. Charles!*"

The second Friday in September Kenny's crew astounded us by finishing the sprinklers, then tested the system as mandated by code. It was positively Orwellian that after the miles of red tape getting the sprinklers approved the code didn't require the presence of a state inspector. Kenny ran the test himself, filling the system with 200 pounds per square inch pressure and holding it there for two hours as his crew inspected the myriad connections in the walls, ceilings, and floors. Nothing leaked, and Kenny filled out a form to be sent to Frankfort — witnessed and signed by *us*. What a bizarre system.

Jo Ann flew in and I showed her the latest changes. "Thank heavens," she said. "You can get this glorious beast open!"

12. Veiled Guests

I dreamed that the Inn had in fact opened and we hosted a wedding reception — with no one on duty but me. Guests swarmed in with flowers and food, women fused over the bride's trousseau, and children scattered in all directions as I chased helplessly after them.

This reflected an urgency that we needed to pull out all the stops to get the remaining jobs done, but we'd already pulled them all out two years earlier, and could do no more than try to keep them open. I devoted myself to putting in the remaining fire-resistant doors, and was working so quickly that I cracked the hammer against my thumb with the full force of my strength. The same thumb I'd hit twice before and I reeled with pain. I soaked it in ice, certain the bone was broken, but was surprised to see a half hour later that it was still in one piece. Four days later I banged my left index finger with the hammer. I'd gotten up at 5:30 after tossing in bed from restlessness and the baying of the caged hound dogs up the street. My left hand was now a mess, with the thumb and two fingers throbbing and the nails an ugly blue, and I was hardly able to lift anything. I swallowed aspirin and kept working.

It was the home stretch, but circumstances had already propelled us into the role of innkeepers in early August when we got a phone call from Carolyn Thompson in Albuquerque, New Mexico. "My husband and I are coming to Augusta, and wonder if we can stay at your place. My husband grew up there!"

My parents took the call and said *Yes!* The Thompsons were due the weekend after our street debate with Kenny, and tensions were as volatile as gasoline on a bonfire. We decided the best room for the Thompsons was the Presidential Suite, and that's where we threw our energies. I was doing final touches in the kitchen while keeping an eye on Bob and Dick. I had misgivings about taking in lodgers before the Inn officially opened, and worried that someone would rat on us to Frankfort. Toward the end of the week dad surged into the kitchen.

"I think you've been spending too much time down here when there's a dozen things to do upstairs. Your mother's been up there for two hours getting the bathroom ready!"

"It so happens mom insisted on being there. And I'm certainly not gonna order her to leave. Besides, how many people do you think we can get into a bathroom at a time?"

"At the moment neither Bob nor Dick are up there. There's plenty they could do in the Suite beside the bathroom!"

I flared up. "We've been in there a dozen times this week! None of us have been sitting around on our hands, for God's sake!"

Dad stepped back. "Well, I know that. I just think we should concentrate on the Suite, and leave other jobs till later."

He went back upstairs while I chewed things over. I was supposed to be managing the place, yet decisions were being made against my wishes. I vowed that if it continued I'd put my foot down and make it clear that *I'd* make operational decisions — not my parents. And if they didn't approve they were welcome to find another manager.

The most important task wasn't done till the afternoon of the Thompsons' arrival, when Bonfield soldered the final coupling and turned on the gas valve of our expensive water heater that had crashed to the floor and had its side dented months earlier. The pilot light ignited and flames roared beneath the boiler, and a few minutes later Bonfield turned a tap in the kitchen as steaming water gushed out.

"Your visitors'll have plenty hot water for their whirlpool tub!"

After two-and-a-half years I could understand nearly everything Bonfield said.

When the Thompsons arrived the Suite was ready. Bob and I took their luggage up, and I saw the ice bucket mom had brought over from the house, resting on a doily on the sitting-room bureau. We showed the Thompsons how to set the air conditioner, then I led the way to the bedroom.

"Closet's here."

Travis Thompson waited with a garment bag, but I hadn't put in a clothes rod and started to apologize when I found myself staring at a newly installed rod — painted and ready for service. Dad had been busier than I'd thought, and I was ashamed for having argued with him.

"Bathroom's this way."

I opened the door for Carolyn and showed her how to work the whirlpool tub — half-expecting to find a hammer lying on the toilet seat. But the room gleamed with everything in order, down to the freshly laundered towels.

"This is fancier than we expected," said Carolyn. "Wait'll people find out about this place!"

The Thompsons left to have dinner at the Beehive. Bob came back to practice his guitar, offering to stay the night in one of the rooms so I could go to my apartment.

"You know," he added. "I noticed how *dark* it is on those steps. They're gonna have a hard time finding their way up them tonight."

Hidden below the brick arch, the entryway was a mass of shadows. I had no idea if dad had wired in the light over the steps, but I found the switch in the service panel and turned it on. A soft glow saturated the entryways, and we were struck by the fact that the front of the Inn was lighted up for the first time in a half century.

"Looks nice," said Bob.

The Thompsons came in for the night.

"The Suite's lovely," said Travis. "And we're glad you didn't put in TVs. We brought some books."

Just the kind of lodgers we'd hoped for.

I took the long way home down Parkview Street. It was dark except for the Inn, where a light glowed in the Presidential Suite as Travis and Carolyn were no doubt enjoying their books. Instead of a work light glaring through a naked window, it was a halo nudging its way through lace curtains. For the first time since the new siding went on two and a half years earlier, I really *saw* the Lamplighter, and God help me, it was enchanting.

13. The Chef

In September we got a letter from the Department of Housing approving our construction plans — authorizing us to *begin* the work we'd started nearly three years earlier. Later the same day Nagy and Kelder stopped in. Nagy stood in the entrance, mesmerized by the transformation.

"Holy shit!"

"Really gorgeous!" said Kelder.

They looked around a while, throwing out compliments, then Kelder cleared his throat.

"There's a new regulation, just came out. I'm afraid you'll have to put sprinklers inside your walk-in box."

"Inside the *walk-in box?*" said dad.

Kelder tucked in his chin to show what he thought of the regulation, and Nagy wandered off to inspect the paint on the wainscoting.

"Good God!" I said. "Is Frankfort afraid the frozen fish will catch fire?"

Nagy laughed and Kelder shrugged. They left, and dad leaned on the front desk.

"To put sprinklers in the walk-in, we'll have to ask Kenny to do more drawings, which Frankfort has to approve. The drawings will go to Lape, then Kenny will need to take measurements, haul down more pipe and round up his crew for another weekend." I nodded and dad continued.

"I guess we'll just wait'll we get a letter from the fire marshal, putting the new regulation in writing."

Maybe the whole thing was Kelder's idea of a joke, but if it was it backfired because we refused to bite.

The plumbing was finished and Bonfield's bill totaled $7,500 — $2,000 below the lowest bid we'd received from the other plumbers. For once we'd saved money, and Jo Ann threw a "stop work" dinner to celebrate. She dressed up the apartment with balloons and served pasta salad, sloppy joes, and peanut-butter ice cream pie.

Then Wince suggested we have dinner at the Excelsior to refine our opening strategy. Jo Ann put on a lovely evening dress, and I got into a jacket and tie after bandaging my bruised and purple fingers. Mom and dad looked positively swank in a suit and cocktail dress. The Excelsior was a restaurant on the grand scale, what you'd expect to find in Palm Springs or Miami. Marble floors, fountains, terraces smothered with shrubbery, multilevel banquet rooms, pearl-white baby grand piano floating above a sleek bar. Wince was regal in his snowy chef's jacket, toque, and checked trousers, and watched his servers with the assured eye of Diocletian reviewing the Praetorian Guard. He let us glimpse the kitchen, glimmering like an operating room of Everest proportions.

"We've gotta draw a lot of people. The owners spent four million on this place." He accepted a cup of coffee from a server. "I'll give notice here in two weeks, and we'll have the St. Charles open in mid-November."

Wince returned to Augusta to interview cooks and servers, asking questions and jotting notes about things I'd never have noticed: Clean fingernails. Scuffed shoes. Doesn't know meat cuts. He learned names quickly and told several of the men and women he'd want them for a second interview in a few weeks.

"This is the countdown," said mom, as we walked Wince to his Cadillac. "Next time you come down we'll have lunch."

"And I'll cook it!" Wince laughed and gave mom a hug.

A few days later a woman called from a realty company in Brooksville. "We'd like to hold our Christmas dinner at your place. You gonna be open?"

"We certainly will!" My heart raced as I copied the details and told her our chef would call her about the menu. Then I spread the news. "Got our first banquet!"

Other people called to ask when our restaurant would open. We'd delayed so long it was almost a joke around town, and I was tempted to say we enjoyed working on the Inn so much we'd decided not to open at all. The media was also heaping on the pressure. A Cincinnati TV station filmed a 10-minute documentary on the Augusta renaissance, focused mostly on the Lamplighter. The camera caught me pretending to hammer a nail into the lobby stairway — where I was careful to avoid hitting my fingers — and the producer interviewed dad at length. The documentary aired, bringing more phone calls, but we were distracted from them by a thunderbolt of bad news. On October 13, a month before our opening, Wince was on the phone.

"This was the hardest decision I've ever had to make," he said, as his voice cracked. "After I gave my notice, the owners here spent most of the day talking it over with me. They kept coming back with better offers and gave me a big salary increase. It's a great place to work, and I guess I've just gotta stay."

Although we didn't know Wince's salary, it was clear we couldn't match it. After we got over the shock of losing him, we realized how generous he'd been, running us around Cincinnati to buy equipment and his many trips to Augusta. He'd helped put the St. Charles on solid footing, and had boosted our morale when it was at rock bottom with his laughter and optimism about what the St. Charles could be. He'd proven to be a good friend, and before hanging up he said, "I wish you folks Godspeed!"

We were searching through the chef résumés we'd gotten when Del called. "Got someone who's experienced, bright, and very excited about the Inn. You gotta see him!"

Hayden Roberts came the next day, and by the time he left I was certain he was the chef for us. He was mid-30s, easygoing with striking black hair and nicely dressed in a tweed suit. He gazed in amazement at the lobby.

"I had no idea there was something like this in this part of Kentucky. It's obvious you guys have done a mountain-load of work!" Hayden looked over every inch of the kitchen and explained what he'd do at the St. Charles. He was banquet chef at a Cincinnati hotel, but said he wanted to put his stamp on his own place. "I'm very keen on regional American recipes."

He'd trained in the South and in Portugal and told us he felt a special kinship for country cooking, and for Kentucky dishes in particular. He ran his hand over the oak mantelpiece.

"You oughta capitalize on the *uniqueness* of this place. Make corn bread and country stew, Kentucky hot browns, that sort of thing. There's so many foods that evolved in this region. People can get a steak anywhere, but there aren't many places that'll fix indigenous dishes."

Hayden lived in Milford, Ohio, an hour's drive by way of the ferry. But if the ferry was closed the drive was twice as long.

"Would you consider moving to Augusta?" I asked.

Hayden pondered. "I just got divorced, and have custody of my two daughters." He said the oldest had just entered first grade, and he was reluctant to have her change schools.

But he came down next day and met some of the teachers. As we walked back to the Inn he confided, "I've got reservations about the school, but I'm mad about the town."

He returned the following day — straight from a banquet in his soiled whites — and handed me some schedules he'd worked up showing how he proposed to deploy the kitchen staff. He also gave me a letter thanking us for giving him so much of our time, and pointing out that, although he wanted to remain in Milford for the current school year, he felt he could make the St. Charles a success.

14. Home Stretch

We found Hayden the last second before midnight. Expenditures were overwhelming us and I found it harder each week to keep a rosy attitude. I awoke from another dream where dad was paying Kenny Bratton for the sprinkler system with a stack of one-hundred-thousand-dollar bills.

Our opening was now set for November 21 — three weeks away and probably the seventh or eighth time we'd change it — and we still had major purchases to make. In addition to what we owed Kenny for the sprinklers, there was carpeting to buy and thousands of dollars of food and beverages to order. We needed more glassware and cutlery, more pots, pans, and cookware, and everything from garbage cans to napkins. We needed a cash register, commercial grade vacuum sweeper, and menus. Fees were due the city and county, and the phone company would have to be reimbursed when the pay phone was installed. We had to have shelves for the walk-in box, floor mats for the entrances, and more cleaning supplies. New items appeared on the list almost hourly. Eighteen thousand dollars remained in our line of credit, and my estimates showed that all but $1,000 would be spent by opening day.

Hayden came in like a whirlwind, checking our inventory of china and flatware, drawing up lists of things to buy, outlining schedules, and drafting menus. He found the cooks and servers he wanted, most of whom had been Wince's choices. ARA/Cory set up our coffee machines and the Pepsi man brought soft-drink equipment. A salesman from Kerns Meats in Brooksville brought his price list. We rushed the completion of the conference room, and Hayden made repeated trips there amid the hammering and sawing to confer with us, a pencil shoved through his unruly hair.

"I'd like to link the entrées with the guest rooms. Country ham for the Bluegrass Room and baked sole for the Starboard Berth."

"Shouldn't the ham go with the Actors' Room?" said dad.

Hayden laughed. "Hollywood strip steak." Mom asked about desserts, and he smiled. "I'll be baking pies every day." He said he was doing a separate menu for breakfast and lunch, including Bavarian waffles, French onion soup, catfish, and a rich Kentucky burgoo. "I'll run daily specials, and items for kids."

We tore around Cincinnati for baking pans, trays, warming dishes, ladles, steak knives, and aprons. Hayden sailed down aisles stacked to the ceiling with used equipment, his eyes darting around the heaps of cookware. He pulled out a cast-iron baking pan with corn-cob shaped molds.

"This'll give a nice brown crust." He noticed the expression on my face. "How we doing?"

"I *think* we're still solvent."

Hayden squeezed my arm. "We're almost finished."

We ate at an Italian restaurant where Hayden knew the chef. We ordered pasta and Hayden ate deliberately, focusing entirely on the food as the lines of his eyes mirrored his response to the flavors and textures.

"Not a bad sauce." He sipped his wine and reached for the bread. His fingertips absorbed the texture of the crust as he broke the bread and held it to his nose. "Oh, no." He signaled for the server. "This isn't fresh. When was it baked?" The server dashed off for another basket of bread, and Hayden winked. "Gotta keep 'em honest."

The final week before opening was so hectic I felt I no longer had even a token control of events, swept along in a raging river of preparations. One of our cooks changed her mind and went to work at a factory, and another cook muttered doubts about leaving her job at a diner in Maysville.

MONDAY, SEVEN DAYS BEFORE OPENING, another cook appeared, Grace, whom Hayden hired in place of the woman who'd abandoned us for the factory. "I'd like to put you on afternoon and evenings," he said.

"Anything but weekend nights," she replied.

Hayden was also uncovering equipment problems. The deep-fryer turned out to be smaller than the one specified in our contract, and after several days' delay Alpha Supply replaced it. The range had several fire bricks missing, and when Hayden tried it out, he found that the oven was a half inch too narrow for the dozens of baking sheets we'd bought at the auction. Poring over my figures that night I estimated that even if we had good business our first week, we'd need another $5,000 by mid-December.

TUESDAY, SIX DAYS BEFORE OPENING, carpet man "Toad" Bold came by in his van.

"You gotta pick new carpet. The supplier sold the ones you wanted 'fore I could get back to him." He opened his van. "Lookee these wonderful patterns!"

We swallowed our disappointment and made new selections, and a few days later Toad brought his crew to begin work. The wine salesman conferred with Hayden, who chose a variety of California labels — Beringer, Kendall Jackson, Konocti — and we held a training session for our servers. To underscore his regional cooking, Hayden complimented the wines with locally brewed beer from the highly regarded Oldenburg

Brewery in Northern Kentucky and Christian Morlein in Cincinnati. We solicited bids for signs to hang in front of the Inn, and I wrote our first newspaper advertisement.

WEDNESDAY, FIVE DAYS TO OPENING, a Thomas-Sysco truck pulled up with our food order. The invoice came to $2,300, but we had ten days to pay. Toad's carpet-layers finished the dining room and moved to the Actors' Room, while Jim Perry made the final plumbing inspection. He handed us the certificate and shook my hand.

"Good luck, Alan. I'll be over to try your food!"

THURSDAY MORNING, FOUR DAYS TO OPENING, the temperature gauge on the walk-in box shot up from zero to 14 degrees F, and we found that the compressor was short-cycling. It was stocked with the thousands of dollars of food we'd just bought and I phoned the repairman in a panic. He solved the problem with a minor adjustment, but I wondered how many more of these shocks we'd have to face.

Toad's carpet-layers moved to the downstairs hall, as Bob helped me assemble the dining room chairs and tables that had been stored in boxes for months. I moved Dick under Hayden's supervision in the kitchen where he cleaned and labeled. Dad hooked up the ice maker and Jo Ann shopped for bedspreads between the dance classes she was giving at school.

FRIDAY, THREE DAYS TO OPENING, I drove around Greater Cincinnati buying shelving, waste cans, bulletin boards, folding step-stools, conference tables, and a rugged vacuum sweeper to maintain our new carpeting. Each time I wrote a check it was like cutting off a piece of my flesh. Jo Ann took the ad I'd written to the Augusta *Times* and *Ledger-Independent*.

THE LAMPLIGHTER INN

Proudly Announces the Opening of the

St. Charles Restaurant

Tuesday, November 22
(Closed Thanksgiving Day)
Serving Breakfast, Lunch & Dinner
~ 7 Days a Week ~
Weekdays 6 a.m.– 8 p.m.
Friday & Saturday 6 a.m. – 9 p.m.
Sunday 7 a.m. – 6 p.m.
Chef Hayden Roberts Welcomes You To
*Old-Fashioned Home Cooking   *Two Elegant Dining Rooms
*Taste-Tempting Daily Specials   *Delectable Desserts from Scratch
*Home-Baked Breads & Biscuits   *Private Banquet Room
*Catering for All Occasions
Reservations Encouraged Weekend Nights @ 756-2603
West 2nd Street   Augusta, KY

SATURDAY, TWO DAYS TO OPENING, Sid and Del joined us, and Rolland returned with Jane and his daughter, Ashley — a budding young dancer and playwright. They stayed through the next day to clean, dust, polish, wax, and vacuum. Our produce was due on another Thomas-Sysco truck, but it failed to arrive, and Hayden scouted out alternative sources. I settled down at the phone in my office with a list of people we knew in the area and dialed the first name, Tom Appleman, who'd been mayor before Ike Weldon.

"Tom? Alan Tongret. You'll be surprised to learn that we're *opening our restaurant!*"

"I may have a heart attack!"

"Hardly believe it, can you? Anyway, we're having a preview for our friends on Monday, starting with breakfast. We'd love to have you come by."

"I'll look forward to it, Alan!"

It was evening when I got to the end of the alphabet — the current mayor, Ike Weldon, whose Eugene Pallette tones rattled the phone.

"I've been runnin' my sporting goods store for a couple years now, and I know how tough it is gettin' into business. If the coffee's hot, I'll be there Monday morning."

Hayden continued his skirmish with the range, whose door refused to close. He was experimenting with muffins and shook his head in dismay. "I've looked all over this thing and can't even find a *name* on it. I can't believe it's a South Bend!"

And the deep-fryer that Alpha Supply had just brought as a replacement disgorged huge tongues of flame up the exhaust stack whenever Hayden turned up the gas. Alpha sent a repairman, who looked it over and shrugged. "Well, don't that beat all!" Thank God we had the Ansul system in place.

SUNDAY, THE DAY BEFORE OPENING, I turned over the children's sermon to Tony. Our newly installed ice maker shut down, and I tore through the manual for a solution before giving up a few hours later. It had also come from Alpha Supply, and I was beginning to mistrust them. Jo Ann went to K-Mart in Maysville to buy a dozen odds and ends, and the rest of the family worked nonstop. That night I reviewed our accounts and noticed the number on the check I was about to write. We'd yet to serve our first meal, but I'd written nine hundred and ten checks since coming to Augusta.

15. The Day We've Hungered For

I tore myself from the sweet envelope of sleep and got to the Inn at 6:00 a.m., my jeans and sweatshirt put aside for a tweed jacket, tie, and wool slacks, and flesh-colored bandages masking the purple nails of my fingers and thumb. A flotilla of clouds emerged in the east on a warm breeze; our mighty Whirlpool furnaces hummed and the Inn stretched its limbs as we readied our first breakfast. Our cash register hadn't come, so I set up a cigar box at the front desk by a copy of the Kentucky sales tax table.

"Morning," said Bob, waving his hand in a benediction as he pushed through the door in a smart blue suit and tie. He staked out a bit of turf behind the front desk as I opened the cigar box. "Fifty dollars in one's and five's, and plenty of change. Yell if you need more."

Hayden galloped in at eight with narrowed eyes. "I don't know if we're gonna make it with that range. I'm having to put biscuits onto those dwarfish trays and it takes forever!"

"What about food deliveries?" I asked.

"Sysco's been promising since Thursday, and I don't know when Kerns is coming. I've called 'em twice. We won't be able to serve half the stuff on the menu."

"Do the servers know what's missing?"

"We'll have a quick review before we start."

The next several hours I shuttled endlessly among the kitchen, office, lobby, and dining room — getting supplies, checking restrooms for paper, helping the servers find things and operate the coffee maker. Kim, Laura, and Lori looked sharp in their servers' black slacks and vests, white blouses, pink cummerbunds, and bow ties. Jo Ann radiated a frilly welcome as hostess in a lavender dress, and Del energized the St. Charles in a black pantsuit as she waited tables and bused dishes. She'd worked at a pancake house in college and ricocheted around the kitchen and dining room like a bullet. Mom vanished into the kitchen to help Dick run the dishwasher, and dad split the day between assisting in the dining room and putting up ceiling tiles in the still unfinished conference room.

School Superintendent Mack Wallace and his wife Wilma came early and dropped their jaws in wonder.

"Wherever did you find that?" said Wilma, running her hand over our hobbit-sized piano. "It's darling!" I took her coat and sat them by the bay window. "I'd like to bring my home economics class to see your rooms!"

Our menu covers hadn't come from the printer and I handed the individual sheets to the Wallaces as Vicky Thornsbury come with her mother in tow. Vicky owned the Lunch Basket, the new cafe, and had taken time to wish us well. I sat them by the fireplace where Vicky could enjoy the activity through the swinging doors of our kitchen.

"Looks busy in there!"

"Chaotic," I said. "Kim will be your server, and thanks again for your help." Our guest checks hadn't come, and Vicky had loaned us several from the Lunch Basket.

I heard more voices and my heart raced as faces crowded the dining room, emblazoned under the bright chandeliers and the blur of the rushing servers. Thelma and Dixie from church; Sharon and Jim Graves from the flower shop. What if everyone hates the food! What if that damned range blows up!

Jo Ann waved encouragement and I took a breath. Concentrate. *This is what you've wanted for three years!*

I floated around the dining room, maitre d' and innkeeper. Laura dashed in with water glasses and orange juice, and Del with a coffeepot in each hand. I glimpsed Hayden through the swinging door, his raven hair tousled below his toque and his jacket unbuttoned at the throat. Steam rose around him in clouds as he bent over the griddle. The air was fragrant with coffee, hot biscuits and sausage, hash brown potatoes, and simmering oatmeal. Sunlight streamed in from the garden, turning the dining room from amber to gold.

Tony materialized by the stained-glass peacock with his girlfriend, Ruthie. "My God! Can you believe *I* painted some of that trim? I musta spent two weeks at the business end of a paint brush, to be sure!" His suit hugged his shoulders, making him look like a retired boxer. "Where do we park ourselves?"

I showed them to one of the ice cream parlor chairs on the stage. "Spotlights might come up, so have a song ready."

Mayor Weldon strode in as he unzipped his sporting-goods jacket.

"Morning, Ace! I knew you Tongrets would get this place open sooner or later. Now this is first rate!" I searched for a place to seat him when Tom Appleman came in. Weldon jerked his thumb. "Why doncha put me with Tom. If he doesn't mind eating with a Republican."

I seated them opposite the Wallaces at the bay window. "Coffee?"

"I like it by the bucket and I like it *hot*," Weldon reminded me.

Del touched my shoulder. "I'll take care of the mayor if you'll find a table for the Lynches."

Lillard and Carol Lynch owned the local home supply store and had sold us most of the paint and wallpaper that had transformed the old hotel into its Cinderella incarnation. I sat them where the light of a chandelier set off Carol's perfectly arranged red hair.

"Now you can see what we did with all of that green paint you mixed for us."

"It goes great with your carpet," said Carol.

Lillard tucked his chin into the menu. "This day was a long time coming, but I betcha feel it was worth it."

Skip Miller, owner of the lumber yard, came with his wife Caroline. In sheer volume we'd used more materials from Miller Lumber than anywhere else, and I wondered how they felt — ordering a meal in a room built almost entirely from supplies that had passed through their hands.

"What's your dad's next project?" Skip asked.

"The rest home," I said.

Halfway through breakfast Parcel Post drove up with our menu covers and we hurried them onto the sheets. The nuns from St. Augustine paraded in and Jo Ann put them at the last remaining table. Then Herb Nagy popped in the door and waved a stack of official looking papers.

"Need to do the final inspection," he said.

"*Now?*" I started to tell him to go jump in the deepest part of the river he could find.

"I'll handle this," said dad.

It was the culminating inspection, capping off every bit of work done the last three years, and an hour later dad returned.

"That's it. Nagy's filling out his forms."

"We passed?" Dad nodded. "Did he mention putting sprinklers in the walk-in box?"

"Not a word. You know, we probably won't see him anymore, and I don't think he's done such a bad job. Why don't we give him breakfast?"

We seated Nagy at an ice cream parlor table that had been vacated and he scarfed down the St. Charles' first complimentary meal. Dad was right that Nagy had steered a difficult channel, but at the moment I wanted nothing more to do with Frankfort. I noticed that the cups were empty at one of the tables, and I found Kim hovering over the toaster.

"Coffee at table number three!"

"Sorry!"

Hayden tossed a smile at me over the steam table. "Goin' great guns!"

"They love your biscuits!"

Hayden beamed. "By the way. Sysco didn't send my grille brick. Can you get me one?" I stared blankly. "Abrasive material, shaped like a brick. Try the pizza parlor."

"And we're outta ice!" said Laura.

Our costly ice maker was still acting up, so I hazarded the dismal confines of McCracken's Bar to buy two bags before crossing the street to Carota's Pizza, where owner Connie Bolin handed me a grille brick.

"Keep it," she said. "My husband and I will be over as soon as we can."

After three hours breakfast thinned out and the servers prepared salad ingredients for lunch. Hayden cleaned the grille with the brick, then made Kentucky burgoo and French onion soup. Our mid-day patrons trotted in, John and Elizabeth Parker from the funeral home, choir director Cathy Riebel and husband Jerry, and Lois Greene — who ran the Piedmont Art Gallery. At four o'clock Adrienne and Susan replaced the other servers, wearing black bow ties instead of pink, and set up dinner by lighting the oil lamps and dimming the chandeliers and wall sconces. Nearly everyone we'd invited had already come for breakfast or lunch, and we had only a couple of tables for dinner, just enough to give Adrienne and Susan a tip or two. The curtain came down on our Open House and thirty minutes later a Kerns Meat truck pulled up.

Hayden clenched his teeth. "*There's* our damn delivery!"

We collapsed with the cigar box in the lobby to count the take, which came to $270.

"Not bad," said Bob.

I loosened my tie. "I guess not." But it seemed as if we'd had more people than that.

"Think of it this way," said dad as he sank into a armchair by the fireplace under the stone carved with 1800. "For the first time in three years it's money coming *in*!"

Tuesday, our first publicized day of business, I rolled out of bed at 4:45 a.m. to open for breakfast at 6:00 a.m. and worked till 11:00 p.m. Hayden had stayed over in one of our rooms and prepared fresh biscuits and muffins, and had plenty of sausage, bacon, and eggs ready. Kim, Laura, and Lori were punctual at their stations and the aroma of brewing coffee invigorated the St. Charles. But Sharon Graves from the flower shop was our only patron.

"It'll take time for word to get around that we've opened," said dad, as I fumed behind the front desk by an empty till.

Mom agreed. "Most people are probably making plans for Thanksgiving."

At 11:00 a.m. business improved as a troupe of diners traipsed through the St. Charles. The repairman got our ice maker working, and Omer Johnson — the *Kentucky Post* writer who'd written the first story on the Inn two years earlier — interviewed us again. We seated him in the lobby with a plate of fresh muffins.

"Delicious! Now if I can get that pretty gal to warm up my coffee!"

Lori blushed as pink as her bow tie and ran for the pot.

Dinner was slow, but brightened up when Rolland and Jane came for dinner. Rolland put down his napkin. "Great porterhouse. Once word gets around the place will do fine!"

On Wednesday 32 patrons flocked in for dinner, double Tuesday's business and earning us $500. Our alcohol license arrived, followed by our shipment of wine and beer. Laura took the first order for a bottle of Kendall Jackson Cabernet Sauvignon, but since she was underage, I got the wine from our cellar and went to the kitchen for glasses and a tray. I threw a towel over one arm — just like the movies — and was headed to the dining room when I saw something was missing.

Jo Ann looked at me. "Alan?"

"We've spent a fortune setting up this kitchen and don't have anything to open a bottle!"

Everybody broke up, and Jo Ann ran to our apartment for a corkscrew.

Except for a few overnight guests the Lamplighter was quiet on Thanksgiving and we gave the staff the day off. Thanksgiving was also my 41st birthday, and after dinner Jo Ann brought out a cake, aflame with candles.

She hugged me. "Make a wish!"

If a man doesn't have a million dollars by the time he's forty-one he hopes to have the big promotion, a nice car and home, and perhaps children. I had no car or house, and certainly no money. My children were unpublished manuscripts, neglected in the closet. But I had a great wife, a caring family, and a stake in the Inn. I blew out the candles and prayed that the Lamplighter would succeed. After three years we'd realized the dream of opening the Inn, but the dream would be smoke in our fingers if the Inn couldn't earn its keep.

Thanksgiving passed and we navigated our first weekend. I dragged myself out again at 4:45 a.m. and didn't get to bed till midnight on Friday and Saturday. Hayden had urged us to get a custom-made drain shelf for the dishwasher, and I exhausted most of the day driving around southwestern Ohio arranging for the job to be done. It cost $200 and I hoped it would pay for itself. By the time I got back dinner was underway and the St. Charles rocked with patrons. Del and Sid were helping, and I found Sid busing dishes in the kitchen as it bristled with activity.

"Very busy," I said.

Sid had also worked at a restaurant in college, and he hustled to load up the dishwasher as perspiration poured down his face. "You know it! I bet business has doubled!"

Sid was right. The day's earnings passed $1,000. We expected an even better Saturday, but did only half of Friday's business, so we anchored our hopes on Sunday. If we'd learned anything about Augustans, it was that they craved going out for Sunday dinner. They crowded into the tiny restaurant in Germantown 12 miles across the tortuous roads of Bracken County, and marched like lemmings to the restaurants in Maysville and Aberdeen, Ohio. Families thought nothing of driving 45 minutes each way to the Perkins restaurant near the university. With our varied menu and kids' specials, our cheerfully lighted dining room and lobby where patrons could wait for friends, we were certain Sunday would be crammed to the rafters. But no one came for breakfast, and only a few straggled in for lunch and dinner. After a booming start our opening week fizzled out like a cannon primed with wet powder.

16. Our Apprenticeship

Despite the rotten business on Sunday our take for the week approached $3,000 and exceeded the Small Business Center projection. Heartened by this, we threw ourselves into preparing for our Grand Opening, but in the two weeks leading to it we continued stumbling. Monday we had only one person for breakfast, two for lunch, and two for dinner. Something was clearly wrong, and we met in the lobby to brainstorm.

"I talked with Pauline," I said, referring to our morning cook. "She thinks our prices are too high, and that a lotta people feel they have to dress up to come here."

Mom shook her head. "We don't wanna drop prices too much."

Hayden crossed his legs beneath an apron spattered with sauce. "My gut feeling is that it wouldn't hurt to lower some of the items."

"The important thing's to get our volume up so we're breaking even," said dad. "We've gotta get twenty or thirty people coming in for each meal."

We agreed to revise the menu, beginning with breakfast where we lowered prices sharply. Diners could now get two eggs and hot biscuits, home fries, and sausage or bacon for $3.15, or hotcakes for $1.85. Single orders of biscuits were 35 cents and a large glass of orange juice 65 cents. We made even more dramatic changes in our lunch menu by lowering our vegetable plate from $2.25 to 95 cents, and fresh-baked pie from

$2.50 to $1.75. We added soup-of-the-day with salad and homemade bread for $2.95, and increased our sandwich selection. We felt the dinner prices were reasonable, but added a roasted turkey breast entrée.

The St. Charles' atmosphere was more problematic. We'd killed ourselves to make it attractive. We weren't a jacket-and-tie place, but the more we discussed it we realized a lot of townspeople were comparing us with the defunct Yesterdays with its greasy linoleum, or McCracken's Bar — which served meals in a room gloomier than a Camus novel. Farmers and Clopay employees were used to going there in their work clothes, and we could see why anyone who'd glimpsed our chandeliers and stained-glass peacock would think us too elegant for everyday dining.

"I'll make flyers of our new prices," I said, hoping that people would begin to feel more relaxed about the place when they saw how reasonable we were.

The kitchen range was also on the agenda, and I promised Hayden I'd call Alpha Supply. The controls were malfunctioning, the oven door had gone haywire, and the last of the fire bricks had fallen into a tray of Hayden's boysenberry muffins.

Del printed our Grand Opening invitations and Bob addressed them with a flourish. With his archeologist's knack for unearthing what we needed, Sid brought another truckload of conference tables and a huge safe for our office, and we asked no questions. The bids came in for our signs — one each for the Inn and St. Charles — and we chose a husband-and-wife artist team in Maysville to design and fabricate them, based on the logo I'd created of the elegant lamplighter in his long black coat and top hat.

Our employees continued testing my diplomacy skills, beginning with Dick, who confessed he was looking for another job.

"I just can't see spending my days cooped up indoors running a dishwasher!"

"I wish we had yard work for you. But there won't be much till spring."

He wiped his hands on his apron and trudged back to the kitchen. Then Grace — always spotless as a lily — had a running dispute with Jeff, who operated on the sloppy side.

"Look at this mess!" she screamed. "The griddle ain't been cleaned like it oughta, and this floor ain't been touched! Jeff is supposed to sweep the floor and mop it every night before he goes home! And look at these pans!" She lifted the covers on the steam table to reveal a ring of food residue. "He ain't even emptied the water!" She rolled up her sleeves. "Wait'll he comes in today. I'll learn him what a mop is! And what soap and water is!"

Some of the staff groused about their hours, and the younger women campaigned to have weekend nights free for dating. And as meticulous as she was about cleaning, Grace — in her 50s and married — was equally meticulous about avoiding work on weekend nights. "My old man drives a truck all week, and on weekends he wants me home to cook *his* dinner!"

A few hours each day I secluded myself in the office to wade through our financial morass. Invoices were due from food purveyors, but our income was too little to cover them. Our dozen employees had pushed the payroll to the sky, and it took me half a day to do the paychecks. After they were given out Adrienne pounced on the front desk and shoved her envelope under my nose.

"I think you made an error!" She was early 30s, attractive with short brunette hair.

Oh God, I thought. But a glance at her pay stub showed that I'd *overpaid* her. Adrienne was our most experienced, most reliable server, and I wrote her a new check with a sense of relief. "You're very honest!"

She laughed. "I'd have been here all the quicker if you'd *underpaid* me!"

Sid and Del got the lobby aglitter with a Christmas tree, and Jo Ann decorated the display cabinets. The night before I drove her to the airport for her return to Arizona we stayed over in the Actors' Room, christening it on behalf of the many performers we knew. Jo Ann was contracted to choreograph *Perfectly Frank* and *Carousel* and wouldn't be back till the end of March. It would be the longest separation of our marriage, but we sorely needed the money.

With so many things to keep track of I shifted some of it to Bob's shoulders, but it was soon clear that his heart wasn't in the Inn. His jokes were growing more macabre, and he showed little initiative. He usually took a glass of wine with dinner, which I overlooked, and at a certain point one glass became two.

"We'll be getting the cabaret going soon," I said, hoping to perk him up. He nodded and slunk back to the cash register.

December brought a smattering of regular customers. We sold our first take-out orders and booked three more banquets. Alpha Supply finally called about the defective range.

"We can replace it with a new South Bend model," said the manager. "But you'll have to pay the difference."

"No problem," I said.

Then I learned that Alpha was charging us more than other suppliers on the unit. We had to accept, since no other supplier would take the faulty stove off our hands, and the new stove was delivered the day before our Grand Opening.

The phone company also dropped a huge ball by failing to list our number in information as I'd requested weeks earlier, and people told me that since they couldn't get our number, they thought we'd *already gone out of business!* I gave hell to the business manager, who squeaked out a promise to correct the problem.

Despite lower prices our patronage remained sluggish. Our second Friday night only one couple came for dinner — making the place seem frighteningly empty amid all the glowing decor — and we sent a server home early to save on payroll. Mayor Weldon was our only regular breakfast customer. He came in the damp gray of early morning before heading to his sporting goods store in Maysville, insisting that his coffee be "boilin' hot!"

"Put it in the microwave and nuke the daylights out of it," I told Kim. "We can't afford to lose him!"

Where the hell are all the Augustans who yammered on and on over the last three years about how they couldn't wait for us to open!? I wondered. We earned less than half of what we did the first week, and there was $1,000 worth of bills on my desk with only $400 left in our account. Then Kenny phoned from his plant in Ohio.

"Listen, Alan, I'm too old to crawl around buildings with this fat gut of mine, and I'm handing the business over to my sons. I'd like to get squared away on the seventy-five hundred you still owe me on the sprinklers. Do you think you can send a check in a week or so?"

"Oh . . . well . . . we were thinking to pay the remainder next year, like we'd arranged."

"Yeah, I remember. But I tell you what, Alan. I'd like to clear this up for tax purposes, so nothing carries over to next year."

In a way, my chilling dream in which dad passed huge greenbacks to Kenny had come true.

17. Stalking the Rainbow

A stream of diners came on Saturday and Sunday of our second week, but earnings were well below the first week, and the following Monday we grossed only $59.40. I raced around town in a nervous fit with hand-out menus and drafted a big ad for the Augusta *Times*.

The Lamplighter Inn, Augusta, Ky.

GRAND OPENING

Friday & Saturday, Dec. 9th & 10th

1– 4 p.m.

Stop by and See Our Newly Decorated

*Guest Rooms *Restaurant *Banquet Room

Take a Tour and Enjoy Some Refreshments

Visit the

ST. CHARLES RESTAURANT

Breakfast Daily at 6:00 a.m. (7:00 a.m. Sunday)

Also Serving Lunch & Dinner

Carry-out Orders & Catering

756-2603

Everyone Welcome!

I paid invoices and somewhere crossed the line from black ink to red. I couldn't understand why we were laying out so much for meat and produce while selling so few meals. And payroll was equally appalling. Tuesday night there wasn't a soul in the dining room, yet we were paying the cook and server — plus salaries for Hayden, Bob, and Dick, and the gas and electric to keep the St. Charles open. The man who sang bass in the Baptist church choir looked in, and we gave him coffee and pie just to have a warm body in the dining room. It was winter, but there was little ice under our skates.

Among other things, Hayden's contract required us to make a health care plan available and to pay 50% of it beginning January 1.

"Here's some quotes," I told him one day.

I was worried that we wouldn't be able to afford it, whatever Hayden decided. More than money, I was worried about our collective state of mind and body. Bob looked increasingly like a character in *Bleak House*, and mom was pushing herself to clean the guest rooms and wash the Inn laundry. Dad worked nonstop toward the Grand Opening, and my own energy was ebbing away. When I stole an hour at mid-afternoon to go to my apartment for a nap, it was impossible to wrestle my mind away from the Inn. The Lamplighter was my universe. I rarely thought of the purple martins, the possum, or the river. And almost never about my writing.

I broke the news of our financial plight to dad, who focused his tired eyes on the figures and sighed. "I guess we'll have to come up with some money!"

My parents had some AT&T stock, and they decided to sell. My own finances were at rock bottom. I'd used up my savings from teaching and was living off the money Jo Ann and I'd put away to buy a house, of which $100 remained, the $100 I'd given up in my dream weeks earlier to keep the Inn afloat. It was an unspoken understanding between Jo

Ann and me that finding a house was shoved considerably into the future.

Then trouble began with Hayden. Part of his job was to train the servers, but most of his time was monopolized by the kitchen. For the most part the women learned from watching Adrienne. Hayden disliked saying things twice and expected the staff to do their jobs without much trial and error. Occasionally the kitchen shook as he raised his voice, but things appeared to be running well — until a few weeks into our operation when Pauline ran to my office in tears.

"What's going on?" I asked, settling her in a chair.

"I was baking muffins and Hayden yelled at me. If I do it one way, he don't like it. If I do it another way he don't like it either. I'm not gonna put up with this anymore!"

She was too upset to go back to the kitchen, and I told her she might as well go home. I talked to Haydn as he wiped his floury hands on his apron.

"I mighta been a little hard on her, but I need to get things moving. She can be awfully slow at times!"

Next morning Pauline quit. Then Susan, an evening server, stomped to me in a rage, pulling off her bow tie and throwing it on the front desk.

"If he thinks I'm gonna put up with this, he's screwy! I was supposed to work three nights this week, and he's cut me down to two. He can get someone else to fill in the rest of the evening!"

She also quit, taking her expensive uniform with her and never returning it. Hayden admitted it had been necessary to change the schedule, and considering the manner in which Susan left, there was nothing else to be done.

Then Kim came to me in tears the same week. She was one of our novice servers, a freckled 19-year-old working the 6:00 a.m. to 2:00 p.m. shift. She drove in over the dicey roads from Brooksville, but was always punctual and was striving to be good at her work. Her face was blotched with anger.

"He yelled at me for no good reason! I don't take that off nobody!"

"All right," I said. "I'll talk to him."

"You better, or I'm gonna quit!"

I had a chat with mom and dad and we agreed that Hayden was at times impatient and irritable, and could be impolitic with the staff. But dad pointed out that he'd seen Hayden tell some of the staff more than once how to do something.

"Who knows? Maybe Wince has to yell at his cooks once in a while."

I spoke to Hayden as circumspectly as I could, and asked him to be a little gentler. In light of what I was beginning to face with or staff, the turmoil I'd had with *The Calamityville Terror* suddenly seemed rather easy.

The husband-and-wife artists from Maysville hung the gorgeously painted signs in front of the Inn, and on Grand Opening Day the Inn stood out like a jewel. The stately lamplighter raised his torch, right out of the Gay Nineties with his long-tailed coat and top hat, and on the St. Charles a portly chef cradled a steaming platter.

Candles gleamed inside hurricane shades in the lobby and brass chandeliers glinted in the conference room. The Christmas tree towered by the front windows. Del created a winter landscape that sparkled in the lobby display case, and evergreen boughs smothered the oak mirror and mantelpiece. Plants and flowers came from well-wishers, and every surface in the lobby was massed with blossoms and greenery that perfumed the air. Champagne, punch, and hors d'oeuvres burdened a table, and our nine guest rooms rang with the glowing exclamations of men, women, and children running through them for a look.

Friday we hosted a reception for friends and business owners, who praised Jo Ann's painting on the pressed-tin ceiling, and dad's oak woodwork and sculpted tulip — showing that I'd been hasty in my judgment. But despite the compliments, our earnings were only $525.

Saturday we showed off the guest rooms to nearly 200 people, and had our hands full serving dinner and checking in lodgers. I'd intended to have live music, but we'd been too busy to arrange something. Instead of entertaining on his guitar, Bob was confined to the front desk, not so much a character from *Bleak House* as Bob Cratchit in Scrooge's counting house, albeit on full salary since opening day. Our take was over $1,000, but I knew it would be interred beneath an avalanche of bills.

It was Bob's turn to stay over and I went home at midnight. Jo Ann's absence made the apartment seem empty — far more empty and lonely than our dining room on days when no one showed up. Our cupboard with its unread books gleamed under the coats of polyurethane. Some of the aspidistra's leaves had turned brown, and I pinched them off and watered it. I was numb from the endless room tours, and despite the trays of aromatic roast turkey breast, Kentucky hot brows, grilled trout, mashed potatoes, mouth-watering corn bread, and apple pies smothered with brown sugar and whipped cream that Hayden and Grace had sent out from the kitchen over the long evening, I hadn't gotten a moment to eat a single morsel and was famished. I opened my refrigerator and found two shriveled apples and a half carton of orange juice.

18. Holidaze

Christmas and New Year's gave us a final shot at earning some income before winter would set its ponderous boots on our collective necks. Adrienne wasn't on for our first banquet, and the less-experienced servers were so nervous they forgot to set the bread plates till after the diners were seated, and I forgot to light the candles in the centerpiece till the meal was over. Dad and I met with Hayden to do a post-mortem on the Grand Opening. We debated ways to reduce waste and cut down on electricity and gas, and decided to advertise special dinners for Christmas and New Year's Eve.

"We have to cut payroll," I said. I'd learned by now that Hayden sometimes put on more cooks than necessary, and for too many hours. "Why don't you write up the schedule and let's go over it together to make sure it's as lean as possible."

Hayden drummed his foot. "Sure. Whatever I can do to get things rolling."

"And I think it'll help if you'd give the new servers more training. Take them aside when things are slow and spend some time on dining room service."

Hayden swept a hand through his coal-black hair. "I don't know if one or two of them will *ever* learn how to serve!"

"They're doing better," said dad. "Some of them have never been in a full-service restaurant before, much less worked in one. This is pretty new to them."

Monday after Grand Opening an accountant doing the city audit checked in for the week, but when I came back from my errands at the bank and post office Bob told me the man had left.

"But he was registered through Friday!" I protested.

"He said he didn't realize we had no TV. He went to the Ramada Inn in Maysville."

So much for our questionnaire.

"Most bed-and-breakfasts don't cater to business people," said mom. "Someone who's on the road all week wants the same programs he sees at home."

Dad spoke up. "We can't afford to lose any more business travelers. A hundred and fifty bucks just walked out the door with that guy!"

My parents brought their two TVs from the house, and I got mine from the apartment. We needed six more, but couldn't afford them at the moment, and we began playing gypsy TV, moving our three sets wherever they were needed. But it was also clear that the pay phone was inadequate. It was the pre-cell phone era when business travelers camped out at our pay phone for an hour at a time. If others had to make an important call we had no choice but to let them use our office phone — filling the ears of potential patrons with a busy signal. An AT&T veteran, dad priced hotel phone systems, but AT&T's smallest unit was beyond our means at $10,000.

Our precious earnings from the Grand Opening evaporated like dew in Death Valley, and by the time I finished writing paychecks in mid-December I wasn't sure if all of them would clear the bank. Next day my parents went to Cincinnati to sell their AT&T stock, but it would take some days for it to clear and I feared we couldn't hold out long enough. Then the Thomas-Sysco salesman phoned.

"Alan, I gotta ask you to have a check for five hundred and seven dollars ready for the driver, or he can't leave your order. My hands are tied on this."

I promised to have the check ready and hung up in a sweat. Then the postman brought a whopping invoice from Kerns Meat, followed by another call from Kenny about the $7,500 we owed him for the sprinkler system.

"I really wanna get this cleared up, Alan."

I ran a finger around my collar. "I'm working on it, Kenny."

As if money wasn't evaporating quickly enough on bills, we were also soaked with an increasing tide of organizations pleading for donations — everything from bogus retired-police charities, which I was warned away from by Augusta Police Sergeant Gregg Cummings, to a karate studio urging us to help subsidize its trip to a competition in South Korea or God knows where. I got very good at saying NO, but some organizations hinted that if we didn't donate, they wouldn't be able to recommend the Inn to their members. And they had lots and lots of members, hint hint. Did this mean they'd deliberately ask their members *not* to eat at our restaurant or stay in our rooms if we didn't cough up a few hundred bucks? And who were their members, exactly? Half the population in Kentucky? Or was I just getting paranoid? Maybe I was paranoid about getting paranoid. Anyway, Hayden hadn't gotten back to me about the health plan quotes, and I dreaded the thought that we'd soon be shouldering that as well.

The St. Charles was lackluster throughout December — with rare bursts of good business that lured us on like a dog chasing a frankfurter tied to a faster dog's tail. It was all smell and no bite. We got a sprinkling of patrons across the day, making it necessary to keep a server on, but not bringing enough income to diffuse the ticking bomb of bills on my desk. Instead of calling in a replacement when a server phoned in sick, I slipped on an apron and took her place to save on payroll — dragging me away from my other work that I had to make up at night.

When's the last time I even *thought* about writing? I wondered. I had no time to play the trumpet, and was constantly blowing my nose from a cold that wouldn't go away. Christmas was coming, and if Bob was Bob Cratchit, I was Alan Scrooge.

I stayed the night in the Pullman Room and slipped into bed with James M. McPherson's Civil War book, *Battle Cry of Freedom*, which I'd nibbled on for weeks. It was past 11:00 p.m. and I kept yawning as I fought to stay awake. Then after a lapse of what seemed a few seconds I opened my eyes and saw that it was 3:00 a.m. My neck ached from the headboard and I put out the light and fell into a sleep riddled with phone calls from karate gi-clad fund-raisers demanding money.

A snowfall clobbered Augusta, and while dad and I cleared it from the sidewalk, the postman slogged up with an envelope that contained something far more chilling than the stuff on our shovels. Dad read it over before handing it to me.

"Read it and weep!"

It was our electric bill. We expected something around $250, but it was *$1,311*. I looked it over several times for evidence of a typing error. "This has to be a mistake!"

The heavy-duty appliances we'd crammed into the Inn had induced us to sign up for the power company's commercial rate, which would allow us to pay a lower cost per kilowatt hour in exchange for using a larger volume of electricity.

"Maybe they billed us at the residential rate," said dad. "If it's not a mistake we'll be paying $15,000 a year!"

The postman also brought our brochures from the printer, which almost took our minds off the electricity bill. There was our top-coated lamplighter, just as I'd sketched him, smelling of fresh ink on good-quality buff-colored paper. That afternoon a couple came to dinner from Portsmouth, Ohio, and I offered them a brochure as they left.

"Hot off the press."

The woman's face lit up. "Thanks. We'll be back!"

Trying to keep myself respectable for the dribble of patrons coming to the Inn I slipped off for a haircut and was shocked by what I saw in the mirror. My hair was flecked with gray and my face was drawn, bringing to mind McPherson's Civil War book and the "stress fatigue" experienced by Lincoln and the generals of both North and South. I had trouble enough running a country inn and couldn't imagine myself in battle. Or was this a kind of battle?

Hayden was also showing signs of stress, and the weekly schedule began driving a wedge between us. We'd decided to close the St. Charles on Christmas Eve and Christmas Day, allowing the staff to be with their families the whole time. Hayden would have both days off as well, but he scheduled himself an additional day off on the 26th. I pointed out to him that as managing chef he could hardly be absent three days running.

He shook his head. "Those first two days the place is gonna be closed anyway. And I've been working double time since November, practically eighty hours a week."

"Hardly eighty hours, Hayden. You haven't been putting in long days since November. And we've provided your room and meals."

"That's not true. Besides, I made a dental appointment for the twenty-sixth. I can't change it now."

"Change it. For the last three or four weeks you've been working forty hours a week, usually six to seven hours a day. We've gotta have you here. I can't afford to replace you."

He reddened to the roots of his black hair. "Well, I guess you could have me punch a time clock!"

I stared at him in astonishment. "Chefs don't punch time clocks. Only hourly workers. Do you wanna be an hourly worker?"

"You're behaving irrationally," Hayden fired back.

"You're the one who's irrational!"

"Look, Alan, I wanna speak to Charles."

"*I'm* the manager here!" The veins stood out on Hayden's neck, and I wanted to drag him over the front desk and pummel him. "Why don't you just go back to the kitchen!"

Hayden started to blurt out something, then walked away. My face burned at having gotten into such a juvenile debate and I buried myself in paper work. When dad came in I told him what had happened, and he agreed that Hayden's demand was excessive.

"But in the sake of good will, maybe we oughta let him have the extra day."

I poured out my troubles to Jo Ann over the phone, and she tried to console me. "Some chefs are real prima donnas. We had a lulu at the summer theatre once!"

The Maysville *Ledger-Independent* ran a front-page story on us, "The Area's Only True Country Inn." There were photos of me showing off the Starboard Berth Room, conferring with Hayden over the menu in the kitchen as we pretended to be great friends, and one of me posing in front of the Inn with my arms confidently folded as if we were the hottest business in America. My acting experience was paying off. I wore my tweed jacket and corduroy shirt open at the throat, and the camera forgave the ravages my face had shown from the barber's chair. The story came out December 21st, just in time to boost our holiday reservations.

Perked up by this attention, I went to Maysville to get a Christmas present for Jo Ann, and stopped in a gift shop just opened by a friend of mine from college, Philip Manning. He guided me through his aisles of dazzling wares as we exchanged tales about the agonies of opening a business.

Philip smiled wanly. "I wish I could just get *away* for an hour or two! I've got some hired help, but I can't afford someone full time. I'm usually here till midnight doing the accounts. It becomes your whole friggin' life!"

Exactly.

While I was in Maysville Hayden had gotten into a shouting match with Jeff about the automatic dishwasher, and dad barely persuaded Jeff not to quit. I threw down my coat.

"If this keeps up we won't have *anyone* working for us!"

"Yeah, Hayden can be pretty abrasive, but he's not likely to change." Dad gave me a sharp glance. "But you know, *you* can be pretty argumentative too."

The remark stung, but he was right. At the moment I only wanted to put my arms around my parents and walk away from Augusta, leaving our problems behind.

19. End of the Party

Hayden started arriving late, and one day showed up four hours after he was supposed to have come in. He swept by the front desk as if nothing had happened when I asked him what was going on.

"Sorry. I had car trouble, and when I finally got to the river the ferry was closed."

"Well, you better tell Grace you're here. She's anxious to get home."

I was proud that I'd contained my anger, but Hayden had missed calls from suppliers and banquet inquiries, and I was tempted to deduct from his check the extra pay we'd have to give Grace.

Blissfully, we had so many reservations for New Year's Eve dinner that we set up both the dining and conference rooms. I'd finally worked it out for Bob to play his guitar, and we asked a local church pianist, Susie Hamm, to play for after-dinner dancing. We gathered the staff for a pep talk and reminded everyone of the importance of the evening. Hayden intoned a few words of instruction, and I wished everyone luck.

"And although it's New Year's," dad concluded, "keep in mind that the champagne's for our guests. Please remember that there's no drinking on duty."

"Well," said Bob, searching the room in astonishment. "I certainly hope no one's been drinking on duty!"

The staff dispersed to their posts and I touched Bob's arm. "Well, *you've* been taking a glass from time to time."

He looked at me with surprise, then left the room.

It was the busiest night we'd had as we scrambled to seat guests and showcase the Inn. Nick and Nina Clooney and the Wallaces came for dinner, and several Maysville friends. We had a bar at the front desk where dad took the first shift while I kicked off the entertainment in the dining room. Sid ran up the spotlights as I leapt on our little stage.

"Welcome to the Lamplighter! I want you to greet a friend of mine. Some of you have already seen him at the front desk, but now you'll have a chance to *hear* what he does better than anyone else I know. Please welcome Bob Donahoe!"

Bob climbed on the stage to warm applause and nodded appreciatively before saying a few words about the Villa-Lobos piece he was about to play. When he dipped into Villa-Lobos' rich sonorities I surveyed the room. Some of the diners were enraptured by Bob's sensuous playing; others were engrossed in conversation, laughing and smiling. Adrienne, Lori, and Laura radiated pure professionalism in their black attire. Lighted by the candles and chandeliers the room gleamed as I'd imagined it would during our three years of work, and I was thrilled to think how festive it must appear from the street. I didn't give a damn about those who thought we were too elegant. How could an inn be too elegant?

Bob mesmerized the diners for thirty minutes before moving to the conference room, and by the end of dinner had played twice in each room. Susie Hamm struck up the music in the lobby, and the couples flocked in to hear Nick Clooney sing along. A line formed at the bar and others filed up the stairs for a glimpse of the guest rooms that weren't taken. When the dining room finally emptied Bob put away the guitar and came to the front desk.

"Sounded good!" I said.

"They didn't really listen." He seemed preoccupied and hardly glanced my way.

I went out to mingle as the last of the chairs in the lobby were taken. But no one was dancing, and I worked my way over to dad.

"I think everyone's too shy!"

I asked Susie to play something slow. She nodded and I went over to the Wallaces as dad and mom moved onto the floor and began a waltz. A moment later Rolland and Jane joined in.

"I didn't know your parents danced!" said Wilma Wallace.

"They took lessons for years," I said, holding out my hand. "I promise not to murder your toes."

Wilma chuckled and took my hand, and by the end of the number a half-dozen other couples were dancing. Later on I sent Bob on a break and took over at the front desk. It was almost midnight, and the servers broke out the champagne and noise makers. Under this din of celebration I noticed a note pad by the cash register covered with Bob's handwriting and started to read it, since we customarily left notes for each other. Then I saw it was the draft of a letter intended for someone else. I put down the pad, but I'd already read too much. The letter expressed Bob's decision to leave Augusta, referring bitterly to how my family was running the Inn.

Midnight came with the champagne and party whistles, and I hugged family and friends. By 1:00 a.m. the lobby emptied and our overnight guests went up to bed, jubilant and stuffed with food. I shut off the lights, checked the stoves and ovens, freezer doors, thermostats, then went up to sleep in the Pullman Room. I'd phoned Jo Ann earlier in the day, and knew that by this hour she'd have come home from a restaurant with her mother and aunt. The party was over.

* * *

The alarm woke me in the uncanny black of a new year. My head throbbed from lack of sleep and I dreaded the thought of dragging myself downstairs. Hayden had stayed over in one of the other rooms and would be up in an hour to prepare breakfast before turning the kitchen over to Jeff. Hayden wasn't at his best in the morning and some days came in looking like a leopard whose lunch had been stolen.

I got out of bed and went to the bathroom.

It was six weeks since we'd opened and I knew what the next 18 hours would bring. One of the servers would be late, or the afternoon cook would call in sick. I wished I could get through one day without dealing with that kind of thing. Our overnight guests would stir in a couple of hours, running baths and shaving, clumping downstairs for their complimentary breakfasts, asking for the Sunday paper. Dad always bought one or two copies of the Cincinnati *Enquirer* at the corner stand, and I'd endeavor to make conversation.

Sleep OK? Wanna make lunch reservations?

A number of our guests had already eaten at the St. Charles and would ask what *other* restaurants were available, God bless 'em. If several lodgers came down at once I'd help the server. Regular or decaf? Hot cocoa? Tea? We'd put on CDs or the radio to the classical FM station.

I turned on the shower. Not fully awake, I steadied myself against the wall, and felt as if my head was stuffed with something that was beginning to swell.

Our guests would finish breakfast and lounge about with the newspaper, then ask what other places there were to see in the area before driving home. We'd offer them brochures on Old Washington and Ripley. Dad would come in, the lines around his eyes showing that he was also short of sleep, and we'd trade off on the dining room and front desk. When the guests checked out, all three of us would take turns cleaning rooms — hauling mountains of dirty linen down the back staircase and dropping off hats, umbrellas, or other items left by our guests at the front desk.

As the sun reached is meridian beyond the gray we'd serve the first Sunday dinners. Perhaps only a few people would show up, but we had to be prepared for more. Jeff would wrap up the uncooked sausage and bacon, and set up the steam table for the changeover. If the weather was pleasant a few carloads of tourists would venture over on the ferry from Ohio. Some of them might order dinner; others would want only coffee and dessert. Still others would have eaten at the Beehive but would ask to see our rooms. Whoever was free would take them on this well-rehearsed trek and answer questions about the renovation. The tours would be repeated through the day and I'd search for a fresh way to say things. Yes, the cannonball bed is a family antique, made by my great-grandfather. No, we never thought it would take three years to redo the place. On and on it would go.

Steam filled the bathroom as the hot water soaked my hair and beat against my shoulders. I hadn't exercised properly since leaving New York and hated the sight of the softness around my waist.

By late afternoon I'd see off the last of the tourists as the cook banged around the kitchen and scrubbed up. I'd help roll up the anti-fatigue mats and run them through the volcanic heat of the dishwasher as the cook mopped the floor. The servers would wipe down the tables, vacuum the carpeting, and clean the servers' station. I'd haul vats of iced tea to the walk-in box as the cook scraped grease from the grille and stored the soups and other steam table items. The cook would at last wad up her apron, sign out on the sheet, and shut off the kitchen lights, then the vent van would cease roaring as an eerie quiet held the Inn.

I'd spend part of the evening going over the day's proceeds and tallying the week. I'd add in the room receipts, breaking down the income between cash and credit card payments, and filing the registration sheets. I'd make up the weekly statement for our bookkeeper, with breakdowns for carryouts, gift certificates, post cards, banquets, conference rentals, food service, beer and wine sales, and lodging. I'd look at the come-up calendar to see what bills absolutely *had* to be paid on Monday, and which ones could be held at bay a few more days.

I'd make notes of people who'd promised to phone back about banquets, room reservations, or family dinners, or salespeople to call concerning screwed-up deliveries. Tuesday was payday, and I'd review the paperwork Sunday night to see that everything was in order. Tip sheets signed by the servers and initialed by Hayden. One of the women would inevitably forget to write the date or her signature, and I'd try to straighten it out before Tuesday so her paycheck wouldn't be held up.

I let the hot water beat against me, hating what lay ahead over the next days and weeks.

Winter had only begun, bringing months of drizzle and stubborn fog before spring could attract tourists. Before then we'd have a mountain of expenses to scale. All the signs showed we wouldn't make it. I wanted to have a week, a *day* to do nothing but sit in a sunny room and read. I wanted to crawl back in bed, to have Jo Ann with me and find that the last three years were nothing but a bad dream.

My throat tightened. I heaved painfully and started crying. The tears vanished down the drain and I was wracked with sobs. I bent over like a baby, too despairing to strike the shower stall with my fists, and sobbed until I was empty.

Part III

1. Winter

I found Bob's two-weeks' notice at the front desk, and when he came in he went quietly about his work, but as the day wore on the ice between us melted. He joked about something and I laughed, and during his final days some of Bob's arcane humor returned. His last day was to have been Saturday, but he also showed up Sunday.

"Thought you'd be packing," I said.

He went behind the cash register. "I don't have much to pack. Thought I'd round off the week here. Go have your lunch."

The night before we hadn't closed the dining room till 11:30 p.m., and with a server and cook out sick, Bob and I had coped with 40 dinner reservations. We were almost too beat to drag ourselves off to bed.

"There's probably some dessert left," I'd suggested.

Bob's eyes sparkled. "Good idea!"

We got slices of Dutch apple pie from the cooler and collapsed in the lobby. My parents had said goodbye to Bob earlier, and we included a week's vacation pay in his final check. We munched pie and listened to the Inn settling in for the night as we talked over the music we'd rehearsed in those days when it seemed the Inn would never open.

With Bob gone I covered the front desk from 7:00 a.m. to noon when dad took over, then I moved to the dining room or helped mom clean guest rooms. I stuck around till 2:00 or 3:00 p.m., especially when we had a luncheon or business meeting. The three of us ate our meals whenever circumstances allowed, but rarely at the same time two days running. Frequently we'd be eating when someone checked in or begged to see the rooms, and we'd come back to a plate of cold food.

Mid-afternoon I'd go to the apartment for a few hours' rest, taking time to water the faithful aspidistra and open a book, then retrace my steps to the Inn at 6:00 or 7:00 p.m. to stay the night. If we had a banquet mom and dad pitched in before going home. I stayed at the front desk as late as necessary, and sometimes business travelers checked in well after midnight — usually someone driving in from the Greater Cincinnati Airport 60 miles away who had underestimated the hairpin convolutions of the infamous Route 8. As Nick Clooney once put it, Route 8 was built by pioneers who needed to slow down a band of pursuing Indians.

I slept on the office bunk bed and learned to wake up at the doorknob turning in the lobby. It wasn't unusual for me to get only four hours' sleep, which I tried to remedy with a nap the next afternoon. I joined the Rotary Club in hopes it would boost our business contacts, which took two hours out of each Monday night at Gertrude Schweir's boarding house where the wind-up toys were still knocking down the salt and pepper shakers. And I made it to church once or twice a month by trading off with dad and mom, sometimes to sing with the choir, although I never resumed the children's sermons. Time was even more golden to me than silence. Somerset Maugham wrote in *The Summing Up* that if he had life to live over he'd wish for better health and greater intelligence. My wish is to get by on less sleep.

With winter making large numbers of tourists unlikely, we simply had to cut expenses, and Bob's departure was a chance to save $1,200 a month in salary and taxes by taking on his duties myself. I paid myself only what I needed for essentials while sending a few dollars to Jo Ann from time to time. Our house purchase account was as dead as my writing career. We put our brains through a wringer searching for ways to cut costs, and Hayden suggested eliminating one or two of the staff who weren't pulling their weight.

"Missy dresses like a slob and she's absent once or twice a week. If I correct her she's insolent. Sure as shooting we're gonna have a repeat of that breakfast fiasco!"

Missy had been cooking breakfast when Tom Appleman ordered pancakes, and she whipped up the last of the mix she had handy into three tiny pancakes instead of getting a fresh box of mix from the stock room. Appleman was flabbergasted by the Lilliputian pancakes but said nothing until after he left the St. Charles, and pretty soon word spread that we served the smallest pancakes in Kentucky. I was vexed at Appleman because he'd known my parents for ten years and hadn't shown the courtesy of talking to us about his meal before joking about it around Augusta. But I was angrier at Missy, and after she came in late again a few days later I fired her.

"Why doncha shove it!" she screamed, slamming the door on her way out. Her husband threatened to beat up Hayden until Police Sergeant Gregg Cummins told him to cool off.

One of our dishwashers didn't know her left hand from her right and took forever getting a tray of dirty dishes filled up, so we decided to let her go as well. But she suddenly stopped coming to work and saved me the joy of firing her.

But our expenses continued swelling like cancer run amok. We had a $300 gas bill due, a quarterly federal withholding payment of $2,700, and a $4,000 bill for carpeting. The bank finally processed our third loan, charging us $283 in closing costs and $3,700 in interest on the advance notes already paid out. The loan had been dribbled out in these notes over the past several months, and all that remained was $1,000.

Kenny was finally off our back on the sprinkler system because my parents had made another deposit to pay him the $7,500. The gargantuan electric bill had also been resolved when we learned it was a quarterly rather than monthly bill.

A shred of good news, but our income had no chance against the growing groundswell of expenses. We rented several rooms to a team of Clopay engineers and catered one of their dinners, but their work ended two days sooner than planned and they checked out, leaving us a couple of hundred dollars short of our projection for the week. Moreover, one engineer had nosebleed, but rather than mention it, he went away and left us with a set of ruined linens.

Then the unemployment office in Maysville notified us that our kitchen helper, Dick, had filed for benefits. An increase in our unemployment rates would have been another nail in our coffin, so I drove to Maysville through a cold rain and sat opposite Dick in a hearing room. The case worker mused over our respective statements, asked some questions, then said we'd get the decision in the mail. As I splashed my way back through the drizzle to the car Dick caught up with me, ducking his head in the rain.

"I'm sorry about this, Alan. I didn't know they'd make you come all the way down here!"

"You know, Dick, the job's still there."

Dick hunched his shoulders. "I just gotta find something else."

The unemployment office ruled in our favor. Dick and his wife had a second baby on the way, and I occasionally saw him weaving around Augusta in the city cruiser as he hustled a living as a part-time policeman.

Despite some spurts of business January went out with a whimper. We were casting out $1,000 a week on food and supplies but hauling in too little to stay solvent. Weekdays were especially slow, and one Tuesday we earned less than $20 — what you'd expect from a lemonade stand but with considerably higher expenses! We did more brain cudgeling and got the idea to improve business with $5.95 "Cabin Fever Specials," with chicken and dumplings Monday nights, roast pork tenderloin on Tuesday, lasagna with broccoli Florentine on Wednesday. I wrote up ads to run in the *Times* through the end of March, but after the first ad appeared only two people showed up.

"What's wrong with people!" I exclaimed to my parents. "They'll drive forty miles to McDonald's, and they don't even get a waitress!"

"Give it some time," said dad.

I spent the next morning over a strong pot of Earl Gray tea trying to slash expenses even further and writing up a leaner schedule for the St. Charles. We had so few breakfast customers that I shifted Kim from 7:00 a.m. to 10:00 a.m., waiting tables myself when people came in early — since I was already handling breakfast for our occasional lodgers. I softened the blow on Kim by giving her an extra hour in the afternoon when tourists were more likely to appear, who usually tipped better than the locals. The shift saved us another $170 a month, which was rather like attacking a forest fire with a plant mister.

Then I prepared the daily bank deposit. Hardly enough cash sat in our safe to make the walk across the street worthwhile, but I hungered to get outdoors with whatever scrap of paper I could muster to convince myself the place was surviving. I opened our check register and the balance told me how badly off we were. Even with the deposit I was about to make, it would only be a few dollars above the red, and tomorrow was payday. We wouldn't make it.

I reached back in the safe for an envelope Rolland had given me the beginning of January. It held a $3,000 check to the Inn, but Rolland had told me not to deposit it "unless things get really tough." My stomach filled with nausea as I added the check to the deposit. Things had gotten really tough.

I knew I had to shake myself out of my depression or I wouldn't be any use to the Inn. Most days I felt as if nothing but bits of tape held my body and mind in one piece. I watched Tom Peters' *In Search of Excellence* on PBS and read *The Art of Japanese Management.* I thumbed through my old copy of Norman Vincent Peale's *The Power of Positive Thinking* and tried cramming my mind with cheerful thoughts when I dropped into bed at night. I reminded myself how good it was to live near my parents in the country, and how lucky I was to have Jo Ann. I tried to be thankful that the Inn had finally opened and that we had at least some money coming in. But I woke most mornings without inspiration and my thoughts were suicidal.

By the end of January things were bad enough that we reluctantly agreed to begin serving at 11:00 a.m. instead of 7:00 a.m. — shutting down most of our breakfast service, except for overnight guests. When I told Kim I was cutting her back another hour each day she shrugged it off. "I'm just glad to have a job!" She shook her long, sandy hair and hiked back to the kitchen. Mayor Weldon would have to go elsewhere for his boilin' hot coffee.

We moved Grace from morning to afternoons, the spot vacated when I'd fired Missy-the-miniature-pancake-maker, allowing us to cut back on kitchen utilities. Our automatic dishwasher and food warmer digested electricity in whale-size mouthfuls. The dishwasher alone had six elements operating at 2,500 watts each, and I estimated that the reductions in payroll, gas, and electricity would save an additional $800 a month.

Cash flow was another torment. Our suppliers required payment within a week of delivery, and with deliveries coming every few days I was chained to my desk reviewing invoices, writing checks, and posting them to our vendors. We were going through a dizzying number of checks and postage, so I began stretching out the payments to once a month. Most of the vendors went along with it, but resistance was swift from a Maysville supplier whose driver was instructed to collect on delivery. I told him I'd send the check to the office in Maysville, and that afternoon the woman who ran the place growled at me over the phone.

"We're going on monthly payments," I replied.

"No can do. We've gotta have payment now!"

"OK," I said. "You'll have it tomorrow." I paid the invoice, and a week later the driver stopped by on his route through Augusta. "We won't be ordering," I said.

The woman called a few days later to ask why we hadn't ordered anything.

"We'll order when you go to monthly billing," I said. "We have cash flow problems just as you do, and I refuse to stop what I'm doing to make out a check every time your driver comes. The bakery bills us monthly, the Pepsi Company and coffee supplier, the wine salesman, and our paper supplier. We'd like to do business with you, but I won't make exceptions."

The woman hung up and we never ordered from her again.

Then I changed our payday from weekly to biweekly, reducing my paperwork and freeing me for other tasks. But despite these initiatives, sluggish business blew us farther and farther away from reaching more patrons. One evening four of our overnight guests came down to the lobby, two women and two girls from Cincinnati, coifed like models and dressed to the nines to enjoy the night ahead. I was especially pleased when they'd come, since they'd been recommended by friends of theirs who'd particularly liked the food at the St. Charles.

"May I show you to a table?" I asked. Then I noticed that they had their hats and coats, and tried to regain my poise. "Everything OK with your rooms?"

One of the women flashed a smile. "Very comfortable." She turned to the others. "Ready?" They went out the door and drove off.

Adrienne was watching from the dining room door. "No go, huh?"

"They obviously had other plans," I said, not bothering to hide my chagrin.

Adrienne gazed at the street. "That's the problem we always had at the Holiday Inn. No matter how good our food was, overnight guests always wanted to go *elsewhere* to eat. Call it the wanderlust!"

Friday night and our dining room was deserted. Adrienne stifled a yawn as she walked back to her post, glancing at the light splashed by our lampposts onto the empty street. Even when we got people to our rooms, we couldn't sell them dinner.

January expired. Despite mild weather, few people came to our Cabin Fever Specials, and Bonfield sprang out of the mist with $400 in receipts for plumbing supplies he'd never turned in. Bills for $4,000 waited on my desk to be paid by the first few days of February, and the final $1,000 in our checking account was gone. I jotted down the figures and gave them to dad. He smoothed the sheet on the front desk — and for the first time since I'd moved to Augusta his shoulders slumped and something seemed to go out of him.

"What about the three thousand Rolland gave us?"

"Completely gone."

"Looks like we might not make it!" He ran his eyes over the figures, hoping I'd overlooked something as he rubbed his wrist, a habit carried over from when he'd worn the brace. His hand was slightly twisted from the shortened bone that would prevent him from regaining full range of motion without more surgery. "Well, let's not push the panic button yet. Your mother and I have a little more coming in."

They'd sold a piece of property in Indiana some years before and were expecting the final mortgage payment. We broke up our little conference and I went back to the pile of invoices on my desk.

2. Sauces

Getting through February was like a ship trying to escape a fog bank. But there were a few bright moments as we waited for wind to lift our sails. The first occurred when a man and woman who'd dined in the St. Charles asked to see our rooms. They fell in love with the Victorian Room and decided to get married and honeymoon at the Inn. Several phone calls made it clear that none of the local clergy were available, so I sent them to the judge executive in Brooksville, and had a bottle of champagne waiting when they returned as husband and wife.

Our other bit of joy came when a heavy snowstorm canceled a Rosemary Clooney-Debbie Boone concert in Cincinnati — one of several concerts they were doing together in the mid 1980s. They brought their entourage to Augusta to await the thaw. Rosemary stayed at her vacation house on the river, but Debbie Boone checked into the Inn with her husband and children. We had few other guests and the Boone clan spread out in two of our rooms for the next ten days, enjoying a quiet idyll in their busy lives. Debbie's husband Gabriel Ferrer spent most of his time writing and arranging projects by phone with California, while she read in our lobby and played with the children. At night she sang them to sleep in that vibrant and engaging voice that had brought the world "You Light Up My Life." The Boones were courteous and unassuming, more like family than lodgers, and we were sad to see them go. When the world was gray they had indeed lighted up our life.

Hayden's job performance continued to erode and caused us to miss a valuable opportunity with the Maysville Country Club. The Club routinely closed in January, and a number of the members discovered the St. Charles and came two or three times, until an influential woman member complained about the strip steak she'd ordered.

"There's something wrong with the sauce!" she exclaimed to dad. "I had this last time I was here and it was delicious. Isn't it supposed to be béarnaise?"

Dad took her plate back to the kitchen — where Jeff was cooking because Hayden had given himself the night off. Jeff glanced over the steam table. "Looks fine to me!"

Dad put the plate under the warmer where Jeff could take a better look. "Are you sure? It looks awfully red."

Jeff waved the spatula. "That's tomato paste. That's how it's done."

Dad asked the woman if she wanted something else, on the house.

She gave another order, then raised an eyebrow. "Your chef isn't here tonight, is he?"

I looked up béarnaise in one of Hayden's cookbooks and discovered that it didn't use tomato paste. Next morning we asked Hayden about it, and he smiled wryly.

"That's Jeff all over. He decides to try something, and doesn't use his head!"

The others in the woman's party had raved about their meals, but we knew from the episode with Tom Appleman's pip-squeak pancakes that one unhappy customer can overshadow fifty satisfied ones. To prevent a reoccurrence we asked Hayden to arrange the schedule so that, except on his day off, he was always on during dinner. He'd been taking two days off and putting himself on mornings and early afternoons.

"At least till the cooks are better trained," said dad. "They can handle breakfast and lunch, but the dinner menu's more sophisticated. That's when we get our most discriminating guests."

Hayden said flatly, "I can't work six nights a week."

"What do you mean?" I stared at him, and he returned a defiant gaze as I went on. "Our contract calls for you to arrange your schedule around the restaurant. We're not asking you to work more hours, just to be here when you're needed."

"It doesn't matter. I haven't been spending enough time with my daughters."

My blood rose. Only a few days earlier Hayden had scheduled himself off during one of the few banquets we had, and I was running out of patience. "Then why'd you take the job? You told us you'd arrange to have your kids looked after!"

"Look, Alan, I simply can't leave them with sitters the entire week!"

I was out of my chair. "You've misled us about this whole business!"

Dad raised his hand. "This isn't getting anywhere."

We eventually compromised so Hayden would work four evenings and go home early the other two days. I was boiling inside, and when Del came down to lend a hand in the dining room I told her I'd crossed a bridge with Hayden.

"Hang in there," she said.

A few days later I typed up a job evaluation for Hayden and left it at his desk. Trying to be diplomatic I praised his menu creation and cooking, and congratulated him on his imaginative specials — while pointing out that he needed to give the staff more training. I also asked to see his inventory sheets, which he'd yet to show me. My most critical comments regarded scheduling. He was making changes without notifying the employees, and he continued showing up late.

What Hayden thought of the evaluation I never learned, because a few days later he gave two-weeks' notice. I was suddenly relieved, but rather than finish the two weeks, he vanished after two days, leaving a scribbled note: *I consider our employment contract to be null and void due to violation of the provision for health insurance being provided by January 1.*

True, we hadn't begun the insurance, but neither had Hayden given me a decision on which he plan wanted. And I felt his increasing number of late arrivals justified our delay in getting the coverage. At the bottom, both of us were at fault.

In any case it was Friday night and we had no chef. Grace was off sick, and Jeff due to a back problem. Our only other hope was Peggy Habermehl — from the school cafeteria who'd started with us a few days before Hayden left. She was eager to learn and came in early Friday to study the menu. Sleet kept our diners to a handful, and she hauled us through with minor glitches. But we had 38 reservations for Saturday night.

"I'd better send an SOS for Betty," said dad, before calling his sister in Indiana.

Aunt Betty was the eldest of dad's three sisters, and most of her years she'd pioneered at the phone company in Indianapolis as one of the few female supervisors. Then she and her husband built a country house with their own hands in southern Indiana. Renovation runs in the family. Now retired from the phone company, she did yard work, wove on her loom, and served as bookkeeper and manager of the well-known Overlook Restaurant.

"I'll be down tomorrow," she said.

Saturday's skies were clear as cut glass, and when people packed the dining room for breakfast we found out that although Hayden had prepared the servers' schedule he hadn't actually notified the women. Dad and I dove into aprons, and for the first time I prayed for people to come in more slowly. By lunch time the crowds grew heavier and patrons piled onto the Gobelin-tapestried furniture in the lobby until it was standing room only. Peggy kept her poise in the kitchen, working a half-dozen orders at once. Her hands moved deftly over the sizzling pans as I ran in and placed a ticket on the clip.

"OK, I can do that. Just gimme more bread!"

We made coffee as fast as the machine would brew it, heaped lettuce and tomatoes onto the salad cooler, and sprinted to the stock room and walk-in box to replenish muffins and iced tea, catsup and margarine. Dad and I had waited table dozens of times and knew where things were kept, but all of a sudden nothing was where it should be. We searched for tartar sauce and apple pie, salad dressings, and cuts of meat. No one was free to run the dishwasher and by afternoon there was a mountain of dirty china, with over-stacked busing trays on every available surface. By 2:00 p.m. a crowd of hungry people thronged the lobby, and as I went to get the next party my aunt marched in, her five-foot frame bundled against the bitter February air. She shared the same blue eyes and attractive Swedish profile as dad, and when she saw me with the stained apron she laughed in amazement.

"I understand you have an opening for a cook!"

3. Aunt Betty

Aunt Betty grabbed an apron and joined Peggy in the kitchen. "I don't wanna get in your way. Just tell me what I can do." Peggy collapsed against the steam table. "You're not in my way, sweetheart!"

The rush ended and we got Adrienne to cover dinner. Dad and I shuttled the mass of china through the dishwasher as Betty came out of the walk-in box.

"Your chef didn't keep up the ordering. You're out of some of the meats you'll need for tonight!"

There was no way to get a delivery on Saturday night, so dad drove to Kerns Meats in Brooksville and picked up the order himself, while I raided the local stores. While we shopped, Betty secluded herself in the chef's office with the menu. Some of the sauces were standard, but others were open to considerable interpretation, such as the Shaker herb marinade and "Velvet" sauce Hayden had concocted for the roast turkey entrée. Most of the sauces were stored in the cooler, but Hayden had never shown Peggy how to make them. Jeff was still off with a bad back, and in any case the incident with the béarnaise sauce made us leery of depending too heavily on him till he was better trained.

Betty studied me with her blue eyes. "Most of these are no problem, but I don't wanna change something your guests are familiar with." She opened a file drawer, stuffed with folders. "I've found some notes

255

Hayden made about ingredients, and I think I can reconstruct what he was doing. He hadn't kept up his baking. We're almost out of desserts, but I've got three apple pies in the oven right now."

The aroma bathed the kitchen, and my aunt saw how pleased I was. "Now, how are reservations for Sunday?"

"About a dozen."

"If it's as nice as today you'll get more." She picked up some sheets of paper with Hayden's inscrutable handwriting. "He used an awful lot of ingredients on some of these sauces. *Expensive* ingredients. How were your food costs running?"

"We couldn't get him to run the food costs. Our *bills* were out of sight!"

"What about inventory? I couldn't find any lists."

Dad was at the door. "As far as we can tell Hayden never did an inventory."

"We'll see what we can do about that," Betty said with a toss of the head.

We put her up in the Presidential Suite, and when I came down next morning the kitchen piped out the smell of baking muffins and biscuits. When Grace reported for work, my aunt quickly won her confidence with the skill she'd developed as an AT&T supervisor. The two women conferred about the week's meals, then Betty put on coat and gloves and vanished into the arctic regions of the walk-in box. She was in and out all day, making lists, checking stock, and helping Peggy prepare dinner. Then she settled in the lobby to warm up with a cup of coffee.

She patted her note pad. "I've found some of the reasons for your high costs. You don't have liver on the menu, do you?" I shook my head. "Did Hayden ever serve it as a special?" I told her he hadn't and she continued. "He's got twenty-five pounds of liver in the freezer. I didn't think you'd used it, but I asked the girls and they confided that the cooks have been preparing it for their own meals!"

"That's interesting!"

"And he's been ordering *vacuum-packed* beef scraps to make soup. That's an expensive way to do it. What's more, Peggy and Grace said Hayden was ordering them to throw out the scraps they trimmed from the other beef cuts. *That's* what he shoulda been using for soup! He's got oodles of pre-cut vacuum-packed steaks and other meats. Those cost an arm-and-a-leg! Gosh, at the Overlook Restaurant we always cut our own meats. You get the portions you want and it's much more reasonable. And vegetables. There's enough kale and lettuce back there to serve the entire county! How often is your produce delivered?"

"Twice a week."

Betty jabbed the note pad with her pencil. "He's got far too much, and some of it's spoiled. And dry goods. There's enough waffle mix to feed the 82nd Airborne. You can order some of those things in smaller quantities without paying a penalty."

My aunt went down the list: Meats poorly wrapped and items not marked. Enough champagne to go along with the waffles for the 82nd Airborne. The list was extensive. Over the next days Betty spent long hours in the walk-in box and stock room, and inspected our selection of wine and beer in the cellar. She typed up a list of the hundreds of items in our inventory, and other lists of what we needed to order. The rest of her days were spent in the kitchen with Grace and Peggy to create lunch and dinner specials to work off the over-abundance Hayden had ordered. She looked a dozen different directions at once to cut costs and suggest improvements for our menu.

"Your new chef will have his own ideas about what to serve, but there's a lot you can do right now to save money."

Produce was a major expense. Our Hollywood strip steak was served with avocados, which were expensive in winter. And Hayden had been baking both apple and pear pies, but the apple pies were selling better.

"And they're *cheaper*," said Betty. "Your Pullman dish is made with shrimp, which is also expensive, and it has to be carefully thawed each time you get an order. The only alternative is to thaw a quantity ahead of time, and on slow days you have to throw a lot away. It's really a matter of finding the dishes your customers want, with the ingredients you can afford. The girls told me that many of the plates have been coming back with the sauces scraped off. One of these sauces uses *four eggs* for each serving!"

"Should we serve fewer items?"

"That would help. Your dinner menu has nine entrées, and the cooks have to keep all of those items stocked and a quantity thawed out for each meal. That's a nightmare for a small restaurant!"

My aunt's arrival sent the morale soaring in the kitchen, but it was evident that it would take weeks to get the St. Charles turned around — and if anything, February was proving to be even less providential than January. One day only two patrons showed up, and another day we set a record-low income of $9.24 — pathetic for even a lemonade stand. The dishwasher broke down, and our Cabin Fever Specials were doing so dismally that I canceled them. The only achievement I'd made was to badger the phone company into assuming the cost of operating the pay phone. We were paying $40.00 a month in exchange for keeping the money in the coin box — which was nil since business travelers used credit cards.

It was difficult finding positive things to write to Jo Ann, who was absorbed in her production of *Carousel* in Phoenix with Buddy Ebsen. I mentioned that Del had spiced things up by changing our winterscape decor to a Valentine theme, and to cheer me up Jo Ann passed along a story she'd seen about a gingerbread house in Des Moines.

"It's large enough for people to go inside, and the city made them put in a *sprinkler system!*"

As the days fled by we hunted for a new chef. Del replaced the Valentine display with Easter lilies, and a record-warm day drew us out for yard work. We raked the last of the leaves that had blown into our arbor vitae trees, green and pungent, and debated what flowers to plant.

"Maybe we can build a gazebo this summer," dad offered, climbing on the stump of the decayed willow tree we'd cut down the previous year.

"And picnic tables," said mom.

Then the weather went sour and lacquered the yard in sleet. After a series of interviews we hired Dora Conrad, a chef with an invigorating personality from the Maysville Country Club who'd run a couple of her own restaurants and seemed to know half the people in Kentucky. Betty went back to Indiana and Dora torpedoed ahead with a new menu that began to attract a small following around town. Then in less than two weeks Dora quit, blaming her departure on a squabble with Adrienne about salads.

"It was nothing," Adrienne exclaimed. "I'd forgotten all about it!"

Some months later we learned Dora was having problems with alcohol, and not long after she died.

Our restaurant was floundering again as bills filled my office. Résumés from chefs came in while dad and I spent sleepless nights agonizing over whom to hire. We hashed things over at breakfast one morning, and by chance dad put into words what I was thinking.

"Let's call Gregg Ross."

Gregg was one of the chefs whom we'd interviewed before we met Hayden. We liked Gregg, but at 28 he was the least experienced chef we'd seen. He was in charge of training and banquets for a popular restaurant chain in Cincinnati, and had studied under Wince. The one difficulty was that some Augustans were rather backward and Gregg was black. Jeff — who'd finally left to attend the community college — was also black. The staff had shown no prejudice against him as far as we knew, but he was their co-worker, whereas Gregg would be their boss. Augusta had a small black community, part of whose heritage was St. Paul Methodist Church. But the black congregation had dwindled and the church was seldom used. I'd had only one black student among my three classes at school, a girl who lived — as Jeff did — with the two or three black families on a street caustically referred to by some locals as "Nigger Alley."

Housing was another concern, but here we held a trump card. One of my parents' apartments on the river had just become vacant, and they decided to offer it to Gregg at a reduced rate. We invited Gregg for a talk, and got a good reference from Wince. We offered Gregg the job and he started the first week of spring. There were banquet inquiries on my desk, and a new cook and server to train. The season of promising weather was on top of us.

4. Music

March came in schizophrenic, sunshine and 70s as wrens battled grackles for nesting space, then sleet that sent the birds underground. I scurried around town with Gregg's new menu and we promoted daily specials on a sandwich-board in front of the Inn. We advertised two-for-the-price-of-one coupons, served a birthday party, a Homemaker's Club banquet, and joined Sharon Graves' flower shop to host Augusta's first bridal show. The pretty young women — some of them my former students — fitted on their gowns in our guest rooms and swept down our staircase to the flashbulbs of the *Times* and *Bracken County News.*

We introduced Gregg to the community with an evening's *Taste of the St. Charles,* treating friends, media, and business owners to a smorgasbord of appetizers and entrées. We printed souvenir menus; Gregg filled the lobby with displays of pâté, vegetables, and fresh fruit, and Susie Hamm beguiled our guests on the piano. Adrienne kept a sharp eye on the serving, and during the three-hour, five-course meal the wine and beer flowed from our cellar.

Gregg had rocketed to a good start, but with tourist season licking at our heels I — the innkeeper — had done little to stimulate our overall business. Jo Ann was back in Augusta, but would have to return to her ailing mother in a few weeks. Our brochure advertised "plays with a professional cast," but had someone phoned for reservations I'd have looked like a charlatan. With Bob's departure and Jo Ann spending more time with her mother, what professionals had I to rely on?

I thought about doing a one-man show on the order of Hal Holbrook's *Mark Twain Tonight*, but who on earth would drive to Augusta to see *me*? But the pressure kept mounting to do something. Winter had devastated our occupancy rate, with 7% in January, 5.5% in February, and 6% in March. More like a ghost house than a B&B. We introduced a business rate of $35 a night and finally put in a phone system we could almost afford for $4,000. We bought six more TVs so all of the rooms had an idiot box, and took ads with several bed-and-breakfast publications. But this new round of spending pushed our reserve from my parents' AT&T stock to the brink of extinction.

More media attention tumbled our way. The *New York Times* travel section ran a story on Augusta, and the Maysville cable TV station taped a fifteen-minute feature on the Inn and transmitted it on their weekly program. The cameraman followed me around the Inn, ending with a shot of me and several patrons devouring chocolate mousse in the St. Charles. Another story was videotaped by a network affiliate in Huntington, West Virginia, and *Good Morning, America* broadcast a segment about Augusta.

Then suddenly we were illuminated by a lightening bolt of a story written by Nick Clooney in his *Kentucky Post* column. A color photo of my parents in front of the Inn covered the page, and the story was titled "Newcomers saw miracles amid decay," written with the sensitivity that made Clooney the region's most respected journalist and personality.

A woman phoned me the morning the story came out. "What a great article! I've gotta schedule a banquet there for my club!"

The phone rang all week, and Sunday dinner was our best ever. Gregg was sprinting ahead in the kitchen, and by the start of spring nearly 2,000 people had toured our rooms. Some of them returned to spend the night, pushing our occupancy rate to 11% in April. But we were still adrift financially and I had to ask my parents to make another deposit before I was able to meet our loan payment.

We were learning hard lessons, one being that we'd dreadfully overestimated the St. Charles' potential, which remained unprofitable despite the severe cuts in waste, labor, utilities, and operating hours. Its moderate capacity meant that getting more banquets helped only marginally, and it was difficult keeping prices competitive with other restaurants in the area which hadn't installed the costly features mandated by our renovation.

"Maybe we should get back to your original idea," I suggested to mom and dad one day. "A bed-and-breakfast with the emphasis on *lodging*."

But how the blazes could we get people to try our lodging?

Augusta had quaint houses and a stunning riverfront, but what was that, stacked up against Bardstown's *Stephen Foster Story*, or Lexington's legendary thoroughbred farms where tourists could see the birthplaces of Man-O-War and Secretariat? Or the Kentucky Derby, the most famous one-minute sporting activity in the universe? If we were going to compete we had to do something *unique*.

"Music's the answer," I told my parents. "We've got the piano, stage, and spotlights, and we might as well use them!"

We knew some local singers, but cabarets need a music director who can play a variety of styles and who's savvy about shaping an evening's entertainment. We felt this was outside Susie Hamm's experience and took out an ad to find someone. A young guy with loads of experience came down from Cincinnati and liked our setup, and we told him we wanted to run each of the cabarets Jo Ann had planned for at least three weekends, two nights each.

"We can pay you between three and five hundred dollars for each cabaret," I said.

The guy let out a hysterical laugh. "Are you kidding? That's what I usually get for a single weekend!"

"Maybe we should forget the cabaret," Jo Ann advised. "Do something simple until you can put the rest of the pieces together."

"I wonder if Susie Hamm would play solo for us?" said dad.

Susie agreed and on her first night in March the dining room was half full. We dimmed the chandeliers and put a candle on the piano before I introduced her. She opened with "Smoke Gets in Your Eyes," and the diners applauded vigorously. She played for thirty minutes, then retired to the lobby where I pressed a glass of iced tea on her.

"How about some chocolate mousse?" I asked.

Susie set down the tea and rubbed her hands. "Later! I can't eat anything now!"

Our refrigerator repairman, David Simons, had serviced one of the coolers and stayed over for dinner. He crept over to Susie.

"I wanna tell you how much I enjoyed that. I was in a terrible mood, and your playing really cheered me up!"

When Susie returned to the piano she found a five-dollar tip Simons had left.

5. Boot Straps

Susie became a regular at the St. Charles, so we gave her billing on our lobby board and ran notices in the *Kentucky Post* entertainment directory. She broadened her repertoire and started playing Saturday nights as well as Friday, getting a whopping $15 an evening plus dinner, although she usually wanted only iced tea. She was attractive with chestnut hair and brown eyes that conveyed enormous warmth, and brightened the evening with her pleasant personality and playful humor. It was a step in the right direction because people had to be *in our dining room* to hear her, which meant they were likely to order something. But a number of restaurants in the area had pianists, and we had to do something more to draw patrons — especially overnight guests.

"What we need is a *combo*," said dad. "Nobody else around here is doing that."

"Fine," said Jo Ann. "But where do we get the musicians?"

"Nothing in Augusta but country-western fiddlers," said mom.

"There are some great players in Cincinnati," I said, "but they'd cost a fortune."

"What about a trumpet player?" said dad. He looked at me, and so did the others.

"Of course!" said mom. "You've been playing at church for a year!"

Jo Ann smiled, but I shook my head. "These people are paying for dinner. The music's gotta be *good*."

"You sound pretty good to me," said dad.

My practicing had become so intermittent that I gave myself a few weeks to shape up. I stole time in the office each day — using a special mute that lowered the sound to a whisper — and practiced on the stage after the restaurant closed. Jo Ann worked with me on piano before returning to Phoenix to do a revue. I finally stepped in front of our diners with "September Song."

As Susie finished the introduction I split in two. Part of me was blowing into the horn, while the other half was thinking how strange it was to be playing *there* — on a stage dad and I had built over the decaying porch of the Parkview Hotel. Where we'd hauled out truck loads of plaster and lath, and Rawley Tate had stumbled in the small hours of the night. Louis Habermehl and his family were dining in the bay window, above the trench that had turned into a muddy crevasse in those endless weeks of our first year. At the other side of the room Adrienne served Dutch apple pie to Tony and Ruthie, where dad had broken his wrist. The room rang with memories, and both realities shimmered in front of me, past and present, and for a moment I dreaded that all of our work would vanish, leaving us in the rubble of the old hotel.

The piece ended and applause brought my two halves slamming back together. Tony raised his glass and Louis Habermehl nodded approval. His daughters smiled over their dessert. A man seated by the fireplace tapped his spoon on his water glass, and a out-of-town couple put down their utensils and clapped vigorously. Mom gave me a motherly look of affection from one of the ice cream parlor tables, and dad — who'd crept away from the front desk to listen — beamed at me.

Susie glanced over her shoulder. "Now that didn't kill you, did it?"

6. Light and Shadow

Susie and I played regularly together and some weeks later dad put my name below hers on the lobby board.

~ Alan Tongret on Trumpet ~

Our circle of weekend regulars began looking forward to the music, but the Inn still wasn't drawing enough guests to stave off collapse, and it was damaging our health. Mom was having worsening side effects from the glaucoma and high blood pressure medication — probably aggravated by our struggle at the Inn, and dad was increasingly on edge with concern. He was also worn out from the three years' renovation, and was taking on too much with the Hydro-Electric Board, and his duties at church and SHARE. And I was undergoing emotional burnout in the pressure cooker of taxes and bills, employees and paperwork, lack of sleep, trying to attend Rotary and SHARE, and the separations from Jo Ann. Some days I thought I was going mad.

Our financial situation grew worse. Gregg attracted new customers in May with Chinese and Mexican food nights, and we distributed discount coupons on the ferry. We held staff meetings to rally spirits, and sponsored an art contest for the annual Sternwheeler Regatta by asking artists to create a sculpture out of driftwood, offering a dinner certificate for two as the prize. The winning artist submitted a lovely carving of an Indian chief, but it was the only entry.

Our occupancy rate rose to 15% in May, but we were still in the red by $3,700. The only good news was that the revue Jo Ann was doing in Arizona closed and she came to Augusta for a month to help me at the front desk and do my mountain of laundry. Business in the St. Charles continued running hot and cold when in June we had our worst Saturday ever with a measly $119.

"And look at this," said dad, holding up a newspaper. "That oughta siphon off the patrons we're just starting to attract!"

It was a front-page picture of a huge riverboat restaurant that had opened near Maysville. Dad's prophecy proved correct, although we got a reprieve when the Regatta committee chose us to provide the official brunch. We were so busy during the two-day event that there was a 90 minute wait to get a table. We earned a bundle of money, but our costs also ballooned.

In the meantime the compressor went out on the walk-in box, and our insurance man told us our Workman's Compensation rate would double over the previous year. We desperately looked for ways to turn the place around. To show our employees how much we valued them I cranked out a staff newsletter. I congratulated Adrienne for taking first place at a horse show in Pennsylvania, and announced that one of our cooks had won a complimentary dinner. I reminded the staff to shut off the coffee maker and chandeliers when not needed, and gave a pep talk about how good service leads to good tips in "The Ole Lamplighter's Corner." One or two servers thought the newsletter was cute, but it generated little *esprit de corps*.

The family gathered over the Fourth of July to hash over the situation.

"Our losses are three thousand a month," said dad. "We've gotta get that down to a thousand dollars or we're going under."

What about cutting expenses?" Leon asked.

"We've cut to the bone," I said.

Dad nodded. "And if we limit the restaurant hours any further we might as well shut down altogether."

"What about operating only weekends?" Rolland suggested.

"Haven't you had some success with the music?" said Sid. "What about expanding?"

"If we add more musicians we'll have to pay them," I retorted. "We can't do that."

"What about doing a play?" said Leon.

"Where do I get the actors? Bob's gone, and so is Jo Ann."

The room lapsed into silence, and Del caught dad's eye. "Realizing it might take another year to make money, do you really wanna stay with it?"

Dad leaned back in his chair. "I'd like to get away from the day-to-day end of it. But not till it's ready to stand on its own feet."

Mom came in. "I'm worried about everyone's health. Alan's put in a lot of time here, and it's gotten to the point that Jo Ann needs him. They haven't had much of a life the last year or two."

Del turned to me. I was thoroughly wrung out, but wanted to say something meaningful. "At least our occupancy's up. I don't wanna spend the rest of my life managing this place, but I'm committed to getting it profitable."

Her eyes stayed on me, and a voice screamed in my head that what I really wanted was to quit the whole thing and run off to Arizona with Jo Ann. I kept imagining that someone in the family would come up with a magical solution, that Rolland would say he'd won the Ohio lottery and had a hundred thousand dollars to invest, or Leon would tell us that a Silicone Valley millionaire wanted to buy the Inn to escape the California rat race. Everyone stared at me, waiting attentively, but offering no miracles. The voice went on inside my head, shouting that I never wanted to pick up another strand of hair in a bathtub, make another bed, or give another room tour as long as I lived. I never wanted to answer another phone or pay another invoice. I wanted to get the hell out.

The conference ended, and a week later we hit bedrock. Our June statement came out showing that, despite a profit of $572 from lodging, the St. Charles had stuck us with an overall loss of $4,695.28. Our food costs were running 70% — double what any restaurant could sustain. The Lamplighter was bleeding to death.

7. Solve a Mystery with a Mystery

I couldn't expect my family to do more than they already had, and a miracle wasn't going to happen. My parents, Del, and brothers had given everything. They'd met their commitment. Their pledge was to renovate the Inn, and it was done. Aunt Margie and Uncle Ray had given of themselves. Aunt Betty had given. Jo Ann had given more than I could measure. It was my turn because, well wasn't I the one responsible? The exhalted innkeeper?!

I'd known for months that it was a foolish thing for me to have done, taking on this job while knowing nothing about restaurants or lodging, but it was done and I was in it up to my neck. I could go on feeling sorry for myself and blaming the bad luck we'd had with the whole train of horrors with Frankfort and Art Taylor's crumbling buildings, the stretches of lousy weather and the locals who begged jobs from us but who never come in for a meal, and a dozen other things. But it wouldn't help.

I had to *do* something, something more than fine-tuning the menu or rallying our staff with pep talks. The July statement would be out in a few weeks and I was terrified that we'd have another mass of red ink. It wasn't the Inn that was bleeding to death, it was my parents, who'd lost a chunk of their life savings and were losing more each month. And did I really want to run off to Arizona with an ugly failure behind me?

A few nights later after the St. Charles had shut down for the evening I sat around gabbing with the four or five guests we had before they went up to their rooms. It was midnight, but I couldn't go to bed because another guest was still out, a young man from out of town who was at a reunion dance with his girlfriend at the school. I got comfortable in front of the fireplace with a novel, then threw it restlessly aside.

Shouldn't I be doing something about the Inn? I thought. We'd tried everything we could think of with the St. Charles and nothing worked, so the solution had to lie with the guest rooms. *But what was it?*

Putting on a play seemed to be the answer, because that was one thing I did know how to do. But we had no money. We'd been over it a hundred times. Even on our minuscule stage, props and scenery would cost something, and I'd have to find the time to design, build, and paint them. And what about costumes and royalties? No, it was a stupid idea and I tried to forget it.

I picked up the novel and tried to lose myself in the pages, then put it down and gazed around the lobby as if seeing it for the first time as an idea struck me. What if we did plays whose settings matched the Lamplighter so we wouldn't need scenery? We could perform in the lobby, with scripts that conformed to the furniture and decor we already had. The place was a veritable antique shop, and there was no need to buy or rent props. We'd find plays whose lighting effects could be satisfied with the chandeliers and table lamps and fireplace. Contemporary plays so our cast could wear their own things, playing characters close to their own personalities so there'd be no need for makeup or stage dialects.

But where to get actors?

I went to the kitchen and made a pot of tea. Supposing I managed to find actors from the Maysville Players and community college, we'd still have to pay them something, and it was hard to believe that we'd squeeze enough audience into the lobby to make a go of it. And how much could we charge, down here in the boondocks?

I was angry and went back to the lobby with the tea. It was insoluble. We couldn't afford actors, and if we had actors who worked for nothing they wouldn't be reliable.

I poured a cup of the Earl Gray tea and dumped myself in an armchair. What we needed, I decided rather cynically, was a dozen apprentices to work 19 hours a day and *pay tuition* in exchange for the chance to play a few parts. Aspiring actors are the only ones who want to act badly enough to pay to do it.

A shiver ran up my spine. I'd found a flaw in my thinking that had paralyzed me for months. There was in fact one other category of human being who'd pay to act. *Non actors*. Which meant nearly everyone on the planet. Real people will pay to act, because that's precisely what they do when they lay out $100 bucks to pretend they hadn't been frightened half to death on a bungee cord, or $5000 bucks to work their tail end off at a dude ranch while playing the role of a cowboy.

I paced around the lobby.

And where would I get these real people? Why, they were upstairs sleeping. Our *overnight guests*. We'd charge them to entertain themselves. The more we charged, the better they'd like it!

But how much? Ten dollars a person? Twenty? With all of our rooms full that would add up, but it would have to be a killer of a play to generate that kind of demand. I pictured our lodgers, the men and women I'd been talking with earlier. What kind of play would they pay to be a part of, given the lobby as the setting? A really killer of a play. . . .

Yes! *A murder mystery*! Offer our guests a chance to be frightened out of their wits and they'd leap at it! I felt giddy and nearly choked on my tea.

But how would we stage it? Some lodgers acting while others watched? No. Everybody plays a part, actor and audience at the same time. Then how do we fit it into the lobby? Or do we really have to? Why not use the entire Inn — lobby, conference room, dining room — everything? Yes! A mobile mystery that flowed from room to room, wherever the action demanded. Keep everybody on their toes. Move the action instead of the scenery!

I imagined our lodgers racing to the dining room for one of the scenes, and there was another thunderclap. They wouldn't just be in the dining room. They'd be *having dinner*, which meant we could solve our long-standing dilemma of losing lodgers to other restaurants! Let the Beehive find its own damn customers. We'd include the cost of dinner in the price to guarantee income from lodging *and food*, plus extra for the mystery. Sell it as a package. We could easily charge $30 a person. Maybe $40!

Hold on a minute. If our guests were working on the mystery during dinner, wouldn't the other diners wonder was going on? Wouldn't it annoy them? Well, we'd just have to tell the other diners that someone had been killed at the Inn, and the overnight guests were trying to get to the bottom of it. It would add suspense, because the mystery guests wouldn't know whether the other diners were innocent bystanders or part of the action. And it would be *free publicity*.

We'd create transitional action to use the Inn to best advantage. Use dad's gorgeous tulip, the oak balustrade, and the pictures we'd hung. Use the hobbit-like closet under the stairway where the vacuum cleaner was stored for hiding evidence. Use the prep room and stock room where limbs could be severed in the meat slicer or bodies concealed between the aisles of pancake mix. Mysteries are supposed to be chillers, so we could include a scene in the walk-in box. Use *everything*, even our wine cellar, where the stones, cobwebs, and musty air were more authentic than anything Vincent Price ever faced on a movie set.

But what exactly would our guests be doing in all these rooms — the conference room, for instance? What do guests normally do there? Have a meeting? Meeting about what? The mystery, of course! They'd go there periodically to update each other on their progress, or to be interrogated. But what about days when outside groups had reserved the conference room? We'd have to re-route the mystery elsewhere. . . .

I sipped more tea.

No! We'd hold a *reception* for our guests and *add it to the cost of the mystery!* Schedule it early in the afternoon when they arrived as a way to introduce everyone and launch the mystery. Brilliant! And that meant we could charge $45 dollars a person. Or $50!

But what if some of them wanted to get out to see the shops and stroll along the river? Hard to keep them cooped up in nice weather.

Again, I'd been thinking too small. We'd include the town in the plot, with places our guests *had* to go to ask questions and dig up evidence. They'd have to leave the Inn to play the game, and Augusta offered some truly atmospheric places to do this — abandoned buildings, galleries and shops, a mile of gorgeous riverfront, and two ancient cemeteries. We'd get the shop owners' permission to leave clues around, a boost to their business by insuring that our lodgers visited their shops. Everybody wins, and we'd have our lodgers turning the town upside down before they were finished. We'd make the *entire town* into a mystery!

But of course there was one place we couldn't include in the mystery, one place that was sacrosanct — the guest rooms. The unwritten code of the lodging industry is that a guest's room is inviolate, his or her castle, not to be intruded upon by anything short of the cleaning maid or a search warrant.

Another shiver rattled my spine. Get a search warrant! If lodgers make reservations to a mystery weekend, aren't they demanding something unusual? Aren't they in effect giving implied consent to have their rooms searched in the interest of finding the killer? A room search would allow our guests to see the unique decor of their fellow lodgers' rooms while involving them more deeply in the mystery. We could plant clues in the rooms to make everyone suspect so the lodgers wouldn't know whom to trust. We'd increase excitement by pitting room against room, husband against wife, friend against friend.

I did a little dance around the lobby.

But what about our staff? They couldn't just pretend not to see and hear our lodgers running around solving a mystery. Again I wanted to smack myself for thinking too unimaginatively. *Make the staff part of the mystery!* Adrienne and Laura, even Gregg and the cooks! They wouldn't have to learn lines or play a "character." They'd be themselves, doing what they were hired to do — including my parents.

There were of course a few practical matters to work out, one of them being the length of the mystery. If it began at two o'clock with the reception and didn't finish until after breakfast the next morning, it meant I had to devise a plot that took 20 hours to unfold. Five times longer than an uncut performance of *Hamlet.* I wasn't sure I was up to that. I poured myself another cup of tea and turned things over in my heated up brain, and it came to me that it really wasn't necessary to fill in every minute. I'd construct a mystery that could be put down and taken up at various times during our lodgers' stay, with peaks of action — between which they could stroll along the river, relax in the lobby or take a nap, even watch those damn TVs. The action could take a major respite when everyone went to bed.

And that led to the greatest problem of all — the script. Who'd get killed and how would it be managed? What was the *plot?* The challenge

I'd taken on was to devise a script carried largely by improvisation because there was no way to let our guests in on the story or rehearse them before coming to the Inn, guests I wouldn't even meet until the performance actually began. The mystery would have to be flexible enough to accommodate the number of reservations we had, and foolproof enough so that it wouldn't be ruined if someone canceled at the last minute, or if we got someone with no talent for improvisation. Where on earth to begin?

I made another pot of tea and threw myself in the armchair, letting my mind roam. What if someone came to the Lamplighter alone, a young woman, say, from out of state? An attractive and rich young woman with a secret. . . ? That was one thread. Then I thought about when I used to go to the Brooklyn Botanic Garden where a forbidding-looking tree was fenced in by itself. The *Varnish* tree, with a skull and crossbones warning that its bark was deadly. I kept that tree in mind, convinced that if I asked enough questions I could find the connection between it and the young woman. I grabbed a note pad and started writing, and as the Inn slept I sketched out a scenario for the mystery.

The lobby door opened and the young man came back from the reunion. "Good night," he said, twirling his carnation and running upstairs.

I glanced out the window as fog blanketed the town. It was 5:45 a.m. and I switched out the lights and slipped onto my office bunk-bed for a nap.

The mystery was finished.

8. A Ladder to Paradise

I called the mystery *The Case of the Wayward Widow*, and when I told my parents and Jo Ann about it the next morning they were exhilarated.

"Sounds like a riot!" said Jo Ann.

"No one around here has done anything like this!" said dad.

"Let's send a notice to the *Post*," mom suggested.

Listings in the *Kentucky Post* were free, so I fired something off, then spent the next several days working out plot details, deciding on clues and red herrings, and inventing character names. An editor at the *Post* interviewed me about the notice and ran a special column on it. We had a read-through, then I took publicity photos using our staff, ran off fliers, and wrote up a letter for travel agents. We decided we needed a minimum of three rooms — three couples or six individuals — to make a go of the mystery.

Then suddenly I found myself unable to go any further. In broad daylight the scenario looked less scintillating than it had in the wee hours the night I wrote it. I'd been worn out after a long week and had become intoxicated with ideas that no longer seemed so brainy. Business in the region was lousy and there was no guarantee that people would fork over 60 bucks apiece — the price I'd finally settled on — for something as whimsical as an overnight whodunit. The floating food palace at Maysville was sucking up every man, woman, and porcupine for miles around and smaller businesses were going under. Mayor Weldon's sporting goods store had sunk below the horizon and Philip Manning's gift shop was gasping for air. If the mystery failed, what would I do then?

"How's publicity coming?" dad asked a week later.

"Not bad," I fibbed.

"Let me know how I can help," said Jo Ann.

I panicked, going into a kind of catatonia as I pretended to develop ads and promotional materials, while oozing through my daily routine, frozen inside as I paid bills out of our moribund account, going through the motions of supervising the staff, and endlessly tinkering with the mystery. I gave a tour to a group of school girls from Taiwan, and visited with college friends I hadn't seen in 20 years who surprised me by staying at the Inn one weekend.

"What a treat!" I said, in shock.

I talked and laughed with them in a mental mist, salivating at their reliable corporate jobs, the Jaguar and medical practice, the sensible, well-ordered lives. Even the news that my favorite actor, Laurence Olivier, had died failed to penetrate my chrysalis of fear. I tossed through sleepless nights, unable to share my fear with Jo Ann and cursing myself for getting everyone's hopes pinned on something so ephemeral as a *play* as means of the Inn's salvation. After all, I couldn't really call myself a playwright. What nerve. The publicity photos gathered dust on my desk, and I hoped someone would give me a fatal knock on the head so I could forget the whole thing. Then the phone rang.

"I saw your notice in the *Post* about the mystery," said a woman.

"Yeah?"

"What a marvelous idea! I'd like to reserve one of your weekends in September."

I fumbled for a pencil. "September. Yes." I wrote down her name and gave her a thumb-nail description of our rooms. "Which one do you want?"

"I'm sorry. I wasn't being clear. I have a lot of crazy friends who have a big bash every year, and this sounds perfect. I want the entire Inn."

For a moment I could think of nothing to say. I was about to tell the woman that we couldn't confirm the mystery unless we had three room reservations. I cleared my throat.

"You want the *entire place?*"

"That's right! How many have you got?"

"Nine rooms."

"Only nine?" Her voice sank. "That's only eighteen people. We've got twenty-three right now, and may have others. Can't you squeeze in a few more?"

I told her the Shaker and Bluegrass rooms had two beds each. "If your friends don't mind sharing."

"Mind? They'd *kill* to sleep together!" She ripped out a raucous laugh. "And there's a couple with a teenage daughter. . . ."

"We have some fold-out cots — "

"We'll take all of them you've got!"

I was writing as fast as I could, but was afraid she'd balk at my next request. "We'll need a non-refundable deposit. Four hundred dollars."

"I've got the checkbook in front of me. What's your address?"

I put down the phone and shouted the news. My parents and Jo Ann congratulated me and we celebrated by having dinner together in the lobby.

"Don't congratulate me till we see if it works," I said.

I could barely believe that it stood the smallest chance of success. Keeping 25 people entertained for an entire weekend! Our read-through was at best a feeble guess at what might happen. I'd made the outline as tight as I could, with clues, character profiles, bits of dialogue, and other hints to help our guests through. But it was a largely improvised work, dependent on our guests' energy and inventiveness. Plays with complete scripts and professional actors fail all the time. Ours was pure gossamer. And if it fell as flat as a buckwheat soufflé would the woman and her friends demand their money back?

"Don't worry," said Jo Ann. "You've got seven weeks to work out the kinks."

Then another woman called who wanted to reserve the entire Inn for a mystery in *two* weeks' time.

9. The Inn Revived

One morning in August I went to the Presidential Suite to help some visitors with their luggage. They were Travis and Carolyn Thompson, who'd stayed with us exactly a year earlier as our first guests before the Inn had officially opened. I put the luggage in their car and Travis offered his hand.

"Won't be long till we're back!"

They were moving to Augusta the following spring.

"And don't forget the brochure," said Carolyn.

In October Augusta would host the first annual Writers' Roundtable. Subsidized by the Kentucky and Ohio arts councils, the Roundtable would feature novelists, poets, and nonfiction writers for readings and workshops, with Ed McClanahan serving as director. Kentucky Educational Television was slated to film the event and headquarters were at the Inn. We were already fully booked for the three-day event.

After seeing the Thompsons off I pitched into the day's work. The town was saturated with sunlight, and the humidity that had dogged us for weeks had left, leaving the hills bright and clear above the river. Gregg came in and we went over the dinner specials.

"Thirty reservations," I said. "And more are likely because of the weather."

"I'll have plenty of steaks," he said, heading off to the kitchen.

My Uncle Chuck and Aunt Faye were visiting from Indiana, and Chuck came in from the yard.

"All right if I mow?" he asked in a drawl.

Chuck was older than dad, with less education and rougher manners. He'd spent most of his 66 years on the farm and was perfectly at home in his overalls and straw hat.

"Go ahead," I said. "Our guests won't be here for a couple of hours."

"Okey-doke!" He whistled and went out the door.

Aunt Faye was cleaning rooms and came down to the landing. "Where to next?"

"The Thompsons have vacated the Suite."

"Pretty day!" She disappeared up the stairway.

At 11:30 our lunch crowd started in, and Pam, our newest server, arrived to help Kim. I finished checking through the reservation book and went to the kitchen to give Jim — our man-of-all-work who'd finally replaced Dick — final instructions for the reception.

At noon I brought my lunch on a tray to the office as an attractive blonde came in the lobby. Ima, who was visiting her aunt in Augusta. Ima's husband — George Plantte — had died a month earlier, leaving her well off, but she was struggling with grief. Her aunt was an invalid and Ima came to the St. Charles for most of her meals. She sat by the fireplace and thumbed through a magazine.

I ate my lunch while a car pulled up and a woman in her 30s hopped out and came inside. She was athletic-looking and wore a khaki pantsuit with a camera slung over her shoulder. She thrust out her hand.

"Alan? Donna Walters. I spoke with you last week about the article?" She looked around the lobby. "I'm not too late, am I?"

"Good heavens, no. Our guests don't arrive for an hour."

Donna filled me in on her plans to include the Lamplighter in a story she was writing for *Southern Living*.

"If you don't mind, I'd like to get some shots outside. You've got a beautiful place!"

She started across the lobby and froze in front of Ima. The two women stared at each other, then Ima buried her face in the magazine as Donna regained her composure and went out to the garden. Forty-five minutes later a caravan of cars stopped out front. I got onto the intercom to the kitchen.

"Jim! Need your help!"

Uncle Chuck rushed in the door. "There's a lot of cars. *City* folk!"

"They're our guests," I said.

Ima took out a compact and touched up her lipstick. Donna had established headquarters at a table in the corner by the stained-glass peacock. She was going over her notes and looked out at the commotion. Men and women thronged in, babbling as Jim helped with the luggage. I rang a bell to get everyone's attention.

"Jim will help you to your rooms, and I wanna remind you that the reception's at two o'clock. And this is Donna Walters." I explained what she was doing for *Southern Living*. "She'll probably want to interview some of you."

Donna was snapping pictures. "Alan's told me about the old house conference you're taking part in, and I promise not to get in the way."

One of the guests, a lawyer in his 50s, sat beside Ima and introduced himself. "And who might you be?"

"Ima Plantte," she said.

"Terrific!" said the lawyer. "I'm a vegetarian!"

At the reception Jim poured wine while Pam passed hors d'oeuvres and Aunt Faye circulated the cheese tray. Donna put a glass of wine in my hand and moved me beside an elderly couple.

"Tell `em about the decor, Alan." Her camera flashed, then she opened her notebook. "Could I have your names?"

A knot of people formed around Ima and listened as she went on about her late husband. It was the most animate I'd seen her, and I was glad she'd come to the reception. The lawyer brought her a glass of iced tea.

"Your husband died in a skiing accident?"

"It was his heart," Ima said, staring down at the ice cubes in the glass.

Jim tapped me on the shoulder. "Everyone's had refills, and I gotta check some things in the kitchen."

Then Uncle Chuck ambled in with a piece of driftwood that he held up for my inspection. "I found this on the river, and I thought these people would wanna see it. Ain't it pretty? I call it 'The Charging Bull.' You can see the bull's horn, right here." Chuck leaned in to me. "What about something to drink?"

"Well, take something with you."

I was annoyed that he'd intruded in the reception, although our guests seemed to be amused. He set the driftwood on a table where they crowded in for a closer look, then poured himself a very full glass of wine.

The lawyer bent over the driftwood. "What the hell is this?"

"Looks like a *dart*," said another man.

Chuck came over. "That wasn't there this morning!"

As the guests stared at the driftwood, Donna slipped over to Ima. "If you haven't the courtesy to speak to me, then maybe you can *read*!" She thrust a note into Ima's lap and walked angrily from the room.

Eyebrows shot up. Ima glanced at the note, then let it fall to the floor where a man picked it up. "You dropped this." Ima's eyes flashed. "It has nothing to do with me. I don't associate with *sluts*."

An embarrassed silence froze the room, which even the music of Glenn Miller coming from the CD player couldn't melt. I whispered to Pam. "Take the tray around again!"

The man brought the note to me. "I think you should see this!"

It read:

You know why I'm here.
Stop pretending you loved him, and *hand it over!*

"What do you think?" the man asked.

"Excuse me," said Ima. "I need some fresh air." She left the room, taking her iced tea with her.

I tapped my glass with a spoon. "If everyone would finish their drinks, it's time for the old house tour!"

We left the Inn and walked up the block to an early 19th-century house that was undergoing renovation. I climbed up the porch and addressed our guests. "We'll go inside in just a moment. But first I wanna point out — "

Someone screamed at the Inn. It was so piercing that one of the women dropped her camera. The screaming dragged on and it sounded like Aunt Faye. I ran toward the Inn with our guests at my heels. Shouts filled the air and people eating lunch in the St. Charles spilled out to see what was happening. I reached the door as Aunt Faye gasped, "At the back!"

I rushed down the hall, passed the kitchen where Gregg and the cooks watched in amazement, and came to the stock room where ice cubes were scattered on the floor. Just inside Ima was lying face down in a pool of tea. I knelt down and felt her neck. There was no pulse, and I called to Chuck over the heads of our guests.

"Get an ambulance! And would everyone please go back to the conference room!"

The lawyer grabbed my arm. "What the hell happened?"

I freed myself. "Just go to the conference room!"

Jim appeared as I herded our bewildered guests back down the hall. "Make sure no one leaves!" I told him.

Inside the conference room I asked Chuck to shut off the music, then I turned to our guests. "Sorry, but we'll have to delay the tour."

Protests rocked the room, and the elderly man stood up. "What about the young woman?"

"She's dead."

There were exclamations of disbelief. "She can't be!" said the lawyer's wife.

"Are you a doctor?" her husband asked.

"I know when someone's dead," I shot back.

The elderly man came forward. "Can we at least go to our room? My wife and I'd like to rest before dinner."

"Not yet." The man scowled as I went to the center of the room. "It makes no sense that a healthy young woman would drop dead like that. A doctor's on the way, but until he gets here everyone will stay put. And I must ask all of you some questions."

The *Case of the Wayward Widow* was underway. As it turned out, Ima had died of poison in her iced tea, and an autopsy revealed that she was nine weeks pregnant. Our guests were shocked by the incident and began hunting for clues and questioning townspeople. That evening we got a warrant and searched their rooms, finding evidence linking several of them to Ima. Inside a panel in the Presidential Suite was a note from Ima to one of the men arranging a "rendezvous" at the boat dock, and similar notes came to light in the other rooms. A small vial of pungent liquid was taped beneath a bed rail in the Bluegrass Room, a knife with a drop of the liquid on its tip was found inside the Shaker Room stove, and other items turned up inside the fainting couch of the Victorian Room. A test at the county lab showed that the liquid was distilled from the rosin of the deadly Varnish tree.

Less than a half hour after the screaming and commotion began, when our guests had dispersed around town to track down clues, a man and woman drove up. The man exclaimed that he was 87 and the woman in her 60s, newlyweds looking for a room.

"Ah!" said the man, taking in our peaceful garden. "Just what we need. *A nice, quiet Inn!*"

Epilogue

The mystery wrapped up Sunday after breakfast, and our guests applauded, filling us with a strange thrill. Because of the *Kentucky Post* article — the weekend entertainment section's lead story — and word-of-mouth publicity, our mystery attracted a surprising amount of attention, and over the next few weeks more groups made reservations. We scheduled mysteries through the fall and into the winter, booking them three and four months ahead.

I suddenly realized I was *writing*. Not the novel or radio script, and certainly nothing I'd want to do the rest of my life. But who made the rules about what I had to write?

Business in the St. Charles continued to seesaw. One Thursday in late August we suffered our worst day ever as no one came in, and we ended the day without making a dime. Then over Labor Day tourists crowded our dining room, earning over $3,000.

I knew from my daily tallies that we were doing better, but when July's statement came we were astounded to see that we'd made a tiny profit, due in large part to the deposits for the mystery. Our occupancy rate rose from 20% in June to 25% in July, and we were getting a regular stream of banquets and dinner parties, capped off when an Augusta High senior class held its 20th reunion at the Inn. Toward the end of the year some of the groups begged us for another mystery and I started a new script. As we approached the first anniversary of our opening our occupancy rate reached 37% — exceeding the break-even point estimated by the Small Business Center. It was a few months shy of four years since I'd left New York, and the red ink was gone.

After our mystery guests went home that Sunday in August, mom and dad — changed out of their Chuck and Faye outfits — relaxed in the lobby with the Sunday paper. They'd performed like real troupers and had infused their parts with comedy.

"You must be bushed," said mom. "What time did you get to bed?"

"Two o'clock. Some of them were still rummaging for clues."

"Why don't you go to Maysville for a movie?" dad suggested.

Dad and I had reached a better understanding of each other, a way to accommodate our differences with fewer barbs. And we made a pretty fair acting team.

"He probably needs a nap," said mom.

"Think I'll take a walk," I said.

"Don't forget your sister's taking over for you tomorrow," mom added.

Del had frequently given up a day to relieve me at the front desk, and she usually managed to wash windows or perform some other task while covering the phone and cash register. I planned to spend the day at the university library and have Chinese food. Del had given a robust performance as Donna Walters from *Southern Living*, opposite murder victim Ima, charmingly played by Lana Spradlin, my hopeful actress from *The Calamityville Terror*.

I went out to the garden where the flowers made a kaleidoscope of lavender, violet, and gold, and the stained-glass lamp in the window was crimson in the sun. Our arbor vitae trees looked down at me, a brotherhood shielding the Inn.

I circled the park where people were playing tennis, and noticed a line of cars in the shade of the SHARE museum by the river. A painting exhibit had opened, and a string trio performed Mozart on the patio. The music made me think of Jo Ann, who was performing in a musical in the Catskills. She'd be back in September, but could only stay a week before returning to her mother in Phoenix. We had no idea when we'd ever celebrate our anniversary together.

The trio finished the Mozart while the ferry — loaded with cars for Ohio — unfurled a wake across the water. I was anxious to see the art exhibit, but after the madness of the mystery weekend I needed to get off by myself for an hour. I hiked up Main Street and crossed the railroad tracks, making my way by the library, past the soiled windows of Mains' grocery and across Route 8 where I started up the hill. With the renovation finished my knees were having an easier time of it, but the thousand days of our labor — more than three and a half years — had exacted a price and I realized I might never again climb quite as fast as I once did. I'd moved to Augusta in the summer of my life and suddenly found myself in autumn.

I reached the top of the hill and gazed out as the ferry reached the Ohio shore and loaded up for the return trip with cars that made colored specks against the river's skin. Grasshoppers thumped in the woods around me, making the town seem to drift away, as if I were seeing it from another dimension. On the east end of town the factories were smokeless on the drowsy Sunday, and freight cars idled on the siding, as if a kid had abandoned a model train set. A pickup truck slipped beneath the canopy of leaves and a lawn mower purred. The clock tower on the school shoved above the trees, and a mist wreathed the steeples on Fourth Street.

At the school house the fall semester had begun. The students from my sophomore class two years earlier had graduated in May, making way for a new crop of seniors who were complete strangers to me. I sat on the hill while darkness inked in the valley. As the street lights came on I studied the houses that seemed to settle into the fatigue of their considerable age. Porch lights made golden pinpoints and there was the sigh of a summer night.

I looked to see if I could find one particular building among the dozens in the center of town. Blue in a vale of green. I found it at last. I was amazed at how small and fragile it was, and my heart trembled as I watched it, shimmering like a dory on a vast sea.

Afterword

To avoid any chance of embarrassing some of the persons who appear in these pages or their families because what I write about them might be deemed unflattering or even critical, I've replaced their real names with fictitious ones. In some cases it wasn't practicable to change names because the individual's actions were public and well known. In all events, everything I've written about really did occur, although in several instances I adhered to the memoirist's liberty of creating or expanding dialog to bring those events more fully to life for my readers.

Twenty years have trotted by since my family began transforming the old Parkview Hotel into the Lamplighter Inn, a generation in which a number of things have changed in Augusta and around the world. For one thing, the current owners of the Inn, the Mohrfields, have *almost* returned the building to the original name, The Parkview Country Inn. But a rose by any other name . . .

Moreover, the dollar has shrunk in value over these two decades, and to fully appreciate my family's struggles one needs to double the figures quoted in my memoir: Consider that the $8,000 I earned for my year of teaching would be $16,000 today, and our debt on the Inn not $300,000 but $600,000. But to end on a positive note, this means that instead of $270 on our first day of business in the restaurant we'd have netted a handsome $540!

A.T.

Acknowledgments

The debt I owe to my wife, Jo Ann, for her unflagging support and inspiration over the years I labored at the Lamplighter and the years I took to write this memoir can never be repaid — nor would she expect them to be. I also want to thank her for being the first and ablest reader of all my books and plays.

I've tried to give a small measure of thanks to my mother and father by dedicating this book to them, and my gratitude extends to my sister Del and brothers Leon, Rolland, and Sid for sharing bravely in the adventure of the Inn. Rolland's wife and daughter, Jane and Ashley, pitched in beyond the call of duty, as did Sid's wife Karen. I'm deeply appreciative of my Aunt Margie and Uncle Ray for lending their time, energy, and good humor to our renovation, and I'm forever obliged to my Aunt Betty for saving our restaurant from certain collapse at our darkest hour.

A huge thanks to Ron Carlson for being a wise and wonderful mentor when I wrote the first draft of my memoir while taking an MFA in creative writing at Arizona State University. I must also acknowledge Mark Harris for his fine assistance, and Janet Pittsley, under whose talented eye I strove to acquire some level of competence when drafting the pen-and-ink illustrations in these pages. I must tip my hat to Dale Wasserman for his generous Foreword and for being such an inspiration to me.

A big handshake of gratitude for Singularity Press publisher Steven Swerdfeger for so cheerfully and wholeheartedly taking on my book, and to Marianne Roccaforte for her expert proofreading. And I'm continually thankful to my colleague Lois Roma-Deeley for her advice and friendship.

A.T.
Phoenix, Arizona

Alan Tongret's plays have been produced in New York, at Alaska's Last Frontier Theatre Festival, and around Arizona, and include *Brontë*, *The World Aflame*, *Memories of the Lost Acres*, *Poor Richard's Revolt*, *Shakespeare and the Gospels: Primetime!*, *Treasure at the Devil's Backbone*, *Aurora*, *Arbor Day*, and others. Tongret earned an MFA in Theatre from Ohio University and acted with the New York Shakespeare Festival, Trinity Square Repertory Theatre, Fords Theatre, Allenberry Playhouse, plus summer stock, dinner theatre, TV, film, and commercials. He was a theatre manager at the Brooklyn Academy of Music for several years before joining his parents to renovate the Lamplighter Inn in Augusta, Kentucky. Tongret returned to school for an MFA in Creative Writing at Arizona State University, and over the last dozen years has headed the theatre program at Paradise Valley Community College in Phoenix, where he's a sometime trumpeter with the jazz band and chaired the planning teams for the new Studio Theatre and Performing Arts Center. He continues to turn out plays, screenplays, novels, and nonfiction, and is an avid practitioner with watercolors, pen-and-ink, and oil pastels. He's married to actress and director Jo Ann Yeoman, and lives in Phoenix with a shady yard that offers plenty of room for his dog Puck to roam about.